Syntax and Pragmatics in Functional Grammar

Functional Grammar Series

This series comprises monographs and collections written in the framework of Functional Grammar.
The aim is to seek explanations for a wide variety of linguistic phenomena, both language specific and cross-linguistic, in terms of the conditions under which and the purposes for which language is used.

Editors:
A. Machtelt Bolkestein
Simon C. Dik
Casper de Groot
J. Lachlan Mackenzie

General address:
Functional Grammar
Spuistraat 210
NL-1012 VT Amsterdam
The Netherlands

Other studies on Functional Grammar include S.C. Dik, *Functional Grammar* (1978), T. Hoekstra et al. (eds.), *Perspectives on Functional Grammar* (1981), S.C. Dik (ed.), *Advances in Functional Grammar* (1983) and A.M. Bolkestein et al. (eds.), *Predicates and Terms in Functional Grammar* (1985), all published by FORIS PUBLICATIONS.

Syntax and Pragmatics in Functional Grammar

A.M. Bolkestein
C. de Groot
J.L. Mackenzie (eds.)

Educational Linguistics/TESOL/ICC
Graduate School of Education
University of Pennsylvania
3700 Walnut Street/Cl
Philadelphia, PA 19104

1985
FORIS PUBLICATIONS
Dordrecht - Holland/Cinnaminson - U.S.A.

Published by:
Foris Publications Holland
P.O. Box 509
3300 AM Dordrecht, The Netherlands

Sole distributor for the U.S.A. and Canada:
Foris Publications U.S.A.
P.O. Box C-50
Cinnaminson N.J. 08077
U.S.A.

CIP-data

ISBN 90 6765 097 8 (Paper)

Printed in the Netherlands by ICG Printing, Dordrecht.

Foreword

Functional Grammar was first given an integrated presentation in Dik (1978).
Since then, Simon Dik and many collaborators across the globe have invested great
energy in developing this theory of grammar. The present volume represents a contribution to this effort. It is also the first of a new series of monographs and
collections entitled Functional Grammar Series, to be published by Foris
Publications. Given the ready availability of many surveys of Functional Grammar,
we will here restrict ourselves to a brief characterization, followed by an indication of the various matters dealt with in this book. Readers interested in a
general introduction to Functional Grammar might consult Dik (1981a: ch. 1).

Functional Grammar is a theory of the organization of natural languages which
takes as its starting-point the hypothesis that the structure of linguistic expressions is not arbitrary but is to a considerable extent influenced by the
communicative purposes of the language-user. The ultimate goal of all work in
Functional Grammar is to reach an understanding of the correlations between the
various structures that linguistic expressions may display and the functions they
fulfil in verbal interaction. It is in contributing to such understanding that
the theory is explanatory. Language is thus seen as an instrument through which
speakers communicate information to addressees with a view to effecting some
change in the knowledge and beliefs (pragmatic information) of those addressees.

In order for information to be communicated verbally, the speaker must choose
appropriate content-elements from his mental dictionary and establish the semantic relations among these. In Functional Grammar, this is reconstructed as the
selection of predicates from the lexicon. These predicates are stored in the
form of predicate-frames, which indicate the nature of the predications that may
be formed around the predicates. The roles that participants play in the states
of affairs designated by the predicate-frames are represented in the latter as
semantic functions (Agent, Goal, Recipient, etc.), whereby each argument of the
predicate is associated with one semantic function.

In many languages, it is possible to present the state of affairs being designated from the perspective or 'camera-angle' of one or more participants. Such
languages are said to permit the assignment of *syntactic functions* (Subject,

Object) to the arguments of predicates. There appear to be three types of language in this respect: those in which both Subject and Object may be assigned (English, Dutch, ...); those in which only Subject may be assigned (French, German, ...); and those in which there is no syntactic function assignment (Hungarian, Serbo-Croatian, ...).

The form of a linguistic expression may be influenced not only by the semantic and syntactic functions borne by the arguments of the various predicates but also by the *pragmatic functions* (Topic, Theme, Focus, Tail, ...) associated with constituents. These pragmatic functions are attributed to constituents in a way that reflects the relation between the information being communicated and the speaker's assessment of the addressee's current pragmatic information. They thereby help to explain those differences between expressions that can be ascribed to the nature of the setting in which they are used.

The twelve chapters in this volume are bound together by a common concern with the matter of syntactic and pragmatic functions and with the interaction between the two. The volume represents an advance on earlier work in Functional Grammar in devoting greater attention to the influence of global discourse on the local structuring of linguistic expressions. The chapters by Bolkestein, Hannay and Pinkster, for example, all stress that the pragmatic functions recognized hitherto in Functional Grammar, while undoubtedly permitting an understanding of many construction-types, will have to be supplemented with both new pragmatic functions (cf. Hannay's sub-Topic) and additional discourse-motivated notions (cf. Bolkestein's 'relatedness'), as well as a realization that the impingement of discourse on the structure of linguistic expressions may be more accurately captured in terms of 'tendencies' than 'rules' (Pinkster). Both Bolkestein and Pinkster are at pains to show that not only pragmatic but also syntactic function assignment is in many cases intimately related to the deployment of information in the ambient discourse. Hannay demonstrates the role of inference in the introduction of entities into the discourse (it is to these that sub-Topic is assigned) and argues that the discourse-dependent relation of 'relevance', needed to link Theme and Predication, is also applicable to sub-Topic assignment.

The volume contains three studies of individual languages, in which the principles of Functional Grammar are applied with both theoretical and empirical advantage. De Vries discusses the notions of topicality and salience in Wambon discourse and relates these to the pragmatic functions Topic and Focus, showing that the assignment of these functions is entirely dependent upon contextual discourse factors and that, under specific circumstances, both functions may be assigned to one and the same constituent. Moutaouakil's contribution is devoted to an analysis of the relevance of the pragmatic function Topic to Arabic: he demonstrates the importance of a Topic-worthiness hierarchy and a referentiality constraint for the appropriate assignment of this function. The chapter by Schachter applies the thinking embodied in Functional Grammar to Toba Batak, arguing that the relevant syntactic functions in that language are Adjunct and Trigger, notions that cannot be equated with Subject and Object; yet Schachter endorses the fundamental claim that the form of linguistic expressions may be determined equally by semantic, syntactic and pragmatic factors.

Three other chapters (those by Bossuyt, Lalleman and De Schutter) deal with aspects of West Germanic. Bossuyt's contribution discusses and supports Dik's (1980a) analysis of the historical development of word-order in Germanic, an analysis which is couched in syntactic terms, but shows that a recognition of pragmatic factors (relating especially to the functions Theme and Focus) allows an understanding of the verb-final order found in the subordinate clauses of German and Dutch. Contemporary Dutch is the language considered by both Lalleman and De Schutter. Lalleman shows that a Functional Grammar approach to spoken Dutch sentence-patterns embraces a large class of acceptable utterances that would otherwise be regarded as ungrammatical and thereby provides a sound basis for the analysis of children's speech, whether Dutch is being learned as a first or second language. De Schutter argues that Dutch sentence-patterns are characterized by as many as four 'special positions' whose function is to strengthen pragmatic relations among constituents; he also claims that all Dutch clauses display a fundamentally SOV-pattern, i.e. that the structural position for the verb is fixed with respect to those for the syntactic functions.

The chapters by Van Buuren, Nuyts and Ziv open up new perspectives for future research. Van Buuren, having presented a concise account of British English intonation, justifiably castigates protagonists of Functional Grammar for giving scant attention to matters of intonation and assuming an all-too-easy correlation between Focus and tonic placement. His aim is to achieve a realistic typology of Focus through an analysis of intonation in terms of tonality and tune. Nuyts explicitly compares Functional Grammar and Transformational Grammar with respect to the 'psychological reality' of each and concludes that Functional Grammar has greater psychological plausibility; yet its possible shortcomings (e.g. the location of pragmatic function assignment in the model) suggests that it should be extended and revised to give what Nuyts dubs a 'Functional Procedural Grammar' in which the work of psycholinguists and functional linguists might be integrated. Ziv's chapter explores new empirical ground, presenting a first attempt to confront Functional Grammar with the problem of parentheticals. Having considered a

number of syntactic, pragmatic and discourse-sensitive characteristics of parentheticals, Ziv considers whether these can be related to the pragmatic function
Tail, and concludes that this is possible, but only at the expense of relaxing
the requirements on the assignment of this function.

All but one of the chapters in this book, that by Moutaouakil, have arisen
from papers presented to the Colloquium on Functional Grammar (Amsterdam, 4-8
June 1984). Many of the other contributions to that Colloquium will be published
in a companion to the present volume, *Predicates and Terms in Functional Grammar*,
with the same editors.

We have pleasure in acknowledging the assistance of Caroline Kroon, Michel
van de Grift and Angeliek van Hout with the proof-reading and indexing of this
volume. Our thanks also go to the Faculty of Letters of the University of Amsterdam for financial undertakings concerning this book. To our typist, with her
unfailing eye for our editorial lapses, we hereby do homage.

Amsterdam   A. Machtelt Bolkestein
Tilburg   Casper de Groot
Amsterdam   J. Lachlan Mackenzie

November 1984

Table of Contents

List of abbreviations and symbols

Semantic functions:

Ag	=	Agent
Go	=	Goal
Rec	=	Recipient
Ben	=	Beneficiary
Instr	=	Instrument
Loc	=	Location
Temp	=	Temporal
Dir	=	Direction
Proc	=	Processed
Fo	=	Force
Po	=	Positioner
Ø	=	Zero function

Syntactic functions:

Subj	=	Subject
Obj	=	Object
DO	=	Direct Object
IO	=	Indirect Object

Pragmatic functions:

Top	=	Topic
Foc	=	Focus

Pragmatic notions:

t^y	=	topicality
TP	=	topic-persistence
RD	=	referential distance
T	=	thematic
R	=	rhematic
N	=	neutral

Categories:

A	=	Adjectival
N	=	Nominal
V	=	Verbal
Vf	=	finite Verb
Vi	=	non-finite Verb
PRO	=	Pronoun
NP	=	Noun Phrase
PP	=	Prepositional Phrase

Rel	=	Relative Pronoun
Sub	=	Subordinator
Co	=	Coordinator
Q	=	Question Word

Term operators:

d	=	definite
i	=	indefinite
1, sg	=	singular
m, pl	=	plural

Morpho-syntactic categories:

p1, p2, p3	=	first, second, third person
act	=	active
pass	=	passive
SS	=	Same Subject
DS	=	Different Subject
SR	=	Switch Reference
pres	=	present
fut	=	future
NF	=	non-future
IRR	=	irrealis
AA	=	Actor-Adjunct
AT	=	Actor-Trigger
perf	=	perfect
part	=	participle

Positions:

S	=	Subject position
O	=	Object position
V	=	Verb position
X	=	neutral position
PØ	=	special position
P1	=	Clause-initial position
P2	=	Theme position
P3	=	Tail position

Cases:

nom = nominative
acc = accusative
gen = genitive
dat = dative
abl = ablative

Constructions and markers:

NcI = Nominativus cum Infinitivo
AcI = Accusativus cum Infinitivo
PM = Personal-name marker
Li = Linker
ThM = Theme marker
STM = Strong Topic marker
TN = Transitional Nasal
RED = Reduplication

Intonational notions:

S = strong stress
W = weak stress
M = medium stress
t = tonic
o = non-tonic
R = rising intonation
F = falling intonation

Hierarchies:

SFH = Semantic Function Hierarchy
TWH = Topic-worthiness Hierarchy

Theories of Grammar:

FG = Functional Grammar
TG = Transformational Grammar
QG = Quantitative Grammar
FPG = Functional Procedural Grammar
UG = Universal Grammar

Languages:

MD = Middle Dutch
MHG = Middle High German
MoD = Modern Dutch
MoE = Modern English
MoHG = Modern High German
OE = Old English
OHG = Old High German
OLG = Old Low German
SAE = Standard Average European

General:

X, Y = arbitrary category or function
$x_1, \ldots, x_n$ = argument variable
$y_1, \ldots, y_n$ = satellite variable
Sat = satellite
SoA = State of Affairs
UoI = Universe of Information
LAD = Language Acquisition Device
AI = Artifical Intelligence
LIPOC = Language-Independent Preferred Order of Constituents

Chapter 1

Cohesiveness and syntactic variation: quantitative vs. qualitative grammar

A. Machtelt Bolkestein
Department of Latin, University of Amsterdam

1. Introduction

In this paper I will confront two different approaches to the study of syntactic variation in languages and of the degree to which the use of a construction can be related to properties of the stretch of discourse in which it occurs, that is, to pragmatic factors.

I will label these two approaches the 'quantitative' and the 'qualitative' approach. Quantitative Grammar (QG) is amply represented in Givón ed. (1983), the qualitative approach is represented by various authors working within the tradition of Functional Grammar (FG), cf. the papers in Bolkestein e.a. (1981), Hannay (to appear) and Mackenzie (1984).

First, by confronting the two approaches I will show that although the results of a quantitative analysis and of a qualitative one may reinforce each other, and heuristically the first may point in the direction of what might qualitatively be the right analysis, this is not always the case: the results may also actually obscure the real functional motivation hidden behind the quantitative data. Furthermore, I will demonstrate that analysis in terms of the FG notions Topic and Focus may provide a deeper insight into the factors motivating the use of a construction, in spite of the fact that in a sense it is the more 'risky' type of approach in having to rely on subjective judgments of the investigator concerning the pragmatic status of the entities involved. Finally, however, it will also be shown that an analysis in which the pragmatic notions Topic and Focus are the only ones used cannot satisfactorily explain the discourse motivation for the use of certain constructions (cf. Hannay (this volume) and Pinkster (this volume) for similar conclusions). The theoretical framework will have to be expanded in order to incorporate a notion of 'relatedness' between constituents.

I will make my point by discussing three different bodies of data, two from Latin, discussed in Bolkestein (1981, 1983, 1984) and one from Chamorro (details in Cooreman 1983, forthcoming and Cooreman, Fox and Givón 1984). First, however, I will make some remarks on the essential characteristics of the two types of analysis.

2. *Quantitative Grammar vs. Functional Grammar*

2.1. *The Quantitative approach*

The type of phenomena discussed in QG as represented in Givón ed. (1983) include variation in voice in a number of languages, and phenomena such as 'dative shifting' or 'Indirect Object promotion'. In FG, such phenomena are candidates for being described as variation in Subj assignment and Obj assignment respectively.[1] In Dik (1978: 99f, 1980a: 29f) such syntactic variation is described as a matter of the choice of 'perspective' from which the speaker wants to present the state of affairs. The notion 'perspective' is not itself given further clarification.

In QG it is demonstrated that in many languages there is a correlation between the selection of a syntactic construction (spoken of as 'syntactic coding points') and the so-called 'degree of topicality' of the constituents involved (spoken of as a 'functional domain'). The QG terminology is somewhat confusing for users of FG, since it suggests that some independent evaluation of the pragmatic status of constituents takes place. However, this is not the case: roughly defined, the degree of topicality of an item is simply computed on the basis of the distribution of coreferent elements in the surrounding discourse, specifically its frequency of occurrence and the distance between the various occurrences. The measurement takes into account both the preceding discourse, counting the referential distance (RD) to earlier occurrences, and the following text, counting the continuity or topic-persistence (TP). By combining these two measures each constituent is assigned a score, the so-called 'degree of topicality' by which it can be compared to other constituents of the same construction or to constituents in other syntactic constructions. Only arguments of predicates (first, second and third arguments) have been subjected to such measurement.

The type of results which such methodology produces may look as follows. In Cooreman, Fox and Givón (1984: 15) it is observed that in the four verb 'voices' possible in the Austronesian language Chamorro, the relative degree of topicality of the Agent and the Goal (Patient), calculated statistically, is as follows:

fig. 1.   antipassive   Ag >> Go

            ergative   Ag   >   Go

            in-passive   Ag   <   Go

            ma-passive   Ag << Go

(> means 'is higher', < means 'is lower in topicality')

No further hypothesis, predictions or claims are set up concerning the question whether or not in individual attestations of these constructions the relative degree of topicality of the two entities involved may be the reverse of that given in fig. 1. I will come back to this question below.

2.2. The Functional approach

In FG, as opposed to QG, pragmatic notions are independently defined. The notion Topic is defined as 'the entity 'about' which the predication predicates something in a given setting', cf. Dik (1978: 14); it does not coincide with syntactic Subj status (1978: 99, 1980a: 29, 39). Focus is defined as 'that constituent which carries the most salient information in a given setting' cf. Dik (1978: 149). For languages which do not have overt marking of Topic, there is no straightforward operational test for determining which is the Topic in a particular sentence, although previous mention, givenness and definiteness are strong indications. The lack of an operational criterion is a 'weakness' of the theory, of course, and has led to many an attempt to modify the notion Topic, defining it more narrowly or more broadly (cf. for instance Hannay this volume).

The operational test for classifying a constituent as Focus is formed by question-answer patterns: Focus is that element in an answering sentence which actually forms the answer to the question posed. In declarative sentences Focus is that element which would be the essential answer if the sentence had been an answer to a question. Thus the linguist must try to determine to what question a sentence under consideration might form an appropriate answer. When studying actual texts, this decision is often a matter of the linguist's subjective judgment concerning the intentions of the speaker, and not at all easy to make, although sometimes some help may be derived from intonation (see, however, Van Buuren this volume) or other overt marking. Again the trouble in identifying Focus has led to several proposals to modify the definition by narrowing it down or broadening it, cf. e.g. Hannay (1983), and De Jong (1981).

In view of the stress laid in QG on the 'functionality' of the notion of degree of topicality (t^y), several basic differences must be pointed out.

2.3. Degree of topicality and pragmatic functions: overlap?

(i)   QG is actually concerned with correlations rather than with conditions. Thus, trustworthy and methodologically sound though the statistical data may be, it is, in itself, not clear whether in Chamorro a high degree of t^y of a Go is a condition *sine qua non* for either optionally or obligatorily expressing the

state of affairs by means of a *ma*-passive construction; nor can it be inferred
from the results whether a *ma*-passive in Chamorro is at all acceptable with an
Agent which has a higher degree of t^y than the Goal.

(ii) Apart from this, a high or low degree of t^y does not necessarily correlate
with Top or Foc status respectively in a sentence, not only when the backward
and forward measures are combined (as in fig. 1), but even when they are kept
separate. First of all, satellites may, of course, be Foc just as readily as
arguments of the predicate. In fact, if they *are* present in a sentence, they
often are the constituent carrying Foc (cf. Panhuis 1982: 19 on the 'communicative dynamism' of such constituents). Moreover, constituents which are Foc in
a particular sentence may either continue to figure, i.e. persist, in the following discourse, or not return at all, especially when they have the status of
a satellite. According to QG they would score higher in degree of t^y in the
former case than in the latter. Thus, as far as the Chamorro data are concerned,
fig. 1. does not tell us e.g. whether in a *ma*-passive construction the Go is
allowed to be Foc as well as Top, nor whether Ag may ever be Top; in short
whether particular constellations of pragmatic and syntactic functions are unacceptable for Chamorro speakers. In fact, a glance at the chunk of discourse
given as an Appendix in Cooreman with respect to the *ma*-passive (1983) shows us
that this is not the case, as appears from sentence (1):

(1)   Pues ma- arekla ginin i   dos saina   na ... i   dos pãra u- man-a'asagwa
        then PAS-arrange from the two parents COMP.. the two FUT-IRR3PL-marry-RED
        'then it was arranged by the two parents that ... the two would get
        married'

        (preceding context: when this woman was still a small girl, her mother

        and father had friends who were rich also and they had a son)

In (1) the Ag constituent, which according to fig. 1. is statistically low in t^y,
may, on the basis of the preceding context, be classified as pragmatically Top;
at the same time the Go constituent, which according to fig. 1. is statistically
high in t^y, is not Top but carries Foc.

   In other words, quantitative differences may well be a consequence of functional differences, but do not tell us what the relevant functional differences
are.[2] Although the latter may offer an explanation for the former, this does not
work the other way round. The observation in Cooreman, Fox and Givón (1984: 28)
that the possibility of a pattern indicates nothing about its probability may
thus just as well be turned round.

Similar evidence for the independence of functional factors and statistical
data is offered by the personal passive construction in classical Latin which is
possible with verba dicendi and sentiendi, as illustrated by (2a and c) vs. (2b):

(2) a. dictator   improbus esse   dicitur
        dictator$_{nom}$ bad$_{nom}$ to-be$_{inf}$ be-said$_{3sg}$ (NcI)

    b. dictatorem   improbum esse   dicitur
        dictator$_{acc}$ bad$_{acc}$ to-be$_{inf}$ be-said$_{3sg}$ (AcI)
        'the dictator is said to be bad'

    c. Caesar   adventare iam   iamque   et adesse   eius
        Caesar$_{nom}$ arrive$_{inf}$ already already-and too to-be-present$_{inf}$ his

        equites   falso   nuntiabantur   (Caes. BC 1, 14, 1)
        horsemen$_{nom}$ wrongly be-told$_{3pl}$
        'Caesar was wrongly told to arrive already and also that already his
        horsemen were present'

In Bolkestein (1981: 90f, 1983) evidence is presented that the so-called Nominativus cum Infinitivo (NcI)-construction in Latin illustrated by (2a) is an optional syntactic alternative to the passive with the whole embedded predication
as Subj (2b); the NcI may be used only under specific pragmatic conditions. On
the basis of various arguments which I will not repeat here, the conclusion is
drawn that the following condition must be satisfied for an NcI to occur: sentential Foc must fall on a constituent of the embedded predication itself (as is the
case in (2c) above); it may not fall on a constituent outside the embedded predication, as in (3):

(3)   FALSO dictatorem$_{acc}$ improbum$_{acc}$ esse dicitur
        'wrongly the dictator is said to be bad'
        (Where Foc is capitalized)

In sentences containing verbs of speech or thought as main verbs Focus quite frequently falls within the embedded predication rather than on a constituent of
the main clause. (In some perceptive traditional grammars of Latin the main
predicate has in such cases been likened to an auxiliary.) Such sentences are
evidence that the observation that embedding and non-finite expression of a
predication is prototypically preserved for backgrounded or presupposed information (cf. Bolinger 1975; Mackenzie 1984) should not be overgeneralized. However,
by having the nominative case-form for its Subj and the main verb agree with it,

the embedded predication indeed has more 'main clause' characteristics than it would have without this raising.

The formulation of the pragmatic condition given above predicts - and is therefore falsifiable - that a sentence such as (4a) does not occur but that (4b) does; and that the NcI-construction (5a) is not a possible alternative to (5b); and that we will not find (6) as an alternative to (3) above:

(4) a. *A QUO dictator$_{nom}$ improbus$_{nom}$ esse dicitur? (NcI)
        By WHOM

    b. A QUO dictatorem improbum esse dicitur? (AcI)
       'By whom is it said that the dictator is bad?'

(5) a. *MIHI dictator improbus esse dicitur (NcI)

       Me$_{dat}$

    b. MIHI dictatorem improbum esse dicitur, sed TIBI ... (AcI)
       'To me it is said that the dictator was bad, but TO YOU ...'

(6)   *FALSO dictator$_{nom}$ improbus$_{nom}$ esse dicitur (NcI)

Similarly, the NcI cannot be used in sentences forming an answer to questions such as (4b) or (5b).

Now, when we apply a QG measurement to the Subj of the NcI and to the accusative Subj of AcI-clauses governed by a passive main verb, statistically, the Subj of an NcI scores much higher in t^y, at least in RD. However, the Subj of the NcI need not be Top in the FG sense. It may just as well be Foc, or be neither Top nor Foc. Consequently, cases exist where the Subj of the NcI has a very low degree of t^y, either on the basis of the anaphoric measure alone, or of the cataphoric one as well, cf. *multa* 'many things' in (7a) and *legio XII* 'the twelfth legion' in its continuation (7b):

(7) a. (Ille ... Athenis non videtur fore)

         Multa   eum   in Asia dicuntur   morari,   maxime   Pharnaces
         many$_{nompl}$ him$_{acc}$ in Asia be-said$_{3pl}$ to-keep$_{inf}$, especially Pharnaces
         '(he ... won't reach Athens) There are said to be many things that keep
         him in A., especially P.', Cic. *Att*. 11, 21, 2

    b.   Legio   XII ... lapidibus egisse   hominem dicitur
         legio$_{nom}$ 12 ... stones$_{abl}$ to-have-driven$_{inf}$ man$_{acc}$ be-said$_{3sg}$
         'the 12th legion is said to have driven him off with stones' (ibid.,
         continuation; no further mention of *Legio XII* in following text)

Thus, the fact that the Subj of the NcI is quite often Top explains the high

degree of t^y, but the latter is not the condition *sine qua non* for the use of
this construction. The relevant condition, outlined above, is the location of
Foc, i.e. of the most salient information, within the embedded predication, and
this cannot be traced by the parameters RD and TP. The QG data are in itself
compatible with the real functional motivation but cannot be inferred from them.
Thus, in order to explain the NcI-construction in Latin as a 'syntactic variant'
of the AcI, the pragmatic notion Focus must be distinguished, in spite of the
occasional problems in identifying it.

3. Reference and relatedness

I will now turn to a third body of data in Latin, where again differences in degree of t^y may well show up without actually revealing the real motivation behind
the choice of a syntactic variant.

   This consists of the behaviour of a class of bitransitive (i.e. three-place)
verbs which may govern two different case patterns, i.e. exhibit phenomena comparable to 'dative shifting' or 'IO-promotion'. The two patterns possible differ
as to which of the three arguments is expressed as accusative Obj (and, consequently, is assigned Subj function when the three-place verb is passivized), cf.
(8a-b):

(8) a.   urbem   fossā   circumdedit
         city$_{acc}$ moat$_{abl}$ have-surrounded$_{3sg}$
         'he surrounds the citadel with a moat'

    b.   fossam   urbi   circumdedit
         moat$_{acc}$ city$_{dat}$ have-surrounded$_{3sg}$

In Bolkestein (1984) it is argued that the variation between the two patterns is
not a matter of a difference in the state of affairs designated (i.e. would have
to be described in terms of predicate formation), but seems to be a difference
in Obj assignment, i.e. to involve a choice of perspective, comparable to the
analysis proposed for *to give* in Dik (1978: 99f, 1980a: 29f). It is shown that in
Latin, this choice of perspective is not random but motivated by properties of
the stretch of discourse, i.e. by pragmatic factors. As opposed to the condition
valid for the use of the NcI-construction discussed in section 2., however, the
condition here cannot be stated in terms of a particular constellation of the
pragmatic functions Top and Foc: the data show that no constellation is excluded
from occurrence (this is different from the findings of Smyth e.a. 1979) for

English, where dative shifting is claimed to be rule-governed by such pragmatic factors; cf. also Hopper and Thompson 1980: 262; Givón 1983b: 57).[3] A number of other factors, partly within the sentences containing the three-place verb, and partly in the surrounding discourse, turn out to influence the selection of pattern. The accusative case-form goes to a constituent when:

(a) it is a relative pronoun, cf. (9) below;

(b) it is the Head of a relative clause, cf. (10);

(c) it is the Head of a complex Modifier, cf. (11);

(d) it occurs in a complex predication in more than one of its clauses, both when the three-place verb figures in a subordinate clause and when it figures in the main clause, cf. (12-13);

(e) it has a coreferential item occurring in the preceding discourse, cf. (14), or

(f) in the following discourse, cf. (15),

(g) and, finally, when the preceding context or the following context contains an item 'related' to it as in (16).

These tendencies are illustrated by (9-16), in which the construction of the a-sentences is preferred to that of the b-sentences (spelled out only in (9-11), but possible in (12-16) as well):

(9) a. urbs quam   fossā   circumdedit
         city which$_{acc}$ moat$_{abl}$ have-surrounded$_{3sg}$

     b. urbs cui$_{(dat)}$ fossam$_{(acc)}$ circumdedit
         'the city which he surrounded with a moat'

(10) a. urbem   quae vicina est   fossā   circumdedit
         city$_{acc}$ which near be$_{3sg}$ moat$_{abl}$ have-surrounded$_{3sg}$

     b. urbi$_{(dat)}$ quae vicina est fossam$_{(acc)}$ circumdedit
         'he surrounded the city which was nearby with a moat'

(11) a. urbem   a Gallis conditam   fossā   circumdedit
         city$_{acc}$ by Galli founded$_{acc}$ moat$_{abl}$ have-surrounded$_{3sg}$

     b. urbi$_{dat}$ a Gallis conditae$_{(dat)}$ fossam$_{(acc)}$ circumdedit
         'he surrounded the city (that was) founded by the Gauls with a moat'

(12)   ubi urbem   fossā   circumdedit,   oppugnare   incipit
         when city$_{acc}$ moat$_{abl}$ have-surrounded$_{3sg}$, to-besiege$_{inf}$ have-begun$_{3sg}$
         'when he had surrounded the city with a moat, he began to besiege it'

(13)   ubi urbem   oppugnare   constituit,   fossā   eam   circumdedit
         when city$_{acc}$ to-besiege$_{inf}$ have-decided, moat$_{abl}$ it$_{acc}$ have-surrounded$_{3sg}$
         'when he had decided to besiege the city, he surrounded it with a moat'

(14)   haec   urbs   in planitie est. Eam   fossā   circumdedit
        this$_{nom}$ city$_{nom}$ on plain   be$_{3sg}$. It$_{acc}$ moat$_{abl}$ have-surrounded$_{3sg}$
        'this city is on a plain. He surrounded it with a moat'

(15)   urbem   fossā   circumdedit.   Deinde oppugnare   incepit
        city$_{acc}$ moat$_{abl}$ have-surrounded$_{3sg}$. Then   to-besiege$_{inf}$ have-begun$_{3sg}$
        'he surrounded the city with a moat. Then he began to besiege it'

(16)   bracchium ei   fractum   est.   Itaque   umerum   lanā
        arm$_{nom}$ him$_{dat}$ broken$_{nom}$ be$_{3sg}$. Therefore shoulder$_{acc}$ wool$_{abl}$

        circumdedit
        have-surrounded$_{3sg}$
        'his arm was broken. Therefore he put wool around the shoulder'

The list of factors illustrated in (9-16) suggests that the constituent selected
as accusative Obj would probably score higher on the t^y scale than the non-
accusative constituent, in agreement with the generalization formulated in Givón
(1983b: 57) to the effect that Obj will score higher than obliques. Some of the
factors will influence the score with respect to RD (such as (a) and (e)), others
with respect to TP (such as (b), (c) and (f)). Factor (d) seems to be neutral
with respect to order. In any case, apparently 'successive reference' to one of
the arguments of the three-place predicate, either anaphorically or cataphoric-
ally, tends to lead to the selection of a perspective in which that argument is
accusative Obj (and, since more than half of the attested instances involve
three-place verbs, Subj). The latter fact contradicts Givón's claim that passivization is more a discontinuity device (1983a: 23, 1983b: 63), cf. Pinksters
observations (this volume).

    Before turning to the notion of successive reference itself, I would like to
offer some additional remarks about each of the factors.

    Tendency (a) is reminiscent of Keenan & Comrie's relativization accessibility
hierarchy (1977); however, Latin allows its relative pronouns to carry any case-
form, and the preference only shows when the choice between two patterns exists.
Factor (b) and (c) may be confronted with the claim in Givón (1983a: 18, 19,
1983b: 63) and Bentivoglio (1983: 294) to the effect that both being restrict-
ively modified *and* the phonological size of a constituent correlate with greater
discontinuity (i.e. with a lower degree of t^y in terms of RD). In Latin, however,
these factors turn out to favour Obj-selection of the constituents involved. In
other words, Obj assignment in Latin correlates with low t^y in some cases, e.g.
(b)-(c), and with high t^y in other cases, e.g. (a), (d), (e), and (f).

    With respect to factor (d), the assignment of Obj appears to differ from

cohesive devices such as the marking of same vs. different Subj in switch-reference languages (SS vs. DS): it seems that in such languages the clause in which
the SS/DS marker occurs can be subordinate to the clause with respect to which
the sameness or difference is marked (the reference or controlling clause), but
not the other way round (cf. Munro 1983: xii). In the case of our Latin verbs,
on the other hand, the hierarchical relation between the two clauses is not
decisive. Factor (f) shows, as is also demonstrated by the existence of antici-
patory SR devices in many languages, that in producing texts speakers plan ahead
when selecting a pattern for the three-place verb. In Reesink (1984: 174) it is
demonstrated that such planning ahead may go further than just the next clause;
sometimes the occurrence of a SS/DS marker is 'controlled' by clauses several
steps away, neglecting less foregrounded material in between. This phenomenon is
parallelled by instances where the selection of pattern for three-place verbs is
determined by the occurrence of a related item several sentences away, cf. (17):

(17)   cum   rex   ... circumdari   *ignes* ... iuberet nisi   inquit
        when king ... be-surrounded fire ... ordered if not ... say$_{3sg}$ ...

        dextramque   *accenso* ... *foculo*   inicit
        righthand$_{acc}$-and lit$_{abl}$ ... hearth$_{abl}$ put-into$_{3sg}$
                          dat$^?$ dat$^?$
        'When the king ordered *fire* to be put around him ..., he said: ...
        and *when the hearth was lit* he put his hand into it', Liv. 2, 12, 12

I will come back to factor (g) below.

   The apparent contradiction between the factors (a) and (d-g) on the one hand
and (b-c) on the other disappears if the notion of 'successive reference' is
somewhat modified: in some of the conditions mentioned there is no actual explicit occurrence of a coreferential item, as in (b), (c) and (d). In QG, only
the latter type of instances seem to be counted as involving $\emptyset$ anaphora, that is,
instances where we are dealing with something like EQUI-NP deletion. In (b) and
(c), however, the decisive factor turns out to be whether or not an argument of
the three-place verb figures once or more than once in the underlying structure
of the sentence, or, in other words, whether it participates in more than one
predication. If it does, it will be coded as accusative Obj or nominative Subj;
if it does not, as an oblique. The fact that such factors influence the choice
of perspective suggests that syntactic function assignment is actually a principle of ease of processing, i.e. a psychological principle. This principle,
called the principle of 'harmony of perspective' in Bolkestein (1984), is a principle of discourse structure, as is shown by (e-g), rather than being limited to

sentence level: the sentence level phenomena are only a particularly obvious
manifestation of the former.

   As observed above, computation of the relative degree of t^y of the accusative
Obj of three-place predicates vs. the oblique argument will produce the result
that statistically the accusative Obj is indeed higher in t^y than the non-accu-
sative, provided that the notion of 'successive reference' is refined in the
above way. However, this does not mean that each individual accusative Obj has
such a high degree of t^y in terms of RD and/or TP. Consider for example (18),
where the acc. Obj *laevam manum* 'left hand' is neither preceded nor followed by
a coreferential expression:

(18)   *laevam manum* ima parte togae circumdedit, sublataque *dextra* proclamavit
         'He put the slip of his toga around *his left hand* (acc), and having
         lifted *his right hand* he proclaimed ...', Val. Max. 3, 2, 17

The above example brings me to a further problem for the quantitative approach,
which, however, at the same time also offers a problem for a FG description of
the relevant phenomena. The list of tendencies (a)-(f) was stated in terms of
'successive reference', albeit not between explicitly expressed constituents,
but between constituents in the underlying predicational structure. Sentence
(18), however, is an instance of tendency (g): an argument of the three-place
verb will be realized as accusative Obj when in the preceding or following discourse an item occurs which is *related* to it. That is, not only the occurrence
of coreferential constituents exercises influence on the selection of perspective,
but the presence of entities having any kind of 'sense-relation' (to use the terminology of Lyons 1977: ch. 9) to one of the arguments of the three-place verb
may do so. The fact that strict coreference is not the only way in which entities
can be conceived of as 'same' is already demonstrated by the existence of a
certain grey area in languages which have switch reference marking devices, cf.
Munro (1983: 11), Comrie (1983: 26), and Reesink (1984: 169): the latter shows
that the condition for SS-marking in the Papuan language Usan includes certain
cases of overlapping reference, and is therefore wider than strict coreference.
Moreover, languages may vary as to what is treated as 'same' in this respect.

   It is not clear how the degree of t^y is to be computed when dealing with other
than strictly coreferential items. Moreover, the parallelism between switch
reference mechanisms and the selection of three-place pattern is far from complete. In the latter case a whole range of semantic relations between entities
seems to be relevant, whereas in the former case the range of possible deviations

from strict coreference occurring with SS is very limited. Some more attested
Latin examples are given in (19):

(19) a. Tum Cassius ... lacernā *caput* circumdedit extentamque *cervicem* ...
   praebuit. Deciderat Cassii *caput*, cum ...   Vell. 2, 70, 2
   'Then C. covered his head (acc) with his cloak (abl) and presented
   his neck. C's head had scarcely fallen, when ...'

   b. Sic ut *a genibus ad umbilicum* ..., *cetera* vestimentis circumdata sint
   Cels. 7, 26, 5C
   'Such that *from the knees to the belly* ..., but that *the other parts*
   (nom) are surrounded with clothes'

   c. siccis   *femina*   adsperguntur;   *epiphoras*   quoque arida
   dried$_{abl}$ thighs$_{nom}$ be-sprinkled$_{3pl}$; eye-ailments too   soften$_{3pl}$
   Plin. *NH* 21, 123
   'with dried ones (rose leaves) the *thighs* are sprinkled; *eye-ailments*
   too dry ones soften'

The relation involved may in fact probably be any type of 'lexical cohesion' distinguished in Lyons (1977: 270f) and Halliday & Hasan (1976: 274f). Consequently,
if the selection of pattern is viewed as a cohesive device, the latter seem to be
right when they observe (1976: 284) 'properly speaking reference is irrelevant
to lexical cohesion'.[4] For similar conclusions cf. Prince (1981), where an
attempt is made to classify entities as Topic on the basis of their 'inferrability' from the preceding discourse or of the degree to which they are 'evoked' in
that discourse and Hannay (this volume). Thus various kinds of near-synonymy, of
contrast (binary or multiple), different types of opposition such as e.g. anto-
nymy, hyponymy, superordinateness, etc. may form the factor influencing the selection of perspective. Moreover, the degree to which entities evoke other entities may be determined not only by their meaning, but also by situational, or
institutional, i.e. pragmatic factors. Such 'relatedness' might be accounted for
in a semantics which contains some sort of 'scripts' or 'frames' approach (cf.
e.g. Dressler and Beaugrande 1981: ch. 5 and De Schutter and Nuyts 1983).

   Givón (1983: 16) seems to realize that not only coreference relations can be
syntactically coded but inferences as well. However, judging (1983: 12) 'the role
of semantic and thematic information in topic (i.e. constituent) identification
to be imponderable', such relations are left out of account in his computation
of the degree of t^y of the constituents involved in syntactic variation (cf.
note 4). Consequently, a constituent will be classed as low in t^y because of the
lack of coreferential entities, even if semantically or pragmatically it is
closely related to other items in the surrounding discourse by way of contrast,

class-membership, etc. Leaving such factors out of account does not do justice
to the fact that in Latin they are important enough to cause the selection of a
pattern in which the 'related' constituent is expressed as an accusative Obj.

This fact throws some doubt on the value of t^y measurements in general. If in
discourse such semantic and pragmatic relations are relevant to the selection of
a syntactic pattern in this particular case in Latin, mightn't they be relevant
with respect to the selection of constructions elsewhere too? (for affirmative
evidence cf. Hannay this volume and Pinkster this volume).

4. Summary and conclusion

Several conclusions arise from the observations made in this paper.

(i) Firstly, pragmatic notions such as the distribution of Topic and Focus over
a predication are sometimes relevant to the assignment of the syntactic function
Subj (i.e. the selection of primary perspective), e.g. in the case of the Latin
NcI-construction.

(ii) Secondly, other discourse factors, different from pragmatic function
arrangement, may also have an explanatory power with respect to the selection of
a syntactic pattern. This is illustrated by the assignment of Obj (i.e. the
selection of secondary perspective) in the case of Latin three-place verbs. These
discourse factors are various types of semantic and pragmatic relations, including coreference, but not limited to it, which hold between entities in a discourse. Such cohesive relations make certain constituents 'important' or 'more
salient' in a way different from the notion Focus as currently used in FG: they
may either be Focus or Topic or neither.

Both the first and the second observation may be considered as evidence in
favour of the claim that the pragmatic component of the grammar plays a more
essential role in the formation of sentences than is suggested in earlier surveys of FG (cf. e.g. Dik 1983: 11). This confirms proposals to this effect made
elsewhere, cf. e.g. Nuyts (this volume) and Gvozdanović (1984).

(iii) Thirdly, in order to describe the input - the semantic and pragmatic
input - for the syntactic rules, the notional apparatus both of the lexicon and
of the pragmatic component of FG must be expanded so as to be able to account for
the phenomena discussed in this paper in a satisfactory way. This might mean that
some sort of script or frame semantics should be developed to provide this input
with the required amount of information.

(iv) Fourthly, the data suggest that the selection of perspective may be due to
a psychological principle, namely that of ease of processing. In a sense, there-

fore, Givón's claim that Subj is not an atomic notion but a discourse pragmatic
entity is confirmed (1982: 104, 1984a: 138, 139f). At the same time, of course,
syntactic functions such as Subj and Obj function as a 'signpost' for the hearer:
his attention is directed to the constituents in these functions, even though
other constituents may be more 'salient' in as far as they may carry 'new' information. Cohesiveness as a factor may well be interfered with by either animacy
or semantic function hierarchies (although evidence for this in the case of the
Latin data was not found): here lies an interesting field for further research,
both linguistic and psycholinguistic, e.g. along the lines of Smyth e.a. (1979).
(v)   Fifthly, speakers plan ahead in producing text, at least to a certain degree, and this planning receives syntactic coding. In this respect the data from
Latin are comparable to the data on switch reference systems. For discourse
analysis purposes the question of individual variation between speakers in coding
backward and forward cohesion and between text-types also invites further research
(vi)   Finally, quantitative studies of the correlation between a syntactic variant
and the distribution of coreferential elements through a discourse may be useful
for corroborating hypotheses about the functional motivation for syntactic variation, but they cannot replace it; nor can the latter be inferred from the statistical results in any direct way.

NOTES

[1]   In FG a distinction is made between the phenomenon of Obj assignment with the
verb *to give* on the one hand, and the phenomenon of predicate formation in
the case of a verb such as *to smear* on the other, cf. Dik (1980a: 31-39).
For discussion of where to class the Latin verbs under consideration cf.
Bolkestein (1984). For suggestions as to the predicate formation type of
verbs in German cf. Brömser (1984).

[2]   From Cooreman (in preparation) it appears that each of the four voices in
Chamorro may be used in ways contrary to what would be expected on the basis
of the purely quantitative data (: 105). Cf. for possible factors section 3.
below.

[3]   With respect to IO-promotion, Givón (1984a: 169f, 1984b)

[4]   Cooreman (in preparation, 105f) recognizes that 'higher discourse organizing
principles' and paragraph level topics may interfere with the topicality
score in the selection of voice in Chamorro. The factor 'relatedness' is
illustrated by her discussion of an example in which the entities involved
are not coreferential, but designate two different Agents which happen to
be brothers (cf. my example (18)).

Chapter 2

The typology of embedded predications and the SOV/SVO shift in Western Germanic

Alain Bossuyt
Institute for General Linguistics, University of Amsterdam

1. Introduction*

Dik (1980a: 159) proposes the following sketch of the transition from VSO to SVO:

(1)	TYPE V1	TYPE V2	TYPE V2s	TYPE V3
	P1VSO	P1VSO	P1VSO	P1SVO
	VSO (dom.)	VSO	–	–
	SVO	SVO (dom.)	SVO (dom.)	SVO (dom.)
	OVS	OVS	OVS	OSV
	XVSO	XVSO	XVSO	XSVO
	QVSO	QVSO	QVSO	QSVO
	RelVSO	RelVSO	RelVSO	RelSVO
	SubVSO	SubVSO	SubVSO	SubSVO

(X = any other constituent than S, O or V; Q = question word;

Rel = Relative; Sub = Subordinator)

Transitions between the different stages are accounted for as follows:

(2) a. V1 > V2 : 'markedness shift'

b. V2 > V2s : 'generalization of V2'

c. V2s > V3 : reinterpretation of P1 & introduction of a new P1

Although Modern English (MoE) can be identified as a V3-language (disregarding some relics of V2-order in WH-questions and negatives), and Modern Dutch (MoD) and Modern High German (MoHG) qualify as V2s-languages as far as their main clause patterns are concerned, some important problems arise if one tries to fit the syntactic evolution of the Germanic languages into this sketch, particularly with regard to subordinate clauses. Firstly, none of the Germanic languages, ancient or modern, qualifies as a V1-language. Indeed, even if most workers in the field accept some variation between SOV-order and orders with the verb more to the front in Proto-Germanic already, there is considerable agreement that SOV was the dominant, unmarked order. We may refer to Hopper (1975) for the argument, and to Gerritsen (1978) and Bean (1983) for a survey of the literature.

Secondly, among the Western Germanic languages, it is only in MoE that the subordinate clauses fit into pattern (1). The V3-order of subordinate MoE clauses does not seem to have arisen through the pattern predicted by (1): SOV subordinate clauses occur in OE; P1VSO subordinate clauses, however, are exceedingly rare in all stages of English (Bean 1983). MoHG and MoD have SOV subordinate clauses. These last observations prompt the question whether the variation postulated for Proto-Germanic already corresponded to the syntactic distinction between main and subordinate clauses. Claims to this effect can be traced back at least as far as Wackernagel (1892). Some such claim is implicit moreover in Dik (1980a) when he restricts the relevance of (1) to the evolution in main clauses in Germanic only. We will argue, however, that, following Hopper (1979), the idea of the pragmatic determination of word order is to be preferred for the older Germanic dialects.

Pragmatic determination of the choice of functional pattern is but one aspect of what has been called the 'pragmatic mode' by Givón (1979), a concept which, in terms of the framework of FG, can be translated into the following character-istics (see Bossuyt, in preparation, for a discussion of these characteristics in respect to Givón's proposals):

(3) a. Frequent use of the positions 'outside the predication', P2 (Theme) and P3 (Tail)

b. A preference for parataxis over subordination

c. Pragmatic determination of the choice of functional patterns

d. No, or restricted use of syntactic function assignment (we will not be able to argue this point here, but we may indicate for instance that Object-assignment is not required for the description of MD, Bossuyt forthcoming).

We will argue that starting from a dominantly SOV or Prefield language, we may account for an immediate transition from verb-final to V2 in the Western Germanic languages and the retention of SOV-order in German and Dutch subordinate clauses if the influence of the pragmatic mode is accepted. With respect to OE, we will argue that the sequence |Verb-final - V3 - V2 - V3| proposed by Bean (1983) can be accounted for by the postulate of the pragmatic mode and flattened out into a sequence |Verb-final - V2 - V3|. The final transition from V2 to V3 in English, and the generalization of V3-order to subordinate clauses, can be accounted for if we accept a return to a more pragmatic mode at the end of the OE period.

We will concentrate on the evolution of embedded predications. From the rela-
tor principles defined by Dik (1983) and the Main Verb Principle[1] (Research
Group FG, forthcoming) the following characteristics can be expected for typical
Prefield and Postfield embedded predications:

(4)   I. PREFIELD   II. POSTFIELD

            a. precedes its center   follows its center
            b. final relator   initial relator
            c. non-main verb   finite verb[2]

With respect to this typological distinction, the reconstruction of Proto-
Germanic as a dominantly Prefield language leads to the following expectations:
(i) We would at least expect some relics of typical Prefield embedded predica-
     tions to be found in the older Germanic dialects.
(ii) Initial relators should be a fairly recent development.
These two hypotheses will be tested in the first two sections of this paper.
Although certain intricate philological problems will prevent us from drawing
any straightforward and firm conclusions, the discussion of both points will
provide indications as to the postulated importance of the pragmatic mode. In the
third and last section, we will try to demonstrate the importance of this pragmatic mode for the evolution of word order in the Western Germanic languages.

2. Absolute and appositive participles

In the older Germanic dialects, the most likely relics of typical Prefield embedded
predications are the so-called absolute (5) and appositive participle constructions (6):

(5) a. jah usgaggandum im   us skipa, sunsaiw   ufkannands ina (Mk 6.54)
        and outgoing   them out ship, immediately recognized   (Gothic)
        'and coming out of the ship, they immediately recognized him'

    b. ettendum   him   onfeng   se hæland hlaf (Mk 14.22 Callaway 1918:2)
        eating$_{datpl}$ they$_{datpl}$ accepted the saviour bread
        'After they had eaten, the saviour accepted bread'

(6) a. atgaggandin in gard   þeinana wato mis ana fotins meinans ni
        coming   in garden yours   water me on feet   mine   neg

        gaft (Luc. 7.44) (Gothic)
        gave
        'When I came to your house, you gave me no water for my feet'

b. dæt hie slogon Gode   gehalgodne kyning (OE Callaway 1901, 174-175)
   that they beat   God$_{dat}$ sanctified king
   'that they beat the king sanctified to God'

Though both construction types, except for (6b), exemplify non-finite embedded
predications (typical of Prefield languages), they fail to show all the required
characteristics. The participle, whose case-ending is supposed to be the relator,
stands at the beginning of the construction. Moreover, the examples selected are
somewhat atypical because more often than not these constructions followed their
centers.

Callaway (1889, 1901 and 1918), who has studied both constructions at great
length in OE (Anglo-Saxon and Northumbrian), argues forcefully that the use of
both constructions is due to Latin influence (or Greek in the case of Gothic).
He concludes that they do not constitute Germanic constructions. Only the
adjectival use of the appositive preterite participle (e.g. (6b)), and what he
calls the 'modal' use of present and past appositive participles (i.e. as a
manner adverbial) does he consider as Germanic in origin.

Although we believe that the nineteenth-century philological tradition tended
to overestimate the influence of Latin originals on Vernacular translations,
Callaway succeeds in showing that in wellnigh all OE examples of both constructions a Latin source can be pointed out. Yet, his conclusions as to the non-
Germanic origin of these constructions have been rejected by Hirt (1934: 178-182),
who points out that participial constructions in Gothic may occur when the Greek
'Vorlage' uses a finite verb (e.g. (6a)), always a strong argument in favour of
genuineness of the construction, considering the slavish way in which the Gothic
Bible follows the Greek text. Moreover, he points out that the construction also
occurs in Old Nordic, with or without a preposition, and without there being any
indications of possible Latin influence:

(7) a.   at   liþnom þrimr vetrom
          after passed three winters
          'after three winters had passed'

    b.   lidnum þeim sjau vetrum
          passed the seven winters
          'after seven winters had passed'

          (From Hirt 1934: 182; no sources indicated)

Again, it should be noticed that the participle stands at the beginning of the
construction, but note:

(8)   þessum þrettan utgengum
        these   three   left
        'after these three had left'

The use of a preposition in (7a) could be seen as an adaptation to Postfield
ordering, and so may the position of the participle. Callaway (1901), in his
study of the Anglo-Saxon appositive participle constructions, observes that in
3.3% of the cases only the participle construction precedes its center. Fronting
of the participle, which contains the relator, may be seen as having resulted
from the relator principles once the construction habitually appeared in the
Postfield.

    Yet, in view of these problems, our conclusions with regard to the participle
constructions as possible relics of Prefield embedded predications must remain
extremely tentative, except perhaps for the point that the construction was
losing ground. Its use, if not necessarily its origin, was restricted to texts
with strong Latin (or Greek) influence, and most often with a direct Latin
source. If they constitute a relict of Prefield characteristics, then we must
conclude that the Germanic languages, from our oldest records onwards, were
rapidly losing this characteristic.

    Before leaving these constructions, however, one more observation of Callaway's
(1889, 1901 and 1918) deserves our attention: in his examination of the renderings
into OE of Latin absolute and appositive participle constructions, he notes that
most frequently they are rendered, firstly, by a finite coordinated or paratactic
construction, and only secondly by a finite subordinate clause. This preference
for the use of coordinated, paratactic constructions constitutes a first indication of the importance of the pragmatic mode (3b).

3. Subordinators resulting from P2-integration

As we had to conclude the preceding section with the observation that, whatever
was left of typical Prefield embedded predication, it was nearly lost at the time
of our oldest records, we may expect that an alternative was already present,
either in the form of paratactic constructions, or Postfield embedded predications.
With respect to the latter, it should be noted that there existed a general subordinator (complementizer), common to the Western Germanic languages: OE þe,
OLG and OHG the. It was used to introduce both relative and subordinate clauses:

(9) a. gesecgan þe   þæt sigorbeacan   meted waere (OE from Delbrück 1909: 675)
        say   that the victory-sign found was
        'say that the victory sign was found'

b. od þone anne dæg þe   he wid   þam wyrme gewegan seolde (Delbrück
    till the one day that he against the dragon fight   shall   1909: 677)
    'until the day that he will fight against the dragon'

c. he for to þæm iglande þe   monn þæt   folc   Mandras hætt   (Delbrück
    he went to the island that one the   people Mandras called 1909: 678)
    'he went to the island the people of which were called Mandras'

The exact origin of this subordinator is lost in the mists of time (though, it
corresponds in its use strictly to Gothic *þei*, the relationship is not altogether
clear (cf. Delbrück 1909: 675)).

If the ultimate origin of initial subordinators can no longer be witnessed in
Germanic or Western Germanic, we may observe a growing diversification and a renewal of the initial subordinators in the Western Germanic languages. An important
mechanism for this diversification and renewal was the attraction of an element
originally belonging to the main clause into the first position of the subordinate
clause. Within FG, this may be characterized as an instance of Theme-integration
into the predication, the 'subordinate clause' being originally related to some
element of the main clause as a predication to its Theme. We may list the following cases:

(i)   The rise of a new general subordinator '*dass*' and '*dat*' in German and
        Dutch, derived from the demonstrative, originally occurring in the main
        clause (Paul 1920, IV: 241-251, Weijnen 1971: 68-69, Bossuyt, in prepa-
        ration).

(10)   joh gizalta in   sar, thiu salida   untar in   was (from Paul 1920,
         and told   them soon that the happiness under them was   IV: 241)
(OHG)   'and he told them soon that happiness was amongst them'

         (Paul's comma reflects the pause in the middle of early Germanic verse).

(11)   Ende doen di   joncfrouwe hoerde dat
         and when the lady   heard that
(MD)
         dat hi dus genade bat   (Riddere metter Mouwen, vs. 275-276)
         that he thus mercy asked
         'And when the lady heard that he prayed for mercy in this way'

(ii)   The origin of the use of the demonstrative as a relative pronoun in OE,
        German and Dutch.
        In the OE 'double-barrelled'complementizer construction', *se-þe*, the in-
        flection of the demonstrative clearly shows that it originally belonged
        to the main clause:

(12) a. and þone   gebringan þe   us beagas geaf (Beowulf 3009; Delbrück 1909:
        and the-one bring   that us rings gave 679)
        'and bring to the one who gave us rings'

     b. un   þæm   þe Cwintus haten wæs (Orosius 138, 1; Delbrück 1909:
        under the-one that Cwintus called was 682)
        'under the one who was called Quintus'

c.   c. sælaca   gefeah   mægenbyrþene þara-þe   him mid hæfde (Beowulf
        sea-booty he-enjoyed great-burden thereof-that him with had   1624)
        'He enjoyed the great burden of sea-booty some of which he carried with
        him'

(iii)   The rise of new subordinators from combinations of a preposition or
        adverb with a demonstrative and/or a subordinator.

(13) a. for þæm þe (because)

(OE)   ær þæm þe (before)

        æfter þæm þe (after) (See Wülfing 1901, II, for an extensive list)

     b. bi daz (while)

(OHG/   âne daz (without which)

 MHG)   auf dass (in order that) (Paul 1920, IV, 251-255 for discussion)

     c. om dat (dat) (because)

(MD)   na dat (after)

Even if we must conclude then that the oldest Western Germanic records do not
allow us to trace the ultimate origin of initial subordinators, we may conclude
that integration of a Theme into the subordinate clause provided an important
source for the diversification and renewal of the set of initial relators. This
also points to the importance of the pragmatic mode in the evolution of subordination in the Western Germanic languages (3a).

4. Changes in functional pattern

Admittedly, the findings of the two preceding sections could be used as an argument against a Prefield reconstruction for Proto-Germanic. There are two arguments to refrain us from doing so:

(i)   If, as is suggested by Dik (1983), LIPOC is an important factor in the
        change from SOV to SVO ('leaking'), then it is only to be expected that
        the position of embedded predications will be the first to switch from
        Prefield to Postfield ordering.

(ii)   As a result of this, one may point to languages such as Hungarian, which
          have fairly consistent Prefield-characteristics (postpositions, etc.),
          but have their embedded predications consistently in the Postfield
          (see Research Group FG, forthcoming).

Whether we are right in refusing to draw the ultimate conclusions from the
extent to which our Prefield-expectations have been disconfirmed with regard to
relicts of Prefield embedded predications and the novelty of initial relators
depends on how good a case can be made for SOV as the (pragmatically) unmarked
order in Germanic.

We will largely restrict our discussion of the evolution of word order patterns to OE, firstly because of lack of space, and secondly because the problems
of OE are the most intricate, if also the best studied. We are fortunate to be
able to rely on Bean (1983). The body of this study consists of a statistical
investigation of word orders to be found in nine chronologically succeeding
sections of the *Chronicle*, ranging from the earliest sections of the first re-
daction (probably based on earlier material) to the post-conquest additions of
the Peterborough manuscript (see Bean 1983: 64-66, for philological justification
of her divisions).

A first argument to be advanced in favour of the unmarked nature of SOV-order
is the point that SOV is the only order to occur in all sentence types, main
declarative, conjunct, relative and subordinate clauses, in all but the very last
section. Its lowest frequency is in main declarative clauses, ranging from 3% at
the lowest to 17% at the highest with an average of 5.2%. Though relatively low,
this frequency is sufficient to support the argument that SOV-order as such
could not serve as a marker of subordination, especially not in view of its high
frequency in conjunct clauses, ranging from 53% down to 3%, and with an average
of 37.5% (calculated on the first eight sections).

A second argument in favour of SOV-order as the unmarked order has been advanced by Hopper (1975) on the basis of the observation that in the plain narrative sequences of the *Chronicle* he studied, SOV-sentences occur consistently
within the narrative sequence.

A third argument may be derived from the point that even Bacquet (1962), who
wishes to set up SVO as the unmarked order for main declarative sentences, has
to admit SOV as the neutral order for sentences containing light adverbials and
pronominals only:

(14)   & he hem it wolde tyþian   (from Bean 1983: 64)
          & he him it wanted to grant
          'and he wanted to grant it to him'

Moreover it may be noted that Bacquet can set up SVO as the unmarked order
for main declarative sentences only at the cost of an extreme fragmentation of
his data into different sentence-types, and a refusal to generalize over different types. Yet he runs into difficulties when trying to establish SOV as a
'marked' sentence type (Bacquet 1963: 617-628; see Bossuyt, in preparation, for
a discussion).

From our first argument it follows that some alternative account of the
selection of functional patterns will have to be sought not involving the distinction between main and subordinate clause.

Hopper (1979) sets up the following pragmatic distribution for sentence
patterns in the OE Chronicle:

(15)   SOV: neutral (in 'foregrounded discourse')

         VSO: 'foregrounding'

         SVO: 'backgrounding'

The notions 'backgrounding' and 'foregrounding' are discourse notions: 'foregrounded discourse' is constituted by passages in which the main events of the
narrative are related, and in which the accent lies on the actions, not on any
one of the participants; 'backgrounded discourse', on the contrary, consists of
passages in which the necessary information concerning surroundings and participants in the narrative is provided - new participants are typically introduced
in 'backgrounded discourse'.

Pleasing as this pragmatic account of word-order distribution may be to our
general contention, we have some doubts as to its applicability to texts other
than plain narratives such as the *Chronicle*. Moreover, the question should be
raised whether SVO and VSO really reflected two different word order patterns in
the earliest OE period, or whether both orders ought to be derived from a P1VSO-
functional pattern.[3] We will claim the latter.

Sentence (16) is sufficient to establish the need for a P1VSO-pattern in OE:

(16)   þy   geare gefuhton Mierce   &   Cantware   æt Ottanforda (from Bean
         that year fought   Mercians and Kent-dwellers at Otford   1983: 60)
         'that year, the Mercians and the Kent-dwellers fought at Otford'

The problem, however, is whether it is necessary to accept a P1SVO-pattern
for the description of OE. Bean (1983) argues that it is, and on the basis of
table (17), she argues that OE evolved from SOV to V3, then to V2 and, ultimately,

back to V3. 'This development', she says, 'causes problems for all the current theories of word order change ... we are dealing with a language which has moved from verb final to verb third with no intervening stages and then switched to verb second. Since then, the language has lost its verb second character and redeveloped into a verb third language. Such a progression is not accounted for by anyone's theory' (Bean 1983: 70).

(17)

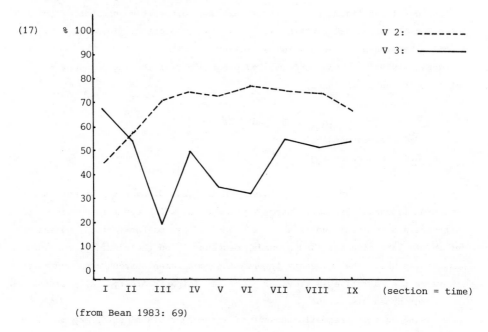

(from Bean 1983: 69)

A first remark to be made with respect to this table is that Bean counts the SVO-sentences as indicative of V3-order, whereas they can in fact be interpreted either way. If we restrict ourselves to actual XSVO-orders, then these orders may be accounted for on the basis of the P2-position and our assumptions concerning the pragmatic mode. Indeed, time and place constituents are very likely to be selected as Themes:

(18) a. As for Paris, the Eiffel Tower is fantastic
     b. In spring, then you should visit Holland

The XVSO-orders which occur in the first section of the *Chronicle* are of the following types:

(19) a. her   Cyneheard ofslog Cynewulf cyning (from Bean 1983: 62)
         in-this-year Cyneheard slew   Cynewulf king
         'In this year, Cyneheard killed King Cynewulf'

   b. & þy ilcan geare Tatwine was gehalgod   to arcebisc   (from Bean 1983:
      & the same year Tatwine was consecrated as archbishop 62)
      'And in the same year, Tatwine was consecrated Archbischop'

In this section, 78 out of 93 XSVO-sentences (83.7%) are of type (19a), while
13 of the rest (14.9%) are of type (19b). As the temporal-locative 'her', and the
introduction 'þy ilcan geare' both belong to a class of likely Theme-candidates,[4]
it is obvious that the XSVO-orders in the earliest OE should be accounted for as
instances of the use of the P2-position. Hence, the number of functional patterns
required for the description of this stage of OE may be reduced to two: P1SOV and
P1VSO. The increase in the use of PVSO-orders in the subsequent section of the
Chronicle (except for section IV), may now be seen as the result of an integration
of the P2-constituent into the P1-position. One indication of this integration is
that in the first section already, 57% of the XVSO-sentences are introduced by
'her', 23% by 'þy ilcan geare' (Bean 1983: 59-85 for the full discussion of the
preceding data).

We have by now reached the preliminary conclusion that the importance of the
pragmatic mode and the P2-position allows us to eliminate the intermediate V3-
stage postulated by Bean (1983). We will now argue that the pragmatic mode may
also help us to account for the apparent absence of a V1-stage.

Starting from a Prefield language with P1SOV-pattern, VSO-patterns may result
from a P1-placement rule by which a Focal verb is placed in P1:

(20)   Focus → P1

Rule (20) neatly accounts for what has been called the 'specialized functions of
the clause-initial verb' in early Germanic by Hopper (1975: 48-50): imperatives,
yes-no questions and conditional clauses. In each of these sentence types, it can
be argued that the verb has been focalised, straightforwardly in the case of
imperatives, in order to bring the truth-value of the whole predication into
focus in the case of yes-no questions and conditionals (i.e. the verb and all its
dependents). This may also account for the use of verb-initial clauses at the
beginning of 'foregrounded discourse' (15).

Of course, a rule like (20) allows for other focal constituents than the verb
to be fronted. This may account for P1VSO-orders resulting from Wackernagel's
law (Wackernagel 1892). Starting from a P1SOV-pattern, P1-placement of a focal

subject on the basis of (20) would require that the P1-position be marked differently from the following S-position. This provides a functional motivation for the tendency to place clitical elements immediately after the P1-position (see e.g. Hopper 1975: 26-36). Wackernagel (1892) argues that light or auxiliary verbs could cliticize to a fronted Subject, thus accounting for early P1VSO-orders. The rise of a P1VSO-pattern may be seen as a result of the operation of rule (20), when both the VSO-orders and the P1VSO-orders resulting from it - the latter in combination with Wackernagel's law - were reinterpreted as an alternative functional pattern.

Unavoidably, the above hypotheses are highly speculative. The following considerations may provide it with some substance:

(i)   The higher frequency of verb-initial sequences in negative than in positive ones (Hopper 1975: 51) can be accounted for along the following lines: P1-placement of a negative in focus combined with Wackernagel's law. This account is moreover crucial in the explanation of the rise of embracing negation (Bossuyt 1982, 1983 and in preparation).

(ii)   The above account would imply that the P1-position, at the earliest stages, was available for focal elements only. In this respect, Bean (1983) notes that in the earliest stages there was a tendency for SVO-order to occur with 'new' subjects, thus confirming Hopper (1979):

(21)   (her   oþiewde cometa se steorra) & Wilfrid biscop was adrifen
        (in-this-year appeared comet the star) & Wilfrid bishop was driven

        of   his bisc dome from Ecgferþe cyninge   (from Bean 1983: 70)
        from his bishopric by   Ecgfrith king
        'In this year a comet appeared, the star, and bishop Wilfrid was driven
        from his bishopric by king Ecgfrith'

        Subsequently, integration of the P2-position into the predication opened up the P1-position for topical elements:

(22)   & hie saldon hiera tuam hefum Stufe & Wihtgare Wiehte ealond (from Bean
        & they sold   their two nephews Stuf & Wihtgar Wight Island 1983: 61)
        'And they sold the Isle of Wight to their two nephews, Stuf & Wihtgar'

        It is the openening up of the P1-position to topical elements through integration into the P1-position which led to the generalization of V2-patterns.

We may summarize our discussion as follows:

(23)   P1VSO + Focus   →   P1: Type V1
                + Pragmatic mode: Type V2

Though it would lead us much too far to pursue this line of thought in this paper, it may be noted that in the Celtic VSO-languages discussed in Dik (1980a), the use of the P1-position seems to be restricted to Focal elements.

If the above account of the early word-order evolution in the Germanic lan-guages is accepted, it follows that the occurrence of P1VSO-patterns was origi-nally restricted to sentences in which Focus-assignment had applied, either to some constituent, or to the whole sentence. The following pragmatic account of the choice of the two functional patterns can then be formulated:

(24)   P1SOV: unmarked

        P1VSO: marked (= Focus or containing the focus of the whole predication)

It would follow from this hypothesis that so-called SVO-patterns in subordinate clauses were restricted to subordinate clauses which were either focal or con-tained the focus of the whole predication. The following observations of Bean's (1983) may substantiate this point:

(i)   When comparing the following sentences, she notes that in the a-sentence, the arrival at Benfleet has been previously mentioned, whereas in the b-sentence, arrival in London has not.

(25) a. ær   Hæsten to Beamflote come
        before Haesten to Benfleet   came
        'before Haesten came to Benfleet'

     b. oþþe hie comon to Lundenbyrg (from Bean 1983: 107)
        until they came to London
        'until they came to London'

(ii)   Bean (1983: 106) notes that throughout the OE period, 'because-clauses' show a tendency towards SVX-order, whereas temporal-locative 'þa-clauses' show a preference for SXV-order. Obviously, the because-clauses are much more likely to be focal or contain the focus of the predication than the temporal-locative clauses which are prime topic or theme candidates.

Bossuyt (in preparation) shows that (24) may also account for the distribution of SVO-patterns in MD subordinate clauses and the few remnants of SOV-order in main clauses. Indeed, with (24) as a starting point, the retention of SOV-orders in Dutch and German as a marker of subordination can be naturally explained: it has been argued (e.g. Sadock 1984) that subordinate clauses tend to contain mainly topical material, which accounts for the dominance of SOV-orders in subordinate clauses from the earliest stages onwards.

5. Conclusions

(i)   The sketch of the transition from VSO to SVO as presented in Dik (1980a) can be maintained as a useful framework within which to discuss the word-order evolution in Germanic, provided we do not see it as a series of stages any language evolving along these lines necessarily has to go through.

(ii)   Hypothesizing an important influence of the pragmatic mode in early (Western) Germanic may account for an immediate transition from Prefield/ SOV to a Type V2-language. It may also account for the retention of SOV as a characteristic of subordination in German and Dutch.

This last part of our conclusion of course raises another problem: how to account for the spread of SVO-patterns in English subordinate clauses and the transition from V2 to V3. Our suggestion would be that towards the end of the OE period, due to an important influx of non-native speakers (Scandinavians in the North and Normans after the Conquest), the pragmatic mode was reintroduced, but we have to refer to Bossuyt (in preparation) for some substantiation of this hypothesis and the analysis of some of its consequences.

One final remark remains to be made. Study of the oldest records and reconstruction are both highly speculative enterprises. Each of the constructions involved is in fact open to multiple analysis, and the crucial evidence for any one of the problems involved is often lacking. The alternative is to decide about each problem with a view to the simplest possible global picture of the changes involved. This paper was devoted to sketching out such a global picture, using general linguistic theory sensitive to different aspects of language use. Even if most of our hypotheses are eventually refuted - and they are certainly desperately in need of further refinements - we hope to have shown that FG, as developed in this volume, may prove a powerful instrument for this type of work.

NOTES

*   This research was supported by the Netherlands Organization for the
    Advancement of Pure Research (ZWO).

[1] The main verb principle states that the first finite verb encountered will
    tend to be interpreted as the main verb.

[2] Strictly, this does not follow from the main verb principle which only pro-
    vides for the tendency for finite verb forms to be avoided if the embedded
    predication precedes its center. Postfield embedded predications may main-
    tain non-main verb forms.

[3] We will not, in this paper, discuss the problem of the brace-pattern
    (P1VfSOVi), nor the problems of 'exbraciation' in OE and ME (see Stockwell
    1977).

[4] The straightforward identification of '*Her*' and '*þy ilcan geare*' as Themes
    is of course not warranted by these two examples, nor by the text-counts of
    Bean (1983); additional textual analysis would be required to strengthen
    this hypothesis. However, the following arguments in favour of this inter-
    pretation may be advanced:

    (i)   at the level of function, by virtue of their temporal semantic function,
          these constituents belong to the class of most likely Theme candidates
          (see Bossuyt, in preparation).
    (ii) at the level of expression, the identification of these elements as
          P2-constituents allows for the most elegant and simple treatment of the
          OE data, and also for the simplest account of the word-order changes in
          OE (cf. the closing remark of the present paper).

Chapter 3

Functional grammar and intonation

Lucas van Buuren
Department of English, University of Amsterdam

0. Introduction and summary

The present paper emerged out of an on-going investigation by the author into the
applicability of Functional Grammar to intonation studies. The research was undertaken because FG appears to be one of the few serious linguistic theories with a
pragmatic component capable, in principle, of incorporating the observations made
by intonationalists over the past half-century. Here, after bringing one intonational analysis in line with it, we shall critically examine the usefulness of
some of the FG pragmatic concepts, especially that of 'focus'. Where such concepts
are felt to be inadequate (or indeed non-existent), positive alternatives will be
suggested, however with the proviso that the specialized nature of our approach
does not permit of sweeping generalisations.

   Part 1 lists different ways of 'packaging' a sentence, concluding that 'intonational prominence' (= tonicity) is the most important variable.

   Part 2 presents an intonational analysis of British English. Sections 2.1. and
2.2. say something about the relationship between intonation and rhythm. In 2.3.
the effect of tonicity is said to create a 'contrast with whatever', thereby
querying the FG notion of 'binary contrast'. Section 2.4. suggests that the
'scope' of the tonic is not confined to either constituent or predication but
takes in different stretches simultaneously. Section 2.5. deals with 'tune', the
well-known distinction between falling and rising intonation patterns, and 2.6.
with 'tonality', the equally well-known differences in tonic movement: high fall,
low fall, rise-fall, fall-rise, etc. So far, neither tune nor tonality have been
taken into consideration in developing FG pragmatic theory.

   Part 3 attempts to identify some of the major obstacles in FG theory to incorporating intonation. While the linguistic relevance of intonation appears obvious
(3.1.), FG theorists do not seem to be able to make up their minds about it, or
about phonology in general (3.2.). Section 3.3. criticizes the inconsistent use
of the Focus function, thereby making it incompatible with any intonational correlate. Other serious obstacles are the crucial role afforded to the 'addressee's
pragmatic knowledge' (3.4.) and the conflation of meaning and interpretation (3.5.)
(3.5.). Consequently, the FG typology of Focus is rejected (3.6.), a more realis-

tic alternative being suggested in our discussion of tune and tonality. Finally,
3.7. proposes that it might be more profitable for FG to approach the 'simplicity'
of Focus types in tone-languages from the known complexity in intonation languages
rather that the other way round as has been done.

1. Content versus expression

If I inform you that Penelope gave your kipper to the cat this morning, you might
well object to what I say, or the way I say it, or to both. The content can be
stated as a predication. Leaving out unnecessary detail:

(1)   Past give$_V$ (Penelope)$_{Ag}$ (your kipper)$_{Go}$ (the cat)$_{Rec}$ (this morning)$_{Temp}$

The way I say it, its expression or 'packaging', depends on the use I make of a
number of strategies at my disposal (cf. Dik 1978: 127). The most important of
these by far is tonicity or 'intonational prominence' (examples 2-7), shown by
capital letters. This is the most versatile strategy and its use is in fact
obligatory in every utterance one utters. The next most important strategies are
probably substitutions and ellipsis (3). In comparison, use of the passive voice
(4) is quite rare. Rarer still are the other strategies exemplified: fronting
(5), left and right dislocation (6), cleaving and pseudo-cleaving (7):

(2) a.   penelope gave your KIPper to the cat this morning

    b.   peNElope gave your kipper to the cat this morning

    c.   penelope GAVE your kipper to the CAT this morning

    d.   peNElope gave YOUR kipper to the cat this MORning

(3) a.   she gave her your KIPper this morning

    b.   she gave it to HER this MORning

    c.   she GAVE it to the cat

    d.   this MORning

    e.   she DID

    f.   HER

    g.   YES

    h.   MM

(4) a.   the CAT was given your kipper by peNElope

    b.   your kipper was given to the cat this MORning

(5) a.   your kipper she gave to the CAT this morning

    b.   this MORning penelope gave your KIPper to the cat

(6) a. your KIPper she gave it to the CAT this morning

   b. the CAT she was GIVen your kipper this morning

   c. peNElope gave it to the CAT your KIPper

   d. she GAVE her your KIPper to the cat

(7) a. it was the CAT she gave your kipper to this morning

   b. it was your KIPper she GAVE to the cat this MORning

   c. it was this morning she gave YOUR kipper to the cat

   d. your KIPper was what she gave to the cat

   e. what she did was give your KIPper to the cat

These 25 different ways of expressing the same state of affairs are merely a
very small selection, and that is not even considering rhythmic and voice
quality variations.

   The following set of examples would presumably be regarded as describing
other states of affairs, i.e. as not having the same truth value (cf. Dik 1978:
71). But it must be said that 'truth value' is apparently not such a clear-cut
criterion, as different languages draw the line in different places.

(8) a. the one/the person who gave your KIPper to the cat was peNElope

   b. what she actually DID do was to give your KIPper to the cat

   c. ALL she did was give your KIPper to the cat this morning

(9) a. she just gave your KIPper to the cat

   b. she only/ALso/ACtually gave your kipper to the CAT

   c. peNElope gave your KIPper to the bloody CAT this morning

   d. all RIGHT she gave your flaming FISH to the flipping cat so WHAT

   One thing should be perfectly clear. One cannot deal with these phenomena if
one cannot handle intonation. Part 2 sets out the intonation of (British) English. The description is a shortened and updated version of Van Buuren (1981).
It has been improved (I hope) on the meaning side as a result of reading the FG
literature on 'Focus' (Dik et al. 1981, De Jong 1980, Hannay 1983), and
Keijsper's work on the meaning of accentuation, especially Keijsper (1983, 1984).

2. Intonation

2.1. Rhythm

If one reads out the following examples on a monotone, as in a prayer, one will
find that the rhythmic differences are preserved. Rhythm, as any drummer will
tell us, is independent of pitch.

(10) a. pe'nelope | 'gave | your 'kipper | to the 'cat | this 'morning |||

　　 b. pe'nelope || gave 'your ,kipper || to the 'cat | this 'morning |||

Phonologically, (10a) is one locution (|||), consisting of 1 piece (||), consist-
ing of 5 bits (|); (10b) is one locution consisting of 3 pieces consisting of 1,
1 and 2 bits respectively. Each bit always has one strongly stressed syllable S,
most other syllables have weak stress W, some may have medium stress M. Bit-
division and stressing are rhythmic matters which should be kept clearly distinct
from intonation.

2.2. Tonicity

Given a particular rhythmic pattern one can take an upward or downward jump in
pitch on each S-syllable, thereby making it tonic (t), or one can not make such
a movement, thereby leaving it non-tonic (o). So there are as many potential
tonics as there are bits/stresses, but there must be (except in prayer) a minimum
of one tonic. Thus, in for example (10a) there are 2x2x2x2x2 = 32 possibilities,
some of which are (11a-e):

(11) a. peNElope gave your kipper to the cat this morning   (toooo)

　　 b. penelope gave your KIPper to the CAT this morning   (ootto)

　　 c. peNElope GAVE your kipper to the CAT this morning   (ttoto)

　　 d. peNElope GAVE your KIPper to the cat this MORning   (tttot)

　　 e. peNElope GAVE your KIPper to the CAT this MORning   (ttttt)

Taking the simplest case of an upward jump followed by a fall on the S-syllable,
the pitch pattern of (11c) would be (12):

(12)   figure 1

As is customary, the dashes are for S-syllables and the dots for W-syllables.
The interval between the two parallel lines is, say, about an octave. At this
point one should read out the other examples in (11) and work out some more.

2.3. Effect of tonicity

Tonicity is a kind of 'vocal pointing'. Say that Samantha and Charlie are in the
same company as myself, and I'm standing at a table laden with goodies. Then I

could say to someone

(13)   give THIS to HER and THAT to HIM

using my index-finger to point out THIS, THAT, HIM and HER. But if I'm in another
room I shall have to say something like

(14)   give some CHOColates to saMANtha and the gorgonZOla to CHARlie

Similarly, if we are all in the same room, I can point my finger at Penelope, the
cat and what is left of your kipper, and say

(15)   SHE gave THAT to HER this morning

Of course one cannot literally point one's finger at non-physical things like
'giving' or 'this morning'. Nevertheless, one observes that people are always
making gestures with their hands, head, eyes and eyebrows on the tonic words,
even if these have abstract referents. In short, tonicity is vocal gesturing,
closely integrated with and supplementing other gestures.

Secondly, it appears to me that the meaning of pointing is 'that rather than
whatever'. What whatever is depends on the circumstances. Pointing at red in a
red-or-green traffic light system means 'red not green': this is a specific
binary contrast. In the usual red-amber-green system it means 'red not amber or
green': a ternary specific contrast. Pointing at red on a colour-chart means
'red, not one of the others', in a toy-shop 'the red item, not one of the others',
in a landscape 'red, not non-red', the latter including the sky, the hills and
the people. The difference between a specific binary contrast and a non-specific
multiple contrast seems very much a matter of degree.

What this all amounts to is that pointing, and thereby tonicity, means 'contrast', however not necessarily in the usual FG sense of binary contrast, but in
the sense of 'contrast with whatever'.

The obvious term for the thing pointed at would be 'focus', and I think this
is more or less what it used to mean. But focus and focusing have now acquired
so many other meanings in Functional Grammar and other approaches that I shall
use 'indicatum' and 'pointing' instead.

2.4. *Scope of the tonic*

Finding 'scope' one of the most difficult aspects of intonation, I can only put forward ideas rather than solutions.

(16) a. she gave your KIPper to the cat

  b. she DID give me some lousy advice

In Functional Grammar (16a) will be regarded as having constituent scope, (16b) as having predication scope (Dik et al. 1981: 52). I would be more inclined to look for a solution in terms of scope 'expanding' from the smallest to the largest. Thus (16a) contrasts, first of all, with *she gave your something else to the cat*, but also, by extension, with *she gave something else to the cat, she did something else for the cat, she did something else, something else happened,* etcetera. Perhaps this is better put like this:

(17)   she gave your KIPper (vs. not: KIPper) to the cat

     she gave your KIPper (vs. not: your KIPper) to the cat

     she gave your KIPper (vs. not: gave your KIPper) to the cat

     she gave your KIPper to the cat (vs. not: gave your KIPper to the cat)

     she gave your KIPper to the cat (vs. not: she gave your KIPper to the cat)

     etc.

In other words, (16a) could be a perfectly acceptable answer (especially on a Rising tune, see below, 2.6.) to any of the following questions: *did she give my goldfish to the cat, did she give her canary to the cat, did she strangle the cat, did she mow the lawn, are you having your breakfast.*

So (16a) doesn't have one particular implication or interpretation, but a whole range of them. The *meaning* of (16a), I feel, is not one of these interpretations, but the whole range. I don't know whether speaker and/or addressee have to commit themselves to only one scope or interpretation on any particular occasion. But in any case, language itself is quite vague in these matters, which is probably just as well. The same argument applies to (16b) which would be regarded in FG as having polarity or predication scope, it being in contrast with *she DIDn't give me some lousy advice*. But that again seems to be confusing meaning with the most likely interpretation, ascribing more precision to language than it has. Especially if said on a Rising tune, (16b) could be a perfectly reasonable answer not only to *didn't she give you some lousy advice* but also to *will*

she give you some lousy advice, wouldn't she offer you some lousy advice,
couldn't she offer you some help, did she say anything, are you all right. See
Smith and Wilson (1979) for comparable ideas on 'semantic entailment'.

2.5. *Tune*

Any piece may be said on a rising (R) or a falling (F) intonation. The phenomenon
is widely known, witness such terms as question and statement intonation. But
these terms are better forgotten, as the choice between F and R has nothing to do
with statements and questions in the usual sense.

    Phonetically, the matter is extremely simple. R tunes end with a rising pitch
on their final syllable, F tunes do not. The difference is also a matter of degree: the rise may be very small, very large, or something in between. Meaning-
wise, F conveys: *alternatives closed*, hence its assertive connotations. It is
used for instance in categorical statements and answers, demanding questions,
rhetorical questions, commands, warnings. R means: *alternatives open*, hence its
inconclusive or querying connotations. It is used in non-final pieces to indicate
that there is more coming, in inconclusive statements and answers, in enquiries,
requests, invitations, vocatives, greetings, in short, when one is appealing to a
listener for his or her attention, response, co-operation and the like.

    A difficult question to answer is: alternatives to what? But I'll try. The
problem is related to that of scope of tonicity. Since tune is a feature of
pieces rather than bits, however, it may be better in this case to think in terms
of contracting rather than expanding scope. The answer, then, seems to be: alternatives to what you please, from the whole predication down to the tonic ele-
ment(s). For example.

(18) ^{R}did peNElope give my KIPper to the cat

can imply that alternatives are being left open to Penelope, to kipper, to both
or to the whole question, so that one might answer it for instance by *no, Charlie;*
no, your canary; no, Charlie gave her your canary; no, she went to the pictures,
and so on.

    Tune can have far-reaching effects on a negative predication like

(19) $^{F/R}$Pe'nelope | 'didn't | 'teach | our 'children | 'anything |||

    With CHILdren tonic, F suggests: it was our children (alternatives closed) she didn't teach anything. R suggests: it wasn't our children (alternatives open) she taught, but other persons.

With a tonic on TEACH, F suggests: it was teaching (no alternatives left open) she didn't do. R suggests: it wasn't teaching (alternatives open) she did to our children, but something quite different.

With a tonic on ANything, F suggests: it was anything you care to name (without any alternatives left open) that she didn't teach them, i.e. she taught them nothing. R suggests: it wasn't just anything you may name (with alternatives left open, i.e. there was something) that she taught them. In other words, she taught them some jolly good stuff, not just any old rubbish.

I am now clearly submitting to the temptation of reading too much meaning into these examples. Again, we are no longer looking at meanings but at interpretations. The meaning difference between F and R is very subtle, very general and very simple: no alternatives left open versus some or many alternatives left open. Perhaps we could refer to this pragmatic strategy as 'conclusiveness' or 'commitment'.

So far, it has not been taken into consideration in the FG literature.

2.6. Tonality

By making different kinds of pitch jumps one can point at an indicatum in different ways. This leads to a sub-division of 'tonic' which I shall call 'tonality'. Note that, in spite of superficial similarities, it has nothing in common with the sub-division of 'Focus' in FG (see 3.6., below).

(20) $^{F/R}$pe'nelope | 'didn't | 'give | your 'KIPper | to the 'cat |||

figure 2

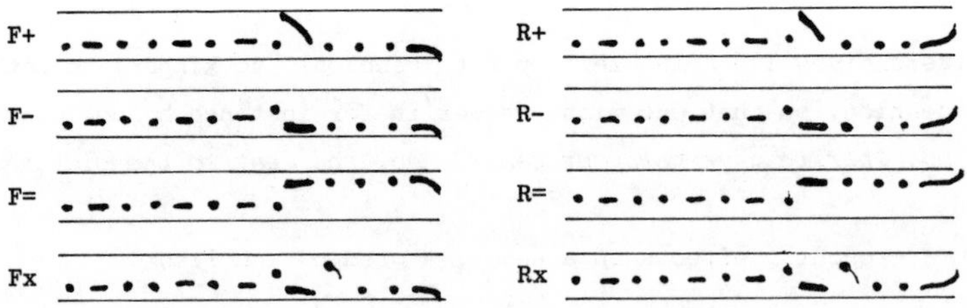

The indicatum of this piece is KIPPER. Then one must take a pitch-jump on the tonic syllable KIP. This can be done in four ways:

(i) *+tonic: preferred alternative*. Upward jump followed by falling movement
during tonic syllable. This option is taken to single out the indicatum rather
than any other alternative: a specific, preferred choice, typically accompanied
by pointing with the index finger. The plus tonic is also the most common and
therefore the neutral one; the next three may be regarded as deviations from it.

(ii) *-tonic: expected alternative*. Downward jump. The indicatum is pointed at
as the expected, remaining or obvious alternative, all other alternatives being
exhausted; typically accompanied by a nod of the head. Minus tonics are very
common on the last indicatum in a series, as in counting. They are also used for
toning down the force of assertions and questions, i.e. for understatement.

(iii)*=tonic: equal or random alternative*. Upward jump. The indicatum is presented as an equivalent or self-evident alternative, the result of an uncommitted,
unconvinced or random selection. It is typically accompanied by a wave of the
hand. R= is common in lists and surprised questions. F= is quite rare in Southern
English, possibly because the combination of random alternative and no alternatives left open is felt to be rather bloody-minded.

(iv) *xtonic: exclusive alternative*. Downward jump followed by a rising-falling
movement. This points out the indicatum as the exclusive or unique alternative,
the speaker having rejected all others. It is very English in the sense that
there seems to be nothing like it in the neighbouring languages, but it is marginal in the sense of being rather restricted in its usage, and sometimes hardly
distinguishable from +tonic. It is most effectively used with emotive words like
beautiful, scandalous, delicious.

　　If all this is not immediately convincing, perhaps this is:

(21)　　$F+$your HOUSE is on fire. Help. Do something

　　　　$F-$your HOUSE is on fire. Just what you might expect

　　　　$F=$your HOUSE is on fire. To mention a random point of interest

　　　　Fxyour HOUSE is on fire. Isn't that fascinating

By making one's pitch-jumps bigger or smaller (within an overall span of about
one octave), one can present the indicatum as more specific, expected, random or
exclusive, or less so. These are all matters of degree. It is interesting to reflect that the distinctions between +/-/=/x are also gradual, but this is an
extra complication that is better ignored for the moment.

　　When there is more than one tonic, the non-final ones can either be ≠tonic
(: unexpected) or -tonic (: expected). By the symbol ≠ I indicate that in such
positions there is no x, and that the distinction +/= is neutralised. In such

non-final positions -tonic is again realised as a downward jump. The realisation
of ≠tonic is a little more complicated: it is like = (upward jump) if the next
tonic is - or x, like + (upward jump plus fall) otherwise (so it is perhaps less
confusing to write = and + respectively instead of ≠, as long as one remembers
that they do not stand for 'equal' and 'preferred' but for something in between:
unexpected).

We can now generate 3x3x3x3x5 = 405 F patterns for our example, and as many R
patterns. All 810 of them are quite common, and they all have different meanings
on the pragmatic level. A few are shown below.

(22)   pe'nelope | 'didn't | 'give | your 'kipper | to the 'cat |||

figure 3

F+oooo	R+oooo
Foo+oo	Ro+oo+
Fo+oo=	R-oo=o
F+=oxo	R=oo-x
F-=-ox	R++=oo
F+++++	R+=-=-
F-----	R----+

3. Some implications for Functional Grammar

3.1. Integrating an intonational analysis into a Functional Grammar framework

So far, I have tried to show that the enormous complexity of English intonation
can be reduced to a few pragmatic choices that have to do with pointing at things
and contrasting them in various ways with their alternatives. My analysis may be
compared to such as those by Halliday (1967), O'Connor and Arnold (1973) and (for
Dutch) Keijsper (1984). In general, the study of intonation would appear to be a
sine qua non for the development of the pragmatic framework of FG. From the point
of view of the intonationalist it is equally desirable to be able to relate one's

work to a theory of language that has a pragmatic component.

As can be seen by comparing the present analysis with earlier work on intonation by myself and others, a number of adjustments have been made to bring it more in line with FG theory. Also, I have touched upon a number of notions central to FG 'pragmatics', such as contrast, scope (both of focus and negation), focus typology, and meaning versus interpretation. It remains to see if and how FG can accommodate an intonational analysis such as this.

The reader will have realised that there remain considerable differences in approach, so that this will be quite a major undertaking. I shall therefore confine myself here to a few comments on what seem to be the most serious obstacles to such an integration, leaving more embracing theoretical considerations in the lap of the future.

3.2. The place of intonation in the theory of Functional Grammar

Until now, FG has made no attempt to account for intonation. Its theorists have taken a rather ambivalent, not to say cavalier attitude to it, witness:

(i)   Intonational prominence is repeatedly mentioned in the literature as the first 'expressive device for signalling Focus', besides constituent ordering, special Focus markers, etc.

(ii)   'Although Focus and primary stress (= tonic, LvB) are not held to coincide, those constituents bearing primary stress will also tend to be assigned Focus function.' (Hannay 1983: 211)

(iii)   'I do not identify Focus with "constituent receiving main stress" (= tonic, LvB), although components with Focus function will often be realised by such constituents.' (Dik 1978: 131)

(iv)   One requires the Focus function 'in order to account for the intonational prominence of these constituents (contrastive stress).' (Dik et al. 1981: 69)

(v)   The terms intonation, tonic, stress, etc. are not to be found in the index to Dik's *Functional Grammar* (1978).

One feels that the linguistic importance of intonation is recognised, but not the necessity to investigate it. Indeed there has been no attempt at all to develop a phonological component. Consequently, linguists working on the phonetics and phonology of language may well tend to turn away from FG, as it offers them no point of contact. If this situation is allowed to persist, I feel that FG could develop into a theory of written language only.

3.3. The use of the Focus function in Functional Grammar

There are two predication-internal pragmatic functions:
'*Focus*: a constituent with Focus function provides the relatively most important or salient information in the given context and situation' (Dik 1978: 93) '... with respect to the pragmatic information of the Speaker and the Addressee' (1978: 92).
'*Topic*: a constituent with Topic function refers to an entity assumed by the speaker to be "known" or "given" to the Addressee, and about which the predication predicates something' (Dik 1978: 92).

Focus is invariably assigned to 'Q-words in Q-word questions, cleft constituents, and constituents presenting contrasted information' (Hannay 1983: 207). It makes no difference whether the constituent in question is tonic or non-tonic. Nor does it matter (which may possibly amount to the same thing) whether it provides the most important information or not.

The rationale for assigning Focus to Q-terms is that its identity 'is the only piece of information belonging to the difference in pragmatic information between Speaker and Addressee, as estimated by the Speaker' (Dik 1978: 150). As pointed out by Hannay (1983: 212) however, when talking about Denis and Margaret Thatcher the most important information in (23a) is provided by the element DENis. Analogically, it is provided by KIPper in (23b, c).

(23) a. why did DENis go to sri lanka
     b. who has eaten up my KIPper
     c. when did you eat up my KIPper

I would go one step further than Hannay, and suggest that the Q-word does not provide the listener with any information at all. Thus, by saying (23c) I'm informing my listener that she ate up my KIPper at a time unknown to me, and that my predication is about that time. If anything, I should think that the Q-word fits the definition of Topic, not of Focus. Cf. Dik (1978: 151). Similarly, in a cleft construction like (7c) Focus would be assigned to the informationally unimportant 'this morning' (Dik: ibid.) rather than to the indicatum 'YOUR (kipper)', unless YOUR is a term in a specific binary contrast (Dik et al. 1980: 58), when it receives Focus as well.

This brings us to the other side of the picture. We have seen that the Focus function is used for elements that do not carry new or important information. Now we also see that it need not be assigned to items that do carry such infor-

mation. More specifically: many indicatums, perhaps the majority of them, will
not receive the Focus function. They will receive it if they are in a specific
binary contrast to something else; they will also receive it if they fill 'a gap
in the pragmatic information of the addressee' (Dik et al. 1981: 60), but not
otherwise. If I say to you

(24)   you're CLEVER

Focus will be assigned to the indicatum if you didn't know, or if you think you
are stupid, but not if you know already that you are clever (or in two minds
about it), no matter how important my information may be to you.

It seems that the Focus function is not being used very consistently as a
result of mixing syntactic, informational and contextual criteria. It is therefore extremely difficult for the student of intonation to relate indicatums,
which are always important information-points, to the FG concept of Focus.

3.4. The status of the speaker's assessment of the addressee's pragmatic knowledge

This turns out to be a crucial criterion in FG. It derives from the view that
'the primary function of a language is communication' (Dik 1978: 5) and that 'the
primary function of communication is to effect changes in the pragmatic information of the other' (1978: 128). Clearly, from the intonationalist's point of view
matters would be considerably simplified if this criterion could be dropped.

An argument in favour is that it gives full weight to the interpersonal and
communicative aspect of language. Indeed the state of the addressee's knowledge
can determine to a considerable extent what a speaker says and how he says it.
But such a view can be taken too far, and it seems to me that that is indeed the
case in the definition of pragmatic functions like Focus.

The addressee's pragmatic knowledge is a feature of the situation, and so is
the speaker's assessment thereof, if he makes one. Neither of them are susceptible
to direct observation. The Focus function, it is said, is 'an underlying function
co-determining the realisation of predications' (Dik 1978: 131). So the way I
understand it, it is meant to predict how a speaker will say something on the
basis of (covert) features of the situation. Now, most linguists will agree nowa-
days that speakers do not react to situations in such a mechanical manner. Except
in the most diabolical situations one always has considerable freedom as to what
one says and how one says it.

Apart from that one may also query the idea that language is primarily a means

for communicating information. Anyone who has asked for the way in a strange
city knows that many people do not succeed very well in communicating the simplest ideas, to say nothing of all those who, throughout the history of mankind,
have preferred war-war-war to jaw-jaw-jaw as a means of explaining their point
of view. This somewhat idealistic view also seems to ignore the many other functions of speech such as lying, cheating, joking, bullying, thinking aloud, expressing one's personality and maintaining relationships. Personally, I feel
that much of the time I'm too busy thinking about myself to assess in such fine
detail how much the other party knows, and sometimes I frankly don't care. The
speaker's assessment of the gaps in the addressee's pragmatic knowledge is not
so crucially important as suggested in the FG literature. In my opinion the criterion should be seriously re-examined.

3.5. Meaning versus use or interpretation

In 2.5. and 2.6. I made a distinction between the rather subtle and general
meanings of tonic placement and tune versus their specific uses or interpretations. From a speaker's point of view the linguistic form 'tonic', meaning 'contrast with whatever' has various specific uses, for an observer various interpretations. If we call it Focus in one case, emphasis in another and nothing in
a third, then we are not dealing with meaning but with uses or interpretations.
It is like saying that the progressive form in English 'means' continuity of
action, determination, descriptiveness, future intention, etc., depending on the
occasion. Indeed, this is what we find - and condemn - in traditional grammars.
But it is precisely what FG does in the way it allocates completive, selective,
expanding, restricting, replacing and parallel Focus, Topic, or nothing at all
to one and the same tonic movement. One wonders why, as it seems at odds with
what Dik was writing in 1968: 'In my view a linguistic description does not describe how a particular speaker-hearer .. uses his language in speaking and
interpreting. Rather, it describes the system of language as such, in abstraction
from how it is known or used, thus providing an answer to the question: what is
the structure of the linguistic expressions of this language.' (Dik 1968: 162)

For the purposes of intonation at least, it would be convenient if FG should
revert to the earlier point of view.

3.6. Types of Focus

The diagram in (25) is a slightly adapted version of that in Dik et al. (1980:
60). In (26) WYT stands for 'What You Thought', WIS for 'What I Say'.

(25)   figure 4

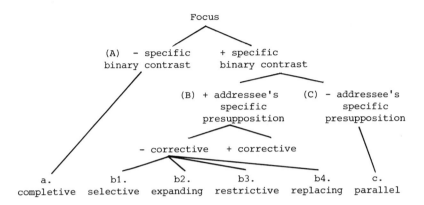

(26) a.   she gave your KIPper (rather than whatever) to the cat

b1. she gave your KIPper (choice from 2 WYTs) to the cat

b2. she gave your KIPper (also, besides WYT) to the cat

b3. she gave your KIPper (only, not the whole WYT) to the cat

b4. she gave your KIPper (instead of WYT) to the cat

c.   she gave (your WIS1 to the WIS2 and) your KIPper to the CAT

As shown, this sub-division of the Focus function is largely on the basis of the addressee's pragmatic information. Note that the various types can not be distinguished in English by the usual pragmatic means of expression: intonation, constituent ordering, special particles, etc. They can only be fully expressed by lexical and syntactic means, in which case they have, I think, different truth values. To my mind, we are not dealing here at all with pragmatic phenomena in the usual sense, but with semantic differences.

This sub-division of Focus, therefore, has nothing in common with tonality, the sub-division of tonic. In order to account for tonality, FG theorists would have to think along the lines of a sub-division of a. (completive) rather than of b. and c.

Also, if the Focus concept is to be kept for various kinds of highlighting as it is at present, rather than merely for 'pointing', one might think of a sub-division on the basis of other formal criteria than intonation. Clearly, the pragmatic functions of ellipsis, passivization, fronting and cleaving (examples 3-7) are quite different from pointing, having to do with such things as explicitness, agent-suppression, point of departure, tracing a path through a predication, and identification. All these things seem to me much more important than the detailed classification of specific binary contrasts, which are perhaps only used in arguments and quarrels. I should like to think that my analysis of tonality and tune may perhaps help to arrive at a more realistic typology of Focus.

3.7. Pointing in tone-languages

The FG classification of Focus types derives immediately from Watters' (1979) analysis of Focus in Aghem, a tone-language spoken in Cameroon. De Jong (1980) also discusses Focus in Efik (Nigeria) and Rendille (Kenya). The trouble with these languages, apart from the fact that most of us do not know them very well, is that some of them do not appear to have any intonation. Watters (1979: 190): 'Note that Aghem does not exploit the phonological structures of the language to mark a focused constituent, as is done in English for example. Thus, Aghem is one of the numerous tone languages in the world which mark the focus by non-phonological means.' If this is so, it would appear that Aghem has an extremely simple system of pragmatic choices in comparison with the complexity of English or Dutch, and then it ought to be the last language to derive a typology of Focus from.

This raises the interesting question if and how pointing, and our different types of pointing, are achieved in tone-languages. After all, there seems to be no shortage of gesturing in these languages, and I personally find it difficult to imagine that there are no linguistic correlates. My own observations on English, Dutch (non-tonal), Norwegian (tonal accent), Chinese (contour tone) and the Nigerian language Yoruba (register tone) suggest that they all use pitch and/or timing for pointing (tonicity) and commitment (tune). Tonality (types of pointing) is most varied in English, less so in Dutch, less so in Norwegian, and I have not been able to discover any of it in Chinese and Yoruba.

There is a great deal of confusion about these things, and a great deal of conflicting evidence. Miller and Tench (1982: 79) state that in Hausa (Nigeria) 'A unit of intonation (or "tone group") does not contain a "tonic" syllable and the notion of "tonicity" does not apply. Hausa intonation manifestly lacks the tonic shifting possibilities that a language like English possesses.' On the other hand, Van den Eynde and Kyota (1984) write about Yaka (Zaire) that 'la flexion tonale du yaka se rapproche d'une structure intonative comme celle décrite pour le néerlandais dans Van Dooren & Van den Eynde (1982, 1983), et pour l'anglais par les mêmes auteurs dans une autre communication au présent colloque.'

For FG linguistics, with its bias towards typological investigation, this would
seem a very worthy area of research. Of course, one would have to be able to
handle pitch and rhythm. It may not be a bad idea at all to take English intonation as a point of departure.

Chapter 4

Inferrability, discourse-boundness, and sub-topics

Mike Hannay
Department of English, Free University of Amsterdam

1. Introduction

While the Topic function in Functional Grammar (henceforth FG) is not given a strictly formal definition but rather a discourse-sensitive one - it is admittedly assigned to a sentence constituent but not to a specific one in the surface linear order; the constituent refers to an entity presented by the speaker and the status of that entity in the discourse setting is crucial - it remains a function which is relevant at sentence-level description. But precisely because it is a discourse-related concept, it must be defined and specified in terms which as precisely as possible relate the individual linguistic expression to the wider discourse setting.

One of the most important tasks in characterising the nature of Topic constituents is thus to specify the necessary contextual conditions which must hold for an entity to be available for Topic selection by the speaker. This will involve investigating the relationship between Topic and given/new information, a relationship which is assumed in FG but left unspecified (cf. Dik 1978: 131; Dik et al. 1981: 44). In what follows I shall first of all sketch a number of minimal assumptions that one can make with respect to the relationship between Topic and Focus on the one hand and given and new information on the other hand. Subsequently I will look at the distinctions made by Prince (1981) with respect to given/new information, paying particular attention to the status of inferrable entities and their claims to Topic candidacy. This will result in the formulation of a rule of sub-Topic formation in FG. Sub-Topic entities differ in kind from 'full' Topics in more or less the same way that inferrables differ from Prince's evoked entity category. Furthermore, I will claim that they have the crucial feature of discourse-boundness in common with evoked entities, their essential dual given/new nature may be reflected in particular settings where, while being involved in the same state of affairs, the speaker appears to have the option of assigning them sub-Topic status or treating them as part of an all-new predication.

2. The Topic function in Functional Grammar

The Topic function is defined as follows (Dik 1978: 130):

(1)   A constituent with Topic function presents the entity 'about' which the
         Predication predicates something in the given setting.

There are two circumstances in which a predication is considered to be Topicless.
The first concerns so-called 'all-new' predications, which may be described as
bare assertions of states of affairs which involve no presuppositions on the part
of the speaker (cf. Dik et al. 1981: 44). The most typical examples of this are
discourse-initial sentences like (2) and replies to *what happened?* questions, as
in (3)[1] (a- and b-sentences in this paper form stretches of coherent discourse):

(2)   This man goes into a shop and ...
(3) a.   What happened?
    b.   The cat broke a vase

Expressions like those in (2) and (3b) may be represented in one of two different
ways. One might either assign Focus function to each constituent in the representation or assign no pragmatic function at all (cf. Dik et al. 1981: 51).
     The second instance of a Topicless predication concerns expressions which do
indeed involve speaker presuppositions, but whose presuppositional content is not
reflected in a term, and of course only terms can be assigned Topic function.
Thus in (4b) the presupposition that someone is ill is involved, but the expression itself does not constitute a predication about that unidentified entity. In
contrast, this is the case in (5), and accordingly (4b) and (5) would be represented as in (6) and (7) respectively:

(4) a.   Who's ill?
    b.   John is ill
(5)   The one who's ill is John
(6) $\text{ill}_A \ (\text{d1x}_i: \text{John}(x_i))_{\emptyset\text{SubjFoc}}$
(7) $(\text{d1x}_j: \text{John}(x_j))_{\text{Foc}} \ \ (\text{d1x}_i: \text{ill}_A \ (x_i))_{\emptyset\text{SubjTop}}$

Both situations mentioned here are accounted for in the Topic definition. With
respect to all-new predications Topiclessness is enforced by the use of the expression 'in the given setting'. The second kind of Topiclessness arises from
the restriction in the definition that Topic status is assigned to entities only.
     There is a strong association between the Topic function on the one hand and
the notion of given information on the other. To set the scene for the later

discussion I am going to assume the following:

(i) It is clear that the Topic-given relation is problematic because givenness itself is open to a number of interpretations. On a first, very broad level, an entity may be seen as given if it is assumed to belong to the pragmatic knowledge of speaker and hearer. At a second, more constrained level a major factor as far as the FG approach is concerned is clearly the given setting, since the definition of Topic in FG implies that for something to be predicable about an entity in the given setting, that entity must in some sense have been introduced in the previous discourse, or in Brown and Yule's (1983: 80) terms, activated. In the rest of the paper I will use the term discourse-bound in this respect. Actually, however, this will not suffice to ensure that an entity when referred to in the discourse will be assigned Topic status: for this an appeal would have to be made to a third, very narrow level of givenness defined on the basis of something like Chafe's (1976) saliency condition, whereby a given entity is an entity which is not only discourse-bound but also in the consciousness of the speaker and hearer at the time of the exchange. However, this has its problems as well, particularly with respect to inferrable entities. For the purposes of this paper I assume that it is at least worth while to specify the conditions required for an entity to be discourse-bound, which I see as a minimal requirement for Topic candidacy.

(ii) An entity which is not discourse-bound can be assumed to be new, and will always have Focushood conferred upon it, since one may further assume that pre-viously unintroduced entities must be salient in the predication in which they are actually mentioned for the first time. Seen from the point of view of Topic, such entities cannot be assigned Topic status since if they do not present in-formation shared by speaker and hearer in the given setting then they cannot have something predicated of them in that setting.

These assumptions can be represented briefly as in (8):

(8)   NEW INFORMATION   (in the sense of   IS FOCUS INFORMATION
                            non-discourse-
                            bound entities)

        GIVEN INFORMATION   (in the sense of   IS EITHER TOPIC INFORMATION
                            discourse-bound   OR FOCUS INFORMATION[2]
                            entities)

3. The status of inferrable entities

On the basis of shared knowledge, or what she calls assumed familiarity, as the central underlying notion, Prince (1981: 237) proposes a taxonomy of given/new

information, which is given in slightly simplified form in (9). An example of
each category is given in (10-15).

(9)   *Assumed familiarity*

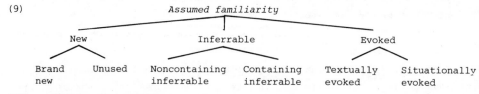

```
              New                  Inferrable              Evoked

    Brand       Unused     Noncontaining   Containing   Textually   Situationally
    new                    inferrable      inferrable   evoked      evoked
```

(10) a. What would you like to eat?

   b. I'd like *a bar of chocolate* (brand new)

(11) a. Why are you crying?

   b. *Princess Grace* has just been killed in a car accident (unused)

(12)   There's a new Rolls out. *The mirror adjustment* is supposed to be computer-
        controlled (noncontaining inferrable)

(13)   I'd like to eat all my chips but *some of them* have gone cold (containing
        inferrable)

(14)   There's a new Woody Allen film out. *It*'s supposed to be his best so far
        (textually evoked)

(15)   (first line of preface to book) *This book* does not claim to be a complete
        and authoritative account of all aspects of Scotch whisky (situationally
        evoked)

Now, evoked entities, like those in (14) and (15) are Topic candidates par ex-
cellence. Given that the previous discourse includes both the verbal and situational context, the entities present therein will have been directly
activated for both speaker and hearer and thus become available to the speaker as
Topic entities. New entities, on the other hand, are according to Prince entities
which are introduced into the discourse for the first time, whether they are in
fact familiar to the hearer or not (the italicized term in (10) is presented as
referring to an unfamiliar, or brand new, entity, while the term italicized in
(11) is presented as being familiar but unused). New entities are thus by definition not discourse-bound, and from a FG point of view terms referring to them
will be assigned Focus function since their being introduced into the discourse
for the first time makes them salient.

   The problem category is that of inferrable entities, and their status as a
discrete class, as well as with respect to Topic candidacy, requires going into
in some detail. Inferrables are entities which in the opinion of the speaker can
be inferred by the hearer 'via logical - or, more commonly, plausible - reasoning,

from entities already Evoked or from other Inferrables' (Prince 1981: 236). The
problem is that although they are presented as a discrete class, Prince also
points out that they may intuitively be classified under either new, since
strictly speaking they are being presented in the discourse for the first time,
or under given, since as Prince puts it 'they are made up of old parts'. It is
the fact that inferrables have both these features that suggest a separate class
of entities. On the one hand they are by definition not brand new since they may
be referred to by definite descriptions, which suggests referent identifiability,
and moreover they differ from unused entities in that unused entities are by
definition not discourse-bound, while inferrables - albeit indirectly - are. On
the other hand they form a class which differs from evoked entities because,
although discourse-bound, they are not referentially identical to entities already present in the linguistic and situational context. What all this does suggest, however, is that they show a stronger affinity to the evoked class, because
of their discourse-bound nature, and in this light it might be reasonably claimed
that they represent a particular class of Topic candidates rather than being seen
as necessarily in Focus.

However, while these features do suggest that they form a particular class of
entities, there are also arguments to suggest that inferrables in fact show a
tendency to shade off, as it were, into evoked entities on the one hand and unused
entities on the other hand. One inferential relation involved is for instance that
of member-set: if a set is introduced into the discourse then one might argue that
this almost entails the members of that set being introduced individually. Obvious
examples are (16-18):

(16)   I went to visit *my parents* yesterday. *My mother* is very ill
(17)   *My brothers* are all very successful. *John*, for example, is an accountant
(18)   I bought *four new books* yesterday. They've gone up in price amazingly
        recently, haven't they, books? *One of them* set me back £25.

Notice that in (18) we also find a case of pronominal reference not to the
referent set introduced in the first sentence but to the whole domain set (the
set of books in the universe of discourse).[3] It appears that the introduction of
a referent set more or less immediately activates (a) any subset of that set and
(b) the whole domain set. Thus it might be said that such 'projections' of the
introduced discourse referent have a rather central place in what Sanford and
Garrod (1981) describe as the 'extended domain of discourse' (see also the discussion on this in Brown and Yule 1983: 260ff), and, although only displaying

partial referential identity, have a highly evoked degree of inferrability.[4]

So much for the relation between inferrable and evoked entities. On the other side of the coin we find cases where the inferencing actually required by the speaker is so complex that one has to ask oneself whether one is not in fact dealing with the introduction of unused, though familiar, entities; in other words that discourse-boundness is difficult to establish. Consider the following example from Werth (forthcoming: 218):

(19)   John and Bill came to see me yesterday. Fred's just acquired a new car

This constitutes a coherent discourse (fragment), but a specific inference is required to ensure that coherence. One possible interpretation offered by Werth is that the second sentence is understood as the gist of something that John and Bill said, from which he concludes that this sentence in fact marks the beginning of a new sub-text, and hence constitutes what in FG terms is an all-new predication. However, another possibility is that a hearer who interprets this as a coherent discourse may additionally see Fred as being 'associated' with John and Bill in some way. In this latter case *Fred* itself refers to an inferrable entity rather than an unused one. Examples like this suggest that one might be concerned with a continuum rather than distinct categories of given/new information (although Prince (1981: 252) argues otherwise).

In other words coherence may be determined in the case of (19) not solely by interpreting the import of the second sentence as a whole - as for instance something said by John and Bill - but also by the inferential relationship of 'association' between John, Bill and Fred. Here again, however, there are degrees of association: mention of John and Bill may for instance for some hearers immediately trigger the entity referred to by *Fred*. Hence in (20) Fred might be seen as almost as strongly activated as *my mother* etc. in (16-18), and at least more overtly so than in (19), if John and Bill, say, always come to visit when Fred, the person they share a flat with, is in a bad mood and starts tearing the place down:

(20) a. John and Bill came to see me yesterday
     b. Oh dear. What's Fred been getting up to now?

The difference between (19) and (20) becomes clear if instead of a familiar entity like *Fred*, a brand new entity is inserted, as in (21) and (22):

(21)   John and Bill came to see me yesterday. Someone Fred knows at work has
        just won half a million on the pools
(22) a. John and Bill came to see me yesterday
     b??Oh dear. What has someone Fred knows at work been getting up to now?

Sentence (22b) is highly marginal because of the presupposition that someone
(known) has been getting up to some (unknown) antic, and the subject term would
be expected to refer to a more discourse-bound entity. Note, for instance, that
Fred in (20b) might be replaced by *he* and the speaker of (20a) might still right-
ly infer that *he* refers to Fred. This would be much less likely in (19) if the
second sentence is interpreted as simply the content of something that John and
Bill said.

A tentative conclusion might then be that although inferrable entities are
more closely associated with evoked entities in that they are discourse-bound,
the demarcation between inferrable and unused is sometimes difficult to establish,
and may require more processing time. However, it must be stressed that inferrables, though discourse-bound, are of a different order than directly evoked
entities, and if they are to be seen as potential Topic candidates then it seems
sensible to try and capture this difference somehow by introducing distinctions
in Topic status.

4. *Inferrables as sub-Topics*

Regarding inferrable entities as discourse-bound, and hence available to the
speaker in the given setting as candidates for Topic selection, does not cause
any specific problems within a FG framework. First it will be noted that in FG
there is no stipulation anyway that coreferentiality with an entity activated in
the setting is a necessary feature of Topic entities, although Dik (1978: 144)
points out that 'more generally, a Topic will be coreferential to a constituent
in a preceding question' (with 'a preceding question' being presumably expandable
to 'the preceding discourse').

Furthermore, from the point of view of discourse coherence in general it makes
sense to consider them as Topic candidates. Within Functional Sentence Perspective,
Daneš(1976: 36) for instance states specifically that a theme (to be understood
slightly differently from Topic, but the differences are not relevant here) may
either be referentially identical or semantically related in a specific way to a
previously introduced discourse referent:

>Das Konzept der TP (=der thematischen Progression, MH) setzt voraus,
>dass die als Thema ausgewählte Bedeutungskomponente (K_2) zu einer
>anderen im vorhergehenden Textabschnitt beinhalteten Bedeutungskom-
>ponente (K_1) in einer spezifischen Beziehung steht; diese Beziehung
>ist entweder eine echte Identitätsrelation oder eine Relation der
>semantischen Verwandtschaft, die es ermöglicht, dass Sprecher und
>Hörer die Komponente K_2 aus dem Kontext heraus als 'bekannt' oder
>'gegeben' betrachten können. Man könnte sagen, dass K_2 durch K_1 an-
>gedeutet wird, dass zwischen K_2 and K_1 die Beziehung einer spezi-
>fierten (direkten oder vermittelten) semantischen Implikation oder
>Inferenz besteht.

Elsewhere, Daneš (1974) sets out how inferrables provide an important means of
thematic progression, which is seen as one of the means of promoting textual cohesion. One example of such a pattern of thematic progression is given in (23),
with Danes' supporting example given in (24):

(23)   *Thematic progression with derived themes*   (th = theme; rh = rheme)

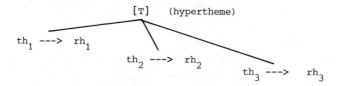

(24)   New Jersey is flat along the coast and southern portion; the north-
       western region is mountainous. The coastal climate is mild, but there
       is considerable cold in the mountain areas during the winter months.
       Summers are fairly hot. The leading industrial production includes
       chemicals, processed food, coal, petroleum, metals and electrical
       equipment. The most important cities are Newark, Jersey City,
       Paterson, Trenton, Camden. Vacation districts include Asbury Park,
       Lakewoods, Cape May, and others.

In this example, various aspects of the 'discourse topic entity' New Jersey are
commented on. As a geo-political unit, New Jersey can be assumed to have a physi-
cal geography, a climate (and various areas of the state may have different
climates), industry, major cities and holiday resorts. Notice also that the so-
called derived themes are related within the paragraph in a certain way. Thus
summers, for instance, may be inferred from *winter months*.

    It seems particularly useful to incorporate these insights into the Functional
Grammar model. Marking the relevant terms for Topic function in cases like (24)

has the particular advantage that it is possible to demonstrate that certain
pieces of information in a predication are relevant with respect to the setting
in a specific way. On the other hand, any set of FG representations for the sentences in a text like (24) would not be able to account in any systematic way
for the coherence and thematic progression in the text if each sentence contained
Focus information only. In fact it may be surprising how much use is actually
made of inferrables as Topic entities. An informal analysis undertaken of random-
ly chosen written texts suggests at least that it may be wise to relativise the
statement by Dik quoted above that Topics will generally be coreferential with
previously mentioned discourse entities. I suspect that this is in fact a genre-
specific feature of discourse.

   In the light of these facts, together with the general conclusion of part 3
above that inferrables should be regarded as displaying a discourse-boundness of
a different order from directly evoked discourse entities, I propose the following pragmatic rule of what I will call sub-Topic formation:

(25)   *Sub-Topic formation*
        If an entity X has been activated in the given setting, then the
        speaker may present an entity Y as a sub-Topic entity, if Y R X,
        where R is a relationship of inference

It is clear that the relation of inference may take a whole host of forms, particularly if one considers situations like that in (19) above. This latter case
is an example of a very general relation of association which is not based on
any specific semantic relation like member-set but rather results from a bridging
assumption (cf. Clark & Haviland 1977). There are also more specifiable relationships, of course, and what I hope is a reasonably comprehensive list of methods
by which strictly unintroduced entities may nevertheless be regarded as discourse-
bound on first mention is given in (26):

(26)   *A specification of the R relation in the rule of sub-Topic formation*
        (i)   part of
        (ii)   member of
        (iii)   subset of
        (iv)   instance of
        (v)   copy of
        (vi)   aspect of
        (vii)   opposite of
        (viii) projection of
        (ix)   associated with

(27)   It's a nice house but *the kitchen* is too small

(28)   The team played quite well I suppose, but *one or two of them* are still a bit unfit

(29)   I was hoping to catch a bus so I could get there on time but when I arrived at the station *one* had just left

(30) a. I've been troubled a lot by sleeplessness recently

     b. That's funny, *sleeplessness*/that has been getting me down too

(31) a. Look, I've just spent all my pocket money on this fantastic Bardot poster!

     b. Oh dear. *The same one*'s going for 50p down the market

(32)   I was hoping for a swinging party but *the atmosphere* was very tense

(33)   Being over-careful has its disadvantages but *carelessness* can be fatal

(34)   I bought Harry a record for his birthday, but *they* are so expensive I nearly had second thoughts

(35)   John and Bill came to see me yesterday. *Fred*'s just acquired a new car

Some of the relations given in (26) are in fact problematic. It is not clear for example whether cases like (30) really do involve inferrable entities and not evoked ones, in the sense that the abstract entity sleeplessness has in fact been directly introduced. The same goes to a certain extent for the 'projection of' relation exemplified by (34): while records have not been introduced into the discourse generically, a set of the domain set has. The point here is that one defining feature of inferrables as I interpret them to be understood by Prince seems to be that they are not co-referential with a previously introduced discourse entity, although they may be definite, and I have assumed this in the proposal of sub-Topic formation. However, one might argue that anaphoricity is not the crucial factor in distinguishing between evoked and inferrable entities – and by extension between Topic and sub-Topic entities – but rather the notion of discourse deixis, particularly since Topic can be viewed as a discourse-deictic function (cf. Levinson 1983: 86-88). In this light phenomena such as lexical repetition and so-called pronouns of laziness clearly present problem cases, but I will not go into this matter any further here.

What is worth looking at is the further relevance of the sub-Topic distinction. First of all the basic effect is that a distinction is possible between sequences like those in (36-38):

(36) a. What happened?

     b. The cat broke the vase

(37) a. Your pets have been troublesome recently, haven't they?

    b. Yes, yesterday the cat broke the vase

(38) a. What did the cat do?

    b. The cat broke the vase

The representations of the (b)-sentences will only differ in respect of pragmatic function assigned to the first argument:

(39) (= 36b) $break_{VFoc}$ $(d1x_i: cat(x_i))_{AgSubjFoc}$ $(d1x_j: vase(x_j))_{GoObjFoc}$

(40) (= 37b) $break_{VFoc}$ $(d1x_i: cat(x_i))_{AgSubjsubTop}$ $(d1x_j: vase(x_j))_{GoObjFoc}$

        $(y_k: yesterday(y_k))_{Temp}$

(41) (= 38b) $break_{VFoc}$ $(d1x_i: cat(x_i))_{AgSubjTop}$ $(d1x_j: vase(x_j))_{GoObjFoc}$

Another advantage of the sub-Topic function emerges when one considers a case like (42):

(42)   I had an easy day at school today. Two of the teachers were ill

What is interesting here is that the second sentence can have two distinct phonological realisations without the setting being interpreted differently. In one, the primary stress falls on the subject term and no other constituent receives phonological prominence. In the other, primary stress falls on the predicate *ill* but secondary stress is also assigned to the subject term. It seems plausible to assume that these two realisations result from two different pragmatic function assignments which are available to the speaker in the given setting. Primary stress falling on the subject term may be seen as the outcome of Focus being assigned to the whole predication as all-new - the entity referred to by *two of the teachers* is indeed inferrable from the setting but the speaker does not select it as Topic entity, preferring to assert a neutral state of affairs which supplies a reason to support the assertion in the first sentence. On the other hand, where primary stress falls on the predicate this can be seen as the outcome of a decision by the speaker to take *two of the teachers* as sub-Topic and to predicate of those entities that they were ill, the predicate *ill* being assigned Focus function in the underlying representation (for a discussion of similar cases within a Hallidayan framework see Kirkwood 1979: 15). The point about all this is that the option of choosing either a Focus-neutral assertion or a predicative statement with a full Topic in this case (I use the term 'full Topic' to correspond with directly evoked entities) is not available to the speaker given one and the same setting.

A similar case involving the optional status of inferrables concerns the following, where the different pragmatic function assignments produce alternative word order patterns:

(43) a. I will now turn my attention to various implications of the analysis
     b. Particularly interesting is its influence on Topic assignment
(44) a. I will now turn my attention to various implications of the analysis
     b. Its influence on Topic assignment is particularly interesting

Although *its influence on Topic assignment* can be inferred from (*implications of*) *the analysis* in the previous sentence, there is of course nothing preventing the speaker from nevertheless introducing it. In (43) this is done by means of a presentative construction. However, given its inferrability it may also be selected as sub-Topic. Rough representations for the b-sentences in (43) and (44) are given in (45) and (46) respectively (the structure of the subject term is based on the proposals in Mackenzie 1983):

(45)   particularly interesting$_A$ (d1x$_i$: {influence$_N$ (it)$_{fo}$ (Topic assignment)$_{go}$}

$^{(x_i)}\emptyset)$ $\emptyset$SubjFoc

(46)   particularly interesting$_{AFoc}$ (d1x$_i$: {influence$_N$ (it)$_{fo}$ (Topic assignment)$_g$}

$^{(x_i)}\emptyset)$ $\emptyset$SubjsubTop

The examples discussed in (42-44) strongly suggest that the blurred status of inferrables with respect to bound and unbound is paralleled somewhat by their ability to be selected by the speaker as either subTopic or Focus in one and the same setting and within one and the same predication. In other words the speaker may in certain cases be free, given a particular state of affairs, to either assume the activatedness of an inferrable entity or not. As such, one might regard such sub-Topic predications as half-way houses between all-new predications and Topic predications.[5]

Finally it will be noted that the relation between evoked discourse entity and sub-Topic entity is paralleled by a particular relation which is assumed in FG between Topic and Theme. Dik (1978: 138) assumes a general relation of relevance between Predication and Theme which he gives as in (47):

(47)   For any pair of Theme T and Predication P to make sense, it must be
         relevant to pronounce P with respect to T.

Coherence in this respect will usually involve, among other things, a relation
of thematic continuity between the Theme and Topic of the predication. The two
relevant entities are often coreferential, but not always. Thus in (48)

(48)   As far as John is concerned, his interests are clearly in another
         direction

John specifies the domain of discourse with respect to which the information in
the predication must be relevant, but the predication itself is about John's
interests. This is precisely the relation which obtains between inferrable entities and the entities which they are 'inferenced off of', as Prince puts it; the
rule of sub-Topic formation, together with the specification of the R relation,
might thus be appealed to in order to specify one area in which the general relation of relevance given in (47) might be secured.

5. Concluding remarks

In the introduction it was pointed out that the value of a discourse-oriented
definition of Topic as a sentence-level function lies in the possibility of
specifying the various relationships which a Topic entity may entertain with
other entities in the given setting. What I have set out to do here is specify
one such relationship, which has been formulated in the rule of sub-Topic
formation. Sub-Topic entities may be complemented by full Topic entities, which
comprise situationally and textually evoked entities, in accordance with Prince's
distinctions, and for which speaker-oriented selection rules may be formulated
similar to that proposed for sub-Topics. These formation rules would impose no
strain on the Topic definition as it stands; rather they would complement the
definition. In this light a broader discourse function of Topic emerges: inferentially, textually and situationally bound entities are available to the speaker
as a means of presenting various types of perspective which allow him to make
relevant contributions to the 'discourse theme', or, to avoid terminological
confusion within a FG framework, what I would label the subject matter of the
discourse. (The perspectives involved here are thus of an informational kind and
are not to be confused with the perspectival function associated with subject
assignment, cf. Van der Auwera's (1981) distinction between pragmatic and

semantic focus).

The relations between individual sentence Topics and the discourse subject matter are vague, as Givón (1983a: 8) points out, and in order to gain insight into these relations it will at least be necessary to specify what the subject matter actually comprises (cf. Brown and Yule's (1983: 75f) notion of topic framework in this respect). However, I would suggest that the three means of providing a perspective are also relevant in gaining insight into these relations.

Finally, further refinements of the Topic system in FG will clearly be required in order to account for the specific status of Topic constituents in the thematic development of a discourse.[6] On the one hand this may involve investigating individual languages with regard to what kinds of Topic function are employed, as De Vries (this volume) suggests; on the other hand, one may wish more generally to distinguish for instance what Dik (forthcoming) calls contrastive and resumed Topics, the former being Topic entities which have the additional 'focus of contrast' feature (cf. Hannay 1983), the latter referring to entities which have been evoked and perhaps also presented as Topic entities in the preceding discourse and are now being picked up again. Note however that such entities must still fulfill the minimum requirement of being inferentially, textually or situationally bound in order to function as Topic entities at sentence level.

NOTES

[*] The research for this paper was carried out within the framework of the conditionally financed research project 'Functional Language Research: Grammar and Pragmatics' at the Free University of Amsterdam. I wish to thank Simon Dik and Lachlan Mackenzie for valuable comments on an earlier version.

[1] It is really only valid to claim that *what happened?* questions produce all-new responses in the minimal settings defined by such constructed examples as (3). It must not be forgotten that *what happened?* may well appear as a question in specific settings where the involvement of particular entities is understood. Thus it will often mean *what happened to you/them* etc., in which case an all-new predication is by no means a guaranteed response.

[2] In fact it may also be neither if only one Topic entity per predication is recognised; thus if *I* is assigned Topic status in (ib) then *it* is not marked for pragmatic function.

(i) a. What did you do with the book?

b. $I_{(Top)}$ burnt$_{(Foc)}$ it

[3] For a brief discussion of the terms 'referent set' and 'domain set' see Brown (1985).

[4] There is a similarity here with what Brown and Yule (1983: 257) call missing links, which unlike true inferences, which have to be made by the hearer, are

seen as gaps in the text. Thus in *I bought a new car yesterday. The windows work automatically,* the sentence *a car has windows* is deemed to be missing from the text.

5   It may be noted in passing that with respect to partitives, which form a specific subset of containing inferrables in Prince's system, there may be another way of capturing representationally the dual bound/unbound nature of inferrables. Since with partitives the whole term actually contains the referent which provides the source of the inference this allows the possibility of capturing the new and evoked parts of the term by assigning pragmatic functions constituent-internally, while the status of the whole constituent - sub-Topic or Focus depending on the setting - can continue to be assigned in the normal way. Thus following the proposals of Brown (1985), whereby the partitive is seen as a term operator, one might represent (i) by (ii). Note that the slash is defined as 'of the'.

(i)   Two of the five elephants have escaped into the bushes

(ii) escape$_V$ $(2_{foc}/5_{top}x_i$: elephant$(x_i))_{AgSubjsubTop}$ $(dmx_j$: bush$(x_j))_{DirFoc}$

It must be added, however, that the matter of constituent-internal pragmatic function assignment is an issue in its own right, as yet not discussed in detail within FG, and I will not go any further into the matter here. See Svoboda (1968) for a treatment of the problem within the theory of Functional Sentence Perspective.

6   If one compares the approach in this paper with regard to specifying the minimum requirements for entities to be used as Topic entitites with the work on thematic paragraphs and topical spans by Givón (1983a) and De Vries (this volume) respectively, then there might appear to be a certain terminological conflict. This should be resolved.

For both Givón and De Vries, a discourse entity on first mention may set up a topical chain or span, and is then seen as a (discourse) topic. It must be stressed that this cannot mean that in FG terms such an entity is necessarily assigned Topic function in the predication in which it is introduced. The beginning of a topical span may be established by the introduction of a brand new (Focus) entity, or by a theme constituent for example (cf. Brown (1983: 323), who mentions existentials and presentatives as topic-marking constructions). De Vries' distinction between strong and weak topics in Wambon is also relevant here: strong topics are entities used in the phase of establishing topicality, while weak topics are used in the phase of maintaining topicality. The functional rather than the formal relation between strong topics, themes and the Topic function clearly requires investigation (cf. De Groot's (1981c) discussion of the status of theme with respect to Hungarian).

Chapter 5

A functional approach to some constructions of spoken Dutch

Josine Lalleman
Institute for General Linguistics, University of Amsterdam

1. Introduction[1]

In Dutch, as in any language, a number of constructions may appear in the speech
of adult native speakers which are accepted as normal in spoken Dutch, but which
do not form part of the grammar of Dutch. For example, in dealing with word
order features of Dutch, De Vooys (1960) mentions a number of sequences which do
not follow the normal ordering pattern of declarative main clauses and states
that:

> In spoken language ['omgangstaal', after Wunderlich, 1894
> 'Umgangssprache'] this phenomenon often occurs: in most
> cases it is a supplement, a correction of something that,
> in hasty speech, did not cross one's mind in time.
>
> (De Vooys 1960: 366; parenthesis and translation mine, JL)

It seems that in grammars of Dutch a borderline is drawn between *correct* and
deviant word order patterns, and that the category *deviant* includes constructions
from spoken Dutch:

(1)   correct / acceptable - incorrect
         ‿‿‿‿‿‿‿‿‿‿‿‿‿‿‿‿‿
                  deviant

If we were to accept this borderline in the field of Language Acquisition, it
would mean applying the norms for (adult) *written* Dutch to the *speech* of children
who are in the process of learning Dutch. The problem of adult norms being used
to decide what is and what is not correct in children's performances is more or
less solved by considering deviations from the adult norm as developmentally
determined: they are *goofs* rather than *errors* (Dulay & Burt 1970). However, if
we want to determine the developmental phases children go through in learning
Dutch, or, at a specific moment in time, we want to determine the level of proficiency a child has reached in Dutch, we should be able to *formally* distinguish
between incorrect word order patterns or developmental goofs and acceptable
spoken Dutch patterns in the following way:

(2)   correct - acceptable / incorrect
                                deviant

In other words, grammatical rules should be formulated in order to distinguish
acceptable spoken Dutch patterns from deviant word order patterns. This is the
topic of this article: I will demonstrate that Functional Grammar offers a
theoretical framework in which the special status of acceptable spoken Dutch
patterns can be formalized by means of optional expression rules.

I will first describe the exact properties of three types of acceptable spoken
Dutch patterns which were found in the speech of Dutch native children and Turkish children who speak Dutch as a second language and who were born and bred in
the Netherlands.

Then I will present the results of a quantitative analysis of the children's
speech, in which the relative frequency of the patterns is calculated. It will
be argued that in view of the regularities in the pragmatic functions of the constituents involved, these patterns *can* be incorporated into the grammar of Dutch,
and because they occur in the speech of all types of speakers of Dutch - native
speakers and second language learners, children and adults - in contrast to
'real' deviations, these patterns *should* be incorporated into the grammar of
Dutch. But first, in the next section, the research questions, the subjects and
the data collection methods will be discussed.

2. Research questions, subjects and data collection

The topic of this article can be put in a wider perspective: the main object is
to collect knowledge about the oral language proficiency of Turkish children,
born and bred in the Netherlands, compared with that of native children at the
moment they start their school 'career'. The subjects are twenty Dutch and twenty
Turkish children, all around six years old. All the children attended nursery
school in Amsterdam, and at the moment the data were gathered, they had all just
entered primary school. Several tests were administered and with each child three
different speech samples were taped: a conversation with an adult, a dialogue
with a class-mate and a story-telling task.

The last-mentioned speech sample will supply the data for the present study.
I call this sample the Picture Sample (PS), because the children were asked to
tell a story about a sequence of events they saw on a number of pictures that
were put in front of them. The resulting speech was analysed with regard to
pragmatic, syntactic and morphological proficiency. In this article, however, I

will restrict myself to the analysis of an aspect of syntactic proficiency: word order in declarative main clauses.

3. Acceptable spoken Dutch patterns

Jansen (1981) discusses in detail a number of word order patterns occurring in the speech of native adults. One of them, the absence, or as Jansen calls it, the deletion of the first constituent of the main clause, will be dealt with here. In terms of Functional Grammar (Dik 1978), we might call this sequence the *Empty P1 Pattern*. The second speech pattern which will be discussed here I will refer to as the *P2 P1 Pattern*: in this type of sequence two constituents appear in front of the finite verb. The third speech pattern to be discussed here, in which a constituent appears to the right of the non-finite verb in a main clause, is referred to as the *P3 Pattern*: a constituent is added to a sentence after a short break in the intonation.

3.1. The Empty P1 Pattern

P1 stands for the initial position in the predication (cf. Dik 1978: 178). In Dutch, P1 is occupied either by members of categories which always must go to this position, such as interrogative words, or by constituents with the pragmatic function of Topic or Focus. When the Subject of the sentence has Topic or Focus function, it may appear either in P1, in front of the finite verb or directly after the finite verb, in S. In the examples given below, *een meisje* (a girl) and *een meneer* (a mister) have Focus function because the child starts his story with these utterances and *de ballon* (the balloon) has Topic function because this constituent was mentioned before:

(3)   *een meisje* had een emmertje   water
         P1 (=SFoc) V_f O

         a   girl   had a   little-bucket water
         'A girl had a bucket of water in her hand'

(4)   en rustig gaat de ballon omhoog
         Co   P1 V_f STop   X

         and quietly goes the balloon up
         'and the balloon rises quietly'

(5)   eerst gaat een meneer een banaan eten
         P1 V_f SFoc   O V_i

         first goes a   mister a   banana eat
         'first a man eats a banana'

Only one constituent can appear in P1: the finite verb consequently always takes
second position in the (main) clause. Nevertheless, an exception to this generalization is found in spoken Dutch: the constituent normally filling P1 is omitted
and the sentence starts with the finite verb.

Jansen (1981: 109-145) discussed this phenomenon in the speech of adult native
speakers. He found that adults often omit pronominal adverbs, adverbs of time and
place, demonstratives and dummy subjects:

Omitted constituent:	*Example:*
(a) pronominal adverbs:	(daar) *wil* ik je over spreken (there) want I you about talk 'I want to talk to you about that'
(b) adverbs of time:	(toen) *ging* ik weg (then) went I away 'Then I went away'
(c) adverbs of place:	(daar) *kwam* ik hem tegen (there) came I him against 'There I met him'
(d) demonstratives:	(die) *zag* ik niet (that) saw I not 'That I didn't see'
(e) dummy subjects:	(d'r) *was* helemaal geen schoolfonds (there) was schoolfund 'there was no schoolfund at all'

In the speech of the children of the present study, pronominal adverbs do not
appear in sentence-initial position. Furthermore, whereas Subject Pronouns are
seldom omitted in first position by adults, the children omit them fairly often.
Because the omission of the Subject Pronoun may also be a feature of simplified
speech, and typical of a rather low level of language proficiency, we need a
criterion by means of which we can distinguish the two types of omission: one
an acceptable spoken Dutch pattern, the other a deviation from the target norm.

This criterion can be formulated in the form of an optional expression rule:

(6) *Optional Expression Rule 1*: P1 may remain empty if the constituent normally
filling this position was mentioned or referred
to in the 'immediate prior' conversation (Jansen
1981: 56)

This criterion also covers the explanation of the phenomenon: a speaker may safely assume that a constituent which was mentioned or referred to shortly before is
easily filled in by the listener. The function of the omission of course is the
shortening of speech: especially in a story-telling task it enlivens a story

when it is told in a quick manner, or at least that is what children (and adults)
often think.

Using (6) as a criterion for acceptable subjectless main clause sequences, we
can distinguish between (7) and (8): the former is an acceptable spoken Dutch
pattern, the latter shows features of simplified speech:

(7)   (EN DE BALLON?) (die) *is* weg in de lucht
        (AND THE BALLOON?) (that) is away in the air
        '(AND WHAT HAPPENED TO THE BALLOON?) It flew off into the air'

(8)   en   daar   gooi   (= zij)/ en   toen schrik   (= hij)
        and there throw (= she)/ and then is-frightened (= he)
        'and there she throws (the water)/ and then he is frightened'

We can distinguish the following types of acceptable verb-initial patterns in
the speech of the children:

Omitted constituent:	*Example:*
(a) demonstratives (Objects):	(EN WAT GEBEURDE ER TOEN? (dat) *weet* ik niet (AND WHAT HAPPENED THERE THEN? (that) know I not '(AND WHAT HAPPENED THEN?) I don't know
(b) adverbs of time:	en dan wil 'ie net iets kopen/ en (dan) and then wants he just something buy/ and (then) *hebt* 'ie geen geld has he no money 'and at that very moment he wants to buy some- thing/ and then he hasn't any money'
(c) adverbs of place:	hier loopt een meisje met haar ballon/ (hier) here walks a girl with her balloon/ (here) *gooit* 'ie z'n banaan leeg throws he his banana empty 'here is a girl walking with her balloon/ here he throws away his banana'
(d) demonstratives (Subjects):	(EN WAAR WERKT JE MOEDER?) (die) *werkt* niet (AND WHERE WORKS YOUR MOTHER?) (that) works not 'Where does your mother work? She doesn't work'
(e) Subject pronouns:	hij koopet iets, die mevrouw/ en hij pakt he buys something, that lady/ and he takes de spaarpot/ (hij (= zij)) *koopt* wat the money-box/ (he (= she)) buys something

There is, however, one thing which remains unclear: why the omission of certain constituents is only possible in P1; in other positions in the sentence it
results in a deviant word order pattern, as in (8). Probably this phenomenon is
another piece of evidence that P1 in fact is a 'special position' (cf. Dik 1978:
178), to which several rules are applied that are restricted to that position.

3.2. The P2 P1 Pattern

In section 3.1. an exception to the requirement that P1 be occupied by one constituent was studied, and the conditions permitting this exception formulated.
There is, however, a second acceptable spoken Dutch pattern to be distinguished,
in which at first sight this requirement is also violated: the P2 P1 Pattern. In
sequences of the following type:

(9)   *dat meisje dat* trapt op de schil
        that girl   that steps on the peel
        'that girl she steps on the peel'

it seems that both the term *dat meisje* and the demonstrative *dat* are placed in
P1. But, given the extended pattern (10):

(10)   P2, P1 V_f S O V_i, P3   (Dik 1978: 153)

we can argue that in these sequences the term is placed in P2, the position for
constituents with the pragmatic function of Theme. In contrast with P3, in which
constituents are placed after a short intonational break, P2 constituents may be
followed by a constituent in P1 *without* a pause.

     If we accept this pattern into the grammar of Dutch, the following optional
expression rule would account for it:

(11)   *Optional Expression Rule 2:* a term may appear in P2, followed by its
                                       corresponding demonstrative in P1. The
                                       latter normally has the syntactic function
                                       of Subject within the predication.[2]

This rule correctly rules out the acceptability of the following utterances:

(12)   **m'n mamma* zit ze alleen ook
        my mommy sits she alone also
        'my mommy is also alone'

(13)   **een meneer hij* was aan 't rijden
        a   mister he was driving
        'a mister was driving'

In (13) a *pronoun* appears in P1, which results in a deviant pattern. In (12) a
pronominal counterpart of the noun appears not in P1 but in S position, so that
this utterance in fact is deviant in two respects.

3.3. The P3 Pattern

Dik (1978: 153-156) argues that given the extended pattern (10) for Dutch main
clauses:

(10)   P2, P1 V$_f$ S O V$_i$, P3

P3 is a special position, which is usually filled by a constituent with the
pragmatic function of Tail. Tail constituents add information to the predication
or part of the predication, but they do not form part of the predication proper:
this is symbolized by the comma.

It seems obvious that this position is extremely useful for a speaker: it
gives him the opportunity to extend his utterance, without really violating the
word order rules. It has not yet been studied whether or not speakers of Dutch
make use of this position in a systematic way, nor is the frequency known with
which adult native speakers of Dutch form sequences of this type.

In the speech of the children that took part in the present study, the following extensions in P3 were found:

Extension in P3   *Example*

(a) clarification of the Subject: en *hij* gaat een boek lezen, *de jongen*
                                        and he goes a   book read, the boy
                                        'and he reads a book, the boy'

(b) correction of the Subject: ennem *die jongen* gaatte nog   ze boom
                                        and   that boy   goes   still the tree

                                        ze achter, *die hond*
                                        his behind, that dog
                                        'and that boy runs behind the tree, that dog'

(c) clarification of the Object: die pakt 'm uit   de zak,   *de*
                                        he takes him out-of the pocket, the

                                        portemonnee
                                        purse
                                        'he takes it out of the pocket, the purse'

(d) clarification of the   hij gaat slapen, *in het bosje*
    predication as a whole: he goes sleep, in the grove
                                        'he is sleeping, in the grove'

                                        die meisje gaat met de ballon spelen,
                                        that girl   goes with the balloon play,

                                        buiten
                                        outside
                                        'that girl plays with her balloon, outside'

                                        nu gaat 'ie weg, met zonder dingen
                                        now goes he away, with without things
                                        'now he leaves, without a thing'

Sometimes it is difficult to distinguish a constituent which is placed in P3 from a normal sequence, if the intonation break is very short. Mostly, however, the pause between the sentence and P3 is obvious. In some cases a child has even begun another sentence and then adds a constituent to the previous sentence:

(14)   en er   zit een jongetje in de zon op het strand te leggen,
          and there sits a boy   in the sun on the beach to lie,

          enne ... op een handdoek
          and ... on a   towel
          'and a boy is lying in the sun on the beach, and ... on a towel'

Naturally, the filling of P3 should be distinguished from those incorrect sequences in which a constituent appears to the right of the non-finite verb *without* a pause, such as:

(15)   *en toen had ze in de zak   gestopt *die   handen*
         Co   X V_f S   PP V_i O
         and then had she in the pocket put   those hands
         'and then she put her hands in her pockets'

We can formulate an optional expression rule to distinguish sequences like (14) from those like (15) in the following way:

(16)   *Optional Expression Rule 3:* a sentence may be followed by any constituent
                                        filling P3, provided that a short break in
                                        the intonation pattern is heard between sen-
                                        tence and added constituent

4. Frequency of occurrence of acceptable spoken Dutch patterns

In the previous section we discussed three types of constructions, each of which at first sight seemed to 'disobey' the word order rules of Dutch, but which are nevertheless accepted as normal in spoken Dutch. These three types do not occur with the same frequency in the speech of the Dutch and Turkish children: whereas the Empty P1 Pattern is found relatively often in the speech of both groups of speakers, the other two constructions appear only once or twice in the speech sample of each child, or, as is the case with the P2 P1 Pattern, in the speech of only some children, and not at all in the speech of the others:

	Empty P1	P2 P1	P3
Dutch	10.3	1.9	2.3
Turkish	8.6	0.6	2

TABLE 1: Percentual number of utterances in the Picture Sample containing acceptable spoken Dutch patterns: (1) Empty P1 Pattern, (2) P2 P1 Pattern, and (3) P3 Pattern

The Empty P1 Pattern is instantiated by more than 20% of all the utterances of two Turkish and four Dutch children. In these cases it is not certain that this construction *always* has the function of enlivening or quickening speech: Schaerlaekens (1977) considers the Empty P1 Pattern as a feature of simplified speech, representing a certain developmental phase in (native speakers') word order acquisition. However, this conclusion would be at least partly in contradiction with the results of the study of Jansen (1981), who found that this pattern occurs rather frequently in the speech of adult native speakers of Dutch.

5. *Discussion*

Spoken Dutch patterns as the three constructions dealt with in this study occur whenever Dutch is spoken, no matter by whom. There is, however, variation in occurrence across speakers and situations, even within the speech of a single speaker. Children, both native and second language speakers, often tend to follow the Empty P1 Pattern, and adults - although no systematic study has been carried out thus far which could verify this claim - seem to follow the P3 Pattern and the P2 P1 Pattern fairly often. Their relative frequency of occurrence, however, is not the most important reason for including spoken Dutch patterns in the grammar of Dutch. It is simply the fact that all (native) speakers of Dutch consider these patterns to be normal. If the function of a grammar of Dutch is to record all the constructions which form part of that language, it is at least strange to exclude specific constructions which occur in the speech of almost every native speaker, and which are regarded as normal by native speakers.

Accepting that speech patterns should form part of the grammar, we must be able to formulate grammatical rules capable of being incorporated. In section 3. we saw that each of the speech patterns that was discussed can be accounted for by Functional Grammar by means of optional expression rules. These expression rules apply to 'special positions', P1, P2 and P3, which refer to pragmatically defined positions in the sentence. These spoken Dutch patterns cannot easily be accommodated in a grammar that contains purely syntactic rules. So, this study indicates that the important role of pragmatic functions in the theory of FG is supported by a word order analysis of the speech of native children and second language learners.

NOTES

[1]   This research was supported by the Foundation for Linguistic Research, which is funded by the Netherlands Organization for the Advancement of Pure Research, ZWO.

[2]   An occasional example of this pattern has been found in the corpus in which the demonstrative has the syntactic function of Object.

Chapter 6

Topics in Arabic: towards a functional analysis

Ahmed Moutaouakil
Faculty of Letters, University Mohamed V, Rabat

0. Introduction and overview of the data

In this article we intend to examine the essential properties of the Topic constituent in Standard Modern Arabic, adopting as our theoretical framework Functional Grammar (FG) as proposed by Dik (1978). Having defined Topic as a pragmatic function assigned to one of the terms of a predication, we will consider the procedure for assigning Topic, the constraints on this procedure and the case-marking and positional properties of the constituent to which Topic is assigned. These properties will be studied with particular reference to one type of sentential structure, the sentence with a verbal predicate.

We consider the italicized constituents in the following sentences to receive the pragmatic function Topic:

(1) a. matā rajaᶜa   *Zaydun?*
         when returned Zayd$_{nom}$
         'When did Zayd return?'

    b. rajaᶜa   *Zaydun* l-bāriḥata
         returned Zayd$_{nom}$ yesterday$_{acc}$
         'Zayd returned yesterday'

(2) a. man qābala *Zaydan*
         who met   Zayd$_{acc}$
         'Who met Zayd?'

    b. qābala *Zaydan* ᶜAmrun
         met   Zayd$_{acc}$ ᶜAmr$_{nom}$
         'ᶜAmr met Zayd'

    c. man rajaᶜa   *l-bāriḥata*
         who returned yesterday$_{acc}$
         'Who returned yesterday?'

    d. rajaᶜa *l-bāriḥata*   Zaydun
         returned yesterday$_{acc}$ Zayd$_{nom}$
         'Zayd returned yesterday'

(3) a. man ʔaᶜtā *Zaydun*   l-kitāba?
         who gave Zayd$_{nom}$ the-book$_{acc}$
         'Who did Zayd give the book to?'

b. ʔa^{c}tā Zaydun l-kitāba ^{c}Amran
    gave Zayd$_{nom}$ the-book$_{acc}$ ^{c}Amran$_{acc}$
    'Zayd gave the book to ^{c}Amr'

(4) a. Kayfa ḥālu Zaydin?
    how state$_{nom}$ Zayd$_{gen}$
    'How is Zayd?'

b. Zaydun marīḍun
    Zayd$_{nom}$ ill$_{nom}$
    'Zayd is ill'

c. ʔayna Zaydun?
    where Zayd$_{nom}$
    'Where is Zayd?'

d. Zaydun fi d-dāri
    Zayd$_{nom}$ in the-house$_{gen}$
    'Zayd is at home'

(5) a. ^{c}indī kitābun
    at-me book$_{nom}$
    'I have a book'

b. fi d-dāri rajulun
    in the-house$_{gen}$ man$_{nom}$

    'A man is at home'

(6) a. mādā fa^{c}alta fi l-laylati l-māḍiyati?
    what you-did in the-night$_{gen}$ the-past$_{gen}$
    'What did you do last night?'

b. fi l-laylati l-māḍiyati qaraʔtu kitāban
    in the-night$_{gen}$ the-past$_{gen}$ I-read book$_{acc}$
    'Last night I read a book'

(7) a. l-laḥmu, r-riṭlu bi ^{c}isrīna dirhaman
    the-meat the-pound$_{nom}$ with twenty dirham$_{acc}$
    'The meat costs twenty dirhams a pound'

b. Zaydun ʔabūhu musāfirun
    Zayd$_{nom}$ brother$_{nom}$ -his travelling$_{nom}$
    'As for Zayd, his brother is travelling'

(8) a. Zaydun, qabaltuhu
    Zayd$_{nom}$ I-met-him
    'As for Zayd, I have met him'

b. l-kitābu qaraʔtuhu
    the-book$_{nom}$ I-read-it
    'As for the book, I have read it'

c. Zaydun, qabala ^{c}Amran
    Zayd$_{nom}$ he-met ^{c}Amr$_{acc}$
    'As for Zayd, he has met ^{c}Amr'

    d. ḍ-ḍuyūfu, jāʔu
       the-guests have-come-they
       'The guests, they have come'

(9) a. *Zaydan* qabaltuhu
      Zayd$_{acc}$ I-met-him
      'I have met Zayd'

    b. *l-kitāba* qara^{c}tuhu
      the book$_{acc}$ I-read-it
      'I have read the book'

1. Definition of Topic

The definition of Topic accepted in FG is that proposed by Dik (1978: 19):

(10)   The Topic presents the entity 'about' which the predication predicates
        something in the given setting.

In all the sentences given above (1-9), the italicized constituent(s) refer(s)
to the entity about which the predication predicates something in the given
setting. Let us consider, for example, (1a) and (1b), repeated here for convenience:

(1) a. matā raja^{c}a *Zaydun*?
      when returned Zayd$_{nom}$
      'When did Zayd return?'

    b. raja^{c}a *Zaydun* l-bāriḥata
      returned Zayd$_{nom}$ yesterday$_{acc}$
      'Zayd returned yesterday'

The constituent *Zaydun* refers to the individual about whom *matā raja^{c}a* is predicated in (1a) and *raja^{c}a l-bāriḥata* in (1b). *Zaydun* is therefore Topic in both
(1a) and (1b). This constituent receives Topic function by virtue of the communicative situation of the speaker uttering (1a) and of the speaker-hearer uttering
(1b) in a conversational exchange. In both sentences, *Zaydun* refers to the entity
'spoken about', although with the difference that in (1a) this constituent refers
to the individual about whom information is being requested whereas in (1b) it
refers to the individual about whom the requested information is being offered.

2. Topic assignment

2.1. The assignment procedure

In FG, syntactic functions (Subject and Object) and pragmatic functions (Focus, Topic, ...) are assigned, under specific conditions, to terms of a predication each of which already bears a semantic function (Agent, Goal, Recipient, ...). Pragmatic function assignment is ordered after syntactic function assignment. Sentence (1a) realizes structure (11), which is specified for functions and in which term (x_1), with the semantic function Agent, is assigned the syntactic function Subject:

(11)   Past raja^c_V (dx$_1$: Zayd(x$_1$))$_{AgSubj}$ (dy$_1$: b$\bar{a}$ri$\d{h}$at(y$_1$))$_{Time}$

(11) represents the result of syntactic function assignment. As for Topic function, it is also assigned, under the pragmatic conditions explained in the previous section, to term (x_1), giving (12):

(12)   Past raja^c_V (dx$_1$: Zayd(x$_1$))$_{AgSubjTop}$ (dy$_1$: b$\bar{a}$ri$\d{h}$at(y$_1$))$_{TimeNew-Focus}$

Structure (12) is realized by the expression rules (see section 3) as (1a).

Let us take (4b) as an example of the type of sentence classifiable as a 'nominal sentence' (i.e. a sentence without any surface verb). In FG, such sentences are considered to have an Adjective or Noun as predicate. Thus, (4b) is of structure (13) prior to syntactic and pragmatic function assignment, in which *mar$\bar{i}\d{d}$* is the predicate (of the category Adjective), with one argument, the term *Zayd* with the semantic function $\emptyset$:

(13)   Pres mar$\bar{i}\d{d}_A$ (dx$_1$: Zayd(x$_1$))$_\emptyset$

The rules of syntactic function assignment allocate Subject to term (x_1), giving (14):

(14)   Pres mar$\bar{i}\d{d}_A$ (dx$_1$: Zayd(x$_1$))$_{\emptyset Subj}$

The pragmatic function Topic is then assigned to the term (x_1), giving (15):

(15)   Pres mar$\bar{i}\d{d}_A$ (dx$_1$: Zayd(x$_1$))$_{\emptyset SubjTop}$

which is converted, by the expression rules, into a pre-phonological representation shown as (4b).

2.2. Constraints on Topic assignment

2.2.1. How many Topics?

Let us recall that one of the constraints imposed on function assignment in FG
is the so-called 'bi-uniqueness' constraint, which we have formulated as follows:

(16)   *Bi-uniqueness constraint*
        The terms in a predication are labelled for semantic, syntactic and
        pragmatic functions in such a way that:
        (i)   no term may have more than one function at each of the three
              functional levels
        (ii) no function may be assigned to more than one term.

If the assignment of semantic and syntactic functions is governed by this constraint, the assignment of pragmatic functions is only partially subject to it:
only one pragmatic function may be assigned to any term in a predication, but
the same pragmatic function may be assigned to more than one term. Thus Topic
may be assigned, under suitable pragmatic conditions, to more than one term in a
predication, witness (3a) and (3b), in which this function is assigned to two
constituents (*Zaydun* and *l-kitāba*). (3b) realizes structure (17), in which Topic
is assigned to both term (x_1) and term (x_2):

(17)   Past $\text{?a}^c\text{tā}_V$ $(dx_1: \text{Zayd } (x_1))_{\text{AgSubjTop}}$ $(dx_2: \text{kitāb}(x_2))_{\text{GoObjTop}}$
        $(dy_1: \text{bāriḥat}(y_1))_{\text{RecNew-Focus}}$

2.2.2. Topic-worthiness

In sentences formed from a predicate (verbal, adjectival or nominal) and a single
argument, Topic function is automatically assigned to the argument irrespective
of its semantic and syntactic functions. Thus, as we saw, the predicate of (4b)
is one-place and the sole argument (*Zaydun*) is automatically assigned Topic
function (cf. 15). On the other hand, in sentences with an n-place predicate, the
question arises whether Topic is assigned to any of the arguments or whether
there is a hierarchy inducing a preference for particular arguments.
    In principle, any argument of a predication can receive Topic function pro-

vided, of course, that it does not already bear a pragmatic function (e.g. Focus). Semantic functions do not seem to play any part in Topic assignment. In (1b), (2b) and (2d), for example, Topic is assigned to the terms *Zaydun, Zaydan l-bārihata*, which have the semantic functions Agent, Goal and Time respectively:

(18)   Past raja^c_V $(dx_1: \text{Zayd}(x_1))_{\text{AgSubjTop}}$ $(dy_1: \text{bārihat}(y_1))_{\text{TimeNew-Focus}}$

(19)   Past qābal$_V$ $(dx_1: {}^c\text{Amr}(x_1))_{\text{AgNew-Focus}}$ $(dx_2: \text{Zayd}(x_2))_{\text{GoObj}}$

(20)   Past raja^c_V $(dx_1: \text{Zayd}(x_1))_{\text{AgSubjNew-Focus}}$ $(dy_1: \text{bārihat}(y_1))_{\text{TimeTop}}$

As to syntactic functions, however, it seems that in Arabic (as in several other natural languages), the term with Subject function is most likely to be Topic.[1] In other words, in an n-argument predication, Topic function is preferentially assigned to the argument to which Subject function has already been assigned. This links up, to a certain extent, with the analysis in the Arabic grammatical tradition according to which the relation of 'l-ʔisnād' (predication) holds, in the verbal sentence, between the predicate of the sentence and the term with the function of Subject. The predicate is called 'musnad' ('predicated about'), and the Subject term is called 'musnad ʔilayh' ('that which is predicated about'). This analysis, although too extreme (since Topic function is assigned neither exclusively nor obligatorily to the Subject), expresses a well-founded intuition about the Subject term's special right to receive Topic function. If the hypothesis of Subject priority is tenable, the following 'Topic-worthiness Hierarchy' (TWH) may be posited:

(21)   *Topic-worthiness hierarchy (TWH)*

$$\text{Subject} > \left\{ \begin{array}{l} \text{Object} \\ \text{Recipient} \\ \text{Beneficiary} \\ \text{Time} \\ \ldots \\ \ldots \\ \text{etc.} \end{array} \right\}$$

3. The nature of the Topic term

3.1. Categories

The term to which Topic is assigned may be an NP, as is shown by the italicized constituents in (1a-b), (2a-d), (3a-b), (4a-d), (5a-b), (7a-b) and (9a-b). It

can also be a prepositional phrase as in (6a-b), or an anaphoric pronoun as in
(8a-d). Nor is it unusual for Topic to be assigned to an entire proposition, as
in (22) and (23):

(22)   ʔan tanāma   bākiran hayrun   laka
        that you-sleep early$_{acc}$ better$_{nom}$ to-you
        'You had better go to bed early'

(23)   l-ladī zāranī   Zaydun
        the-one visited-me Zayd$_{nom}$
        'The one who visited me was Zayd'

3.2. Case-marking

The formal expression of constituents (whether by case-marking, adpositions or a
combination of both) is in FG determined by the functions they fulfil: cases are
attributed on the basis of the semantic, syntactic and pragmatic functions[2]
borne by the various elements of the sentence. The case-form of a constituent that
is part of a predication (i.e. a term (argument or satellite), of a predication)
is determined by its semantic function and, if it has one, by its syntactic
function. The case-form of an 'external' constituent (i.e. the Theme or Tail) is
determined by its pragmatic function alone.[3]

    In Arabic, the 'internal' pragmatic functions (Focus, Topic, ...) are neutral
with respect to the cases borne by the terms to which they are assigned. Thus, a
term receiving an 'internal' pragmatic function displays the case conferred upon
it by its semantic (or possibly syntactic) function. In (1b), (2b), (2d) and
(4b), repeated here for convenience, the italicized constituents take the case-
forms bestown upon them by their functions of Subject, Object, Time and Subject
respectively, as is shown by the underlying representations (24), (25), (26) and
(27):

(1b)   raja^{c}a   *Zaydun* l-bārihata
        returned Zayd$_{nom}$ yesterday$_{acc}$
        'Zayd returned yesterday'

(24)   Past raja$^{c}_{V}$ (dx$_1$: Zayd(x$_1$))$_{AgSubjTop}$ (dy$_1$: bārihat(y$_1$))$_{TimeNew-Focus}$
                                    ⌣⌣⌣   ⌣⌣⌣
                                    NOM   ACC

(2b)   qābala *Zaydan* ^{c}Amrun
        met   Zayd$_{acc}$ ^{c}Amr$_{nom}$
        '^{c}Amr met Zayd'

(25)   Past qābal$_{V}$(dx$_1$: ^{c}Amr(x$_1$))$_{AgSubjNew-Focus}$ (dx$_2$: Zayd(x$_2$))$_{GoObjTop}$
                              ⌣⌣⌣   ⌣⌣⌣
                              NOM   ACC

(2d)   raja^{c}a   *l-bāriḥata*   Zaydun
        returned yesterday$_{acc}$ Zayd$_{nom}$
        'Zayd returned yesterday'

(26)   Past raja^c_V(dx$_1$: Zayd(x$_1$))$_{AgSubjNew\text{-}Focus}$ (dy$_1$: bāriḥat(y$_1$))$_{Time\ Top}$
                                        $\underset{\sim}{\text{NOM}}$ $\underset{\sim}{\text{ACC}}$

(4b)   *Zaydun   marīḍun*
        Zayd$_{nom}$ ill$_{nom}$
        'Zayd is ill'

(27)   Pres marīḍ$_A$ (dx$_1$: Zayd(x$_1$))$_{\emptyset SubjTop}$
                                        $\underset{\sim}{\text{NOM}}$

4. Positioning of the Topic

Let us recall that the order of constituents is co-determined in FG by syntactic
functions, pragmatic functions, the categorial complexity of constituents and,
to a certain, and as yet not clearly determined extent, semantic functions.[4] The
placement rules for a constituent to which Topic has been assigned and the constraints upon these rules differ quite appreciably according as the constituent
occurs in a sentence with a verbal predicate or in a sentence with a non-verbal
predicate (i.e. where the predicate is an adjective, noun or prepositional
phrase). We shall here consider only the positioning of the Topic in verbal sentences.

4.1. Topic placement rules

We have already had occasion to argue[5] for the hypothesis that the constituents
of the Arabic verbal sentence are ordered according to the following pattern:

(28)   P2, P1 P∅ V S (0) (X), P3

Two types of position may be distinguished in this pattern: the 'external' positions (P2 and P3) occupied by constituents that do not belong to the predication
proper (the Theme and the Tail respectively); and the 'internal' positions occupied by constituents that are elements of the predication. As for the latter,
position P1 is generally occupied by complementizers, while P∅ is reserved for
constituents with the pragmatic function of Focus (e.g. interrogative pronouns,
contrastive Focus) or of Topic; positions V, S, (0) and (X) are occupied by the
verb, Subject, Object and any other constituent respectively, such that (X) is
the position for constituents that lack a syntactic or pragmatic function which

could place them in one of the other positions.

A constituent with Topic function may occupy the position corresponding to its syntactic function (i.e. position S or position O) or, if it has no syntactic function, the position conferred upon it by its semantic function. Thus, in (1b) and (2a), the constituents *Zaydun* and *Zaydan* occupy positions S and O respectively, positions corresponding to their syntactic functions of Subject and Object. In (2c), the constituent *l-bārihata* occupies position X by virtue of its semantic function (Time). However, in accordance with a general tendency (a tendency which is not specific to Arabic), the preferred position of the Topic is early in the sentence, witness (6b) and (9a-b).

There is a problem with such cases: what is the exact position occupied by the Topic? In other words, since FG recognizes three clause-initial positions (cf. pattern (28)), does the Topic, when placed at the beginning of the sentence, occupy position P2, position P1 or position PØ? The facts of Arabic suggest the following solution to this problem:

(i) The Topic of (6b) and (9a-b), although placed at the beginning of the sentence, can only occupy a position inside the predication, since it is a term (i.e. an element that receives a given semantic function and to which a syntactic function may be assigned); this emerges clearly from the structure (29) underlying (6b):

(29)   Past qābala$_V$ (dx$_1$: tu(x$_1$))$_{AgSubj}$ (dx$_2$: kitāb(x$_2$))$_{GoObjNew-Focus}$

        (dy$_1$: laylat mādiyat(y$_1$))$_{TimeTop}$

It follows that the Topic cannot be placed in P2, which is one of the positions characterized by being outside the predication proper. One indication that Topic position is inside the predication is that sentences in which the Topic constituent is placed in front of the complementizers (e.g. the interrogative particle *ʔa*) which always occupy absolute initial position in the predication (i.e. position P1) are ungrammatical:

(30) a. fi l-laylati   l-mādiyati ʔa qaraʔta kitāban
        in the-night$_{gen}$ the-past$_{gen}$ Q you-read book$_{acc}$
        'Last night, did you read a book?'

     b. Zaydan   ʔa qābaltahu?
        Zayd$_{acc}$ Q you-met-him
        'Zayd, did you meet him?'

c. l-kitāba   ʔa qaraʔtahu?
   the-book_acc Q you-read-it
   'The book, did you read it?'

(ii) Having concluded that sentence-initial Topic does not occupy P2 but a position inside the predication, we still have to determine if it occupies P1 or PØ. Consider the following sentences:

(31) a. ʔa fi l-laylati   l-mādiyati qaraʔta kitāban?
        Q in the-night_gen the-past_gen you-read book_acc
        'Did you read a book last night?'

     b. ʔa Zaydan   qabaltahu?
        Q Zayd_acc you-met-him
        'Did you meet Zayd?'

In (31a-b), the Topic constituents *fi-laylati l-mādiyati* and *Zaydan* are preceded by the complementizer *ʔa* which, as we have seen, occupies absolute initial position in the predication (i.e. P1). If a position generally cannot be occupied by more than one constituent, position P1 is filled by the complementizer and therefore cannot house another constituent. The Topic consequently occupies the remaining available position, PØ. Thus we may now propose the following rule of Topic placement:

(32)   Topic ----opt----> PØ

4.2. Constraints on the placement of Topic in PØ

A Topic placed in PØ is necessarily a 'referring expression', i.e. an expression conveying information likely to allow the hearer to identify, in a given setting, the entity it refers to. In sentences in which the Topic does not have this property (i.e. is not a referring expression), placement in PØ is blocked, witness the ungrammaticality of (33a-c) as compared to (6b) and (9a-b), repeated here for convenience:

(33) a.*fi laylatin qaraʔtu kitāban
       in night_gen I-read book_acc
       'One night I read a book'

     b.*rajulan qabaltuhu
       man_acc I-met-him
       'A man, I met him'

      c.*kitāban qaraʔtuhu
         book$_{acc}$ I-read-it
         'A book, I read it'

(6) b. fi l-laylati   l-māḍiyati qaraʔtu kitāban
        in the-night$_{gen}$ the-past$_{gen}$ I-read book$_{acc}$
        'Last night I read a book'

(9) a. Zaydan qābaltuhu
        Zayd$_{acc}$ I-met-him
        'I have met Zayd'

      b. l-kitāba   qaraʔtuhu
        the-book$_{acc}$ I-read-it
        'I have read the book'

The referentiality constraint may be formulated as follows:[6]

(34)   *Referentiality Constraint*

        A Topic placed in PØ must be a *referring expression* (i.e. an expression
        conveying information permitting the hearer to identify its referent).

In Arabic, certain constituents cannot be placed in PØ, even if they have the
functions of Topic or Contrastive Focus:
(i) In Arabic, the constituent with the syntactic function Subject is normally
placed after the verb in accordance with the pattern (28), repeated her for convenience:

(28)   P2, P1 PØ V S (0) (X), P3

If it is placed before the verb, it can only occupy position P2, thus becoming a
Theme. Sentence (35), which differs from (1b) in the positioning of the SubjTop
constituent before the verb is to be analysed not as (36) but as (37):

(35)   Zaydun rajaᶜ-a   l-bāriḥata
        Zayd$_{nom}$ returned-he yesterday$_{acc}$
        'Zayd returned yesterday'

(36)   Zaydun (Top) rajaᶜa l-bāriḥata (New-Focus)

(37)   Zaydun (= x_i) (Theme), rajaᶜa (= x_i) (Top) l-bāriḥata (New-Focus)

As is clear from (37), Topic function is assigned in (35) not to *Zaydun*, which,
by virtue of its position outside the predication (P2), is a Theme, but to the

pronoun -*a* which refers back to the Theme from within the verb raja^{c}a. Our conclusion is that the term to which Topic function is assigned, if it is also
Subject, necessarily occupies the position conferred upon it by its syntactic
function, as in (1b), repeated here for convenience:

(1b)   raja^{c}a Zaydun l-bārihata
        returned Zayd$_{nom}$ yesterday$_{acc}$
        'Zayd returned yesterday'

(ii) A constituent with the semantic function Companion,[7] if assigned Topic
function, necessarily occupies the position it has by virtue of its semantic
function. It cannot be placed in PØ because of a syntactic rule of Arabic preventing Companion terms from being positioned before the verb:

(38)   A: man sāfara   wa Zaydan (Top)?
            who travelled and Zayd$_{acc}$
            'Who travelled with Zayd?'
(39)   B: a. sāfara ^{c}Amrun wa Zaydan (Top)
                travelled ^{c}Amr$_{nom}$ and Zayd$_{acc}$

            b. *wa Zaydan sāfara ^{c}Amrun
               and Zayd$_{acc}$ travelled ^{c}Amr$_{nom}$
               '^{c}Amr travelled with Zayd'

(iii) Sentences in which an ObjTop is placed in PØ are, to say the least, marked.
Thus, (42), in which the ObjTop (*Zaydan*) is positioned before the verb, is marked
if not ungrammatical as compared with (41), where the constituent occupies the
position conferred upon it by its syntactic function:

(40)   A: man ra?ā   Zaydan (Top)?
            who has-seen Zayd$_{acc}$
            'Who has seen Zayd?'
(41)   B: ra?ā ^{c}Amrun Zaydan (Top)
            has-seen ^{c}Amr$_{nom}$ Zayd$_{acc}$

(42)   ??Zaydan(Top) ra?ā ^{c}Amrun
        Zayd$_{acc}$ has-seen ^{c}Amr$_{nom}$
        '^{c}Amr has seen Zayd'

Yet sentences like (42) lose their marked character when the Topic placed in PØ
is picked up again by a suffixed anaphoric pronoun in the verb, as in (9a) and

(9b) uttered in response to (43) and (44) respectively:

(43)   A: hal qābalta Zaydan (Top)
             Q   you-met Zayd$_{acc}$
             'Did you meet Zayd?'

(9a)   B: Zaydan (= x_i) (Topic) qābaltuhu (= x_i)
             Zayd$_{acc}$ I-met-him
             'I met Zayd'

(44)   A: hal qaraʔta l-kitāba (Top)
             Q   you-read the-book$_{acc}$
             'Did you read the book?'

(9b)   B: l-kitāba (= x_i) (Top) qaraʔtuhu (= x_i)
             the-book$_{acc}$ I-read-it
             'I read the book'

Moreover, sentences of structure (42) are not problematic if the Object constituent placed sentence-initially is understood as having not Topic function
but Contrastive Focus function, as is shown by (46) uttered as a contrastive
response to (45):

(45)   A: qābalta ^{C}Amran
             you-met ^{C}Amr$_{acc}$
             'You met ^{C}Amr'

(46)   B: Zaydan (Contrastive-Focus) qābaltu (lā ^{C}Amran)
             Zayd$_{acc}$ I-met   not ^{C}Amr$_{acc}$
             'It was Zayd I met (, not ^{C}Amr)'

If this analysis is correct, (42) will tend to be interpreted as a contrastive
response to (47). If so, the Object constituent *Zaydan* will have the pragmatic
function Contrastive Focus, not Topic:

(47)   A: raʔā ^{C}Amrun (Top) Hālidan (Foc)
             has-seen ^{C}Amr$_{nom}$ Hālid$_{acc}$
             '^{C}Amr has seen Hālid'

(48)   B: Zaydan (Contrastive Focus) raʔā ^{C}Amrun (Top) (lā Hālidan)
             Zayd$_{acc}$ has-seen ^{C}Amr$_{nom}$ not Hālid$_{acc}$
             'It is Zayd that ^{C}Amr has seen (, not Halid)'

    Position PØ, as we have pointed out, is one position for a constituent to
which the pragmatic function Topic or Focus has been assigned. This position can

only be occupied by one constituent, i.e. one Topic or one Focus.[8] Sentences
(49a-c) are ungrammatical because PØ is occupied by a Topic *and* a Focus:

(49) a.*man (Foc) l-bāriḥata (Top) ra?ayta?
        who   yesterday$_{acc}$ you-saw
        'Who did you see yesterday?'

     b.*matā (Foc) Zaydan (Top) ?a^{c}tayta kitāban
        when   Zayd$_{acc}$ you-gave book$_{acc}$
        'When did you give Zaydan a book?'

     c.*l-kitāba (Contrastive Focus) Zaydan (Top) ?a^{c}taytu
        the-book$_{acc}$ Zayd$_{acc}$ I-gave
        'It's the book that I gave to Zayd'

If Topic function is assigned to more than one term in a predication, only one
of them may occupy PØ, hence the ungrammaticality of (50c) as compared with (50b):

(50) a. mādā fa^{c}alta l-bāriḥata (Top) fi l-bayti (Top)
        what you-did yesterday$_{acc}$ in the-house$_{gen}$
        'What did you do at home yesterday?'

     b. l-bāriḥata (Top) qara?tu kitāban fi l-bayti (Top)
        yesterday$_{acc}$ I-read book$_{acc}$ in the-house$_{gen}$

     c.*l-bāriḥata (Top) fi l-bayti (Top) qara?tu kitāban
        yesterday$_{acc}$ in the-house$_{gen}$ I-read book$_{acc}$
        'Yesterday I read a book at home'

5. *Conclusions*

The pragmatic function Topic is assigned in Modern Standard Arabic to the constituent referring to the entity 'spoken about' in the predication, in accordance
with the Topic-worthiness Hierarchy giving priority to Subjects. A constituent
to which Topic function is assigned receives the case conferred upon it by its
semantic or syntactic function. In Modern Standard Arabic, the pragmatic function
Topic plays no role in determining the case-form of constituents. The semantic
and syntactic function of the Topic also determine its positioning. However, in
accordance with a general tendency, it frequently occupies a preverbal position:
this is not P1, as the placement rules of FG might lead one to expect, but PØ.
Two fundamental constraints govern the rule placing Topic in PØ, the
'referentiality constraint' and the 'single occupancy constraint'. Other constraints, which we have been unable to examine here for lack of space, must also
be envisaged in this connection, notably 'island constraints' which could be
reformulated, in an FG framework, in terms of constraints on the PØ placement
rule.

NOTES

[1] See, for the tendency for Topic function to be preferentially assigned to Subject, Dik (1978: 143).

[2] Moutaouakil (1983a) studies the interaction of semantic, syntactic and pragmatic functions as determiners of the cases displayed by the terms to which they are assigned and proposes the following hierarchy of decreasing influence:

syntactic functions > semantic functions > pragmatic functions.

[3] See, for the case-marking of the Theme in Arabic, Moutaouakil (1983b).

[4] We believe that the intuition of the ancient Arabic grammarians that semantic functions also determine the order of constituents is not without empirical foundation. It remains to be established, however, to what extent semantic functions influence constituent order and how they interact with syntactic and pragmatic functions in this respect.

[5] See Moutaouakil (1983a) for the arguments motivating the postulation of P∅.

[6] See, for a pragmatic approach to reference, Dik (1978: 55-56).

[7] We shall give the label 'Companion' to the semantic function associated with the constituents called 'Maf^{C}ūl ma^{C}ahu' in the Arabic grammatical tradition.

[8] The constraint which we shall call the 'Single Occupancy Constraint' may be formulated as follows:

Single Occupancy Constraint

Any one position may be occupied by only one constituent.

Chapter 7

Some considerations concerning the notion of 'psychological reality' in functional grammar

Jan Nuyts
Department of Germanic Philology, University of Antwerp

0. Introduction

In this paper, I will be concerned with some aspects of the problems inherent in the notion of psychological adequacy as part of the methodological requirements of Functional Grammar (FG) (Dik 1978 : 7ff, 1983: 6ff). Introducing this notion implies associating the model in one way or other with the study of the 'psychological reality' of language, and this association is important on the one hand for the discussion between FG and a competing model like Transformational Grammar (TG), and on the other hand for future perspectives and developments of FG. My aim is to investigate the plausibility in this respect, first of the functional view of language in general, as opposed to the formal view inherent in TG, and second of the FG model in particular. More precisely, I want to sketch the motivation for the introduction of what I will call a 'Functional Procedural Grammar' (FPG) (see De Schutter and Nuyts 1983). In order to do this, however, I will have to start by making some remarks on the notion of 'psychological reality' in general.[1]

1. Linguistic and psycholinguistic models and 'psychological reality'

1.1. Process models

Des Tombe (1976) makes a distinction between two basic types of models, each having a different status in the study of language, viz. taxonomic models and process models. A taxonomy is any model that gives 'an enumeration of all possible acts of behaviour and their mutual relations' (Des Tombe 1976: 131; my translation), i.e. it is a model of the structure of linguistic utterances. A process model, on the other hand, is also a taxonomy, since it enumerates all possible acts of behaviour as well, but not in any ad hoc manner: it aims at describing the factual performance processes involved in the behaviour under consideration. Or, put differently, it aims at 'psychological reality'.

Now, we might wonder what makes a particular model a process model. Or, alternatively, how can we gain insight into the performance processes, the psychological reality of language? Since the failure of behaviorism, no one will doubt the necessity of accepting the existence of complex systems of rules underlying this behaviour, giving it the meaningfulness we all know it has. Nevertheless, the problem remains that the human mind is indeed a 'black box', to which there is no direct access. We cannot observe in any way the processes and systems about which we have to hypothesize in order to explain language use. Of course, the mind has a material aspect, since it is a function of the neurophysiology of the brain. But this fact is not very helpful, for we do not know what (sort of) function is concerned. In the case of language, we have fairly good notions of the neurophysiology of speech and hearing, but how the psychological mechanisms of language are engaged in these processes is still one big question. And it will remain one as long as neurolinguists cannot make use of well-motivated hypotheses about the mental structures of language. Obviously, the construction of such hypotheses cannot ignore what is known about the neurophysiology of the brain, but these matters can only restrict the number of possibilities.[2]

Thus, in language, only the effects of the performance processes are observable, i.e. linguistic utterances used in particular environments as acoustic strings with a particular syntactic organization on different levels, and the meanings of parts of these utterances and the utterances as a whole, in isolation and in context; moreover, different types of intuitive reflections on these utterances (on their form, meaning, way of being used, etc.) and other types of indirect behavioral clues accompanying the linguistic behaviour. Gaining insight into the performance processes can therefore never be a direct matter, it will always depend on indirectly trying to account for the data of linguistic behaviour.[3] The matter is to fill in what we all know must happen somehow, viz. a connection of the sound pattern we observe and of the meaning we know it has, in two directions depending on whether we produce or interpret the utterance; a connection on which we can moreover reflect somehow in judging the utterance in question. Only if we are able to develop one coherent system for these performance processes which can account for the whole variety of linguistic behavioral acts (i.e., that is able to predict the behaviour of a normal speaker/hearer in a particular situation in a way that is moreover compatible with insights gained into the acquisition, pathological disturbances, genetics, phylogeny, etc. of language) can we have certainty that our guesswork has been adequate.

It should be clear then, that the distinction between process models and non-process models cannot be made on any a priori basis, in the sense that each would take into account other (types of) data. Or, as Chomsky (1980: 107) puts it, there is no 'psychological data' and 'other data', there is only 'data'. The question whether a particular model can be considered to be a process model will therefore simply depend on a negative argumentation: is there any good reason to say that the model under consideration is not adequate? That is to say, a model has to fulfil one preliminary condition in order to be considered for this title. Obviously, a descriptive system that is content to merely inventory and order 'possible acts of behaviour and their relations' on a purely inductive basis, without using any deductive principles explaining these acts and their relations, will certainly not provide any insights into the performance processes. A process model will always have to be developed on the basis of deductive reasoning, creating a theoretical framework that determines the choice and ordering of types and systems of rules necessary to treat the behavioral data. As Des Tombe says, a process model necessarily takes the form of a simulating device. Once this condition is fulfilled, however, there are two types of questions that have to be put, in order to consider the 'psychological reality' of a particular model: on the one hand, there is the criterion of observational adequacy (or 'external descriptive adequacy') within the domain of aspects of the linguistic behavioral data the model wants to account for; on the other hand, there is the compatibility of the general premises on which the particular model is developed, with insights gained into other aspects of linguistic behaviour, or more generally, with widely accepted and well-motivated views on what we can expect to be the nature of the performance processes (i.e. 'internal descriptive adequacy'). If there is no reason to reject the model in one of these respects, then we may call it a process model. A process model, then, is any model for which there have not yet been found any arguments to refute it.

1.2. Linguistics and psycholinguistics

At this point, an excursion into the relation between linguistics and psycholinguistics seems necessary. It follows from the above exposition that there is no reason to believe that only psycholinguistic models can be models of the performance processes. We can only agree with Ryle's (1949: 308) criticism of the view 'that psychology is the sole empirical study of people's mental powers, propensities and performances', and with Katz' (1964) and Chomsky's (passim) defence of a mentalistic view of linguistics. Indeed, models like TG or FG certainly fulfil the preliminary condition for being considered as a candidate for a process model, since they both use deductive ways of reasoning, in the above sense.

But obviously, their deductive systems are restricted: they certainly cannot be conceived of as models for the full variety of aspects that we can expect to be involved in the performance processes. They are only intended to treat the syntactic organization of utterances at the sentence level, and they are not able to treat the syntax of the text or discourse. And though the attitude toward the role of semantic and pragmatic aspects in the understanding and treatment of the syntactic organization of utterances is completely different in both models (a difference that is reflected immediately in the concepts used to explain the sur- face organization of utterances), neither of them describe the semantic (or knowledge-based) and pragmatic systems involved in linguistic performance (e.g. such matters as presupposition, metaphor, speech acts, etc. do not belong to the domain of these models). It is precisely here that one of the main differences between these linguistic models and (theoretical) psycholinguistic models (in- cluding artificial intelligence models) can be found: these linguistic models primarily concentrate on the syntactic aspects of linguistic behaviour, and they depend as much as possible on data within their specific domain of inquiry, thus attaining a considerable amount of precision in their concepts and rules; psycho- linguists on the other hand rather theorize on the whole system of performance processes, thus developing models that are much less detailed and complete on each level, but which give a much better idea of the general concept of these processes, and of the interaction of the different levels within them (a classic- al example from AI is Winograd 1972, a more recent one from theoretical psycho- linguistics is Schlesinger 1977). Of course, there are also differences between these 'disciplines': linguists typically use idealized data (complete and in- tuitively well-formed sentences, written language, etc.), whereas psycholinguists are concerned with 'real' behaviour (spoken phrases, including error performances) moreover, the latter use experimental techniques for data-gathering and hypothesis testing, whereas the former do not. Although (above all functional) linguists are clearly changing their attitude in these respects: much more attention is being paid to experimental data-gathering, to the analysis of spoken language, etc.

Anyhow, it seems clear that the difference between linguistics and psycholin- guistics is only a matter of orientation, and both 'disciplines' appear to be com- plementary. There is consequently every reason to try and reach a greater integra- tion of both. Yet it is clear that this opens important perspectives for evaluating and selecting models within linguistics. For we have to take Katz (1964: 133f) at his word when he says that 'since the psychologist and the mentalistic linguist are constructing theories of the same kind, [...] it follows that the linguist's theory is subject to the requirement that it harmonize with the psychologist's theories', and thus, this 'requirement enables us to refute a linguistic theory

if we can find psychological theories or facts that are inconsistent with it'.
(See Watt 1974 from the psycholinguistic perspective). More specifically, we can
expect linguistic models to be integrable into a complete process model of the
type developed in psycholinguistics. If they are not, they should be rejected.

2. Functionalism versus formalism and psychological validity

2.1. The functionalism/formalism distinction

The difference between the functional paradigm (to which FG belongs) and the
formal paradigm (of which TG is the most outstanding exponent) in linguistics
concentrates on one question: is the fact that language is used by its owner,
man, to perform activities that are subsumed under the heading of 'communication'
and thus also the fact that language fulfils particular functions in this
respect, taken into account or not, in analysing the syntax of linguistic utterances? (For an analysis of the notion of 'language function', see Nuyts 1984 and
Nuyts in preparation). At first sight, the difference might appear to be a methodological one: formalists analyse syntax in a pure form, abstracting away from
the fact that the utterances are meaningful in the context in which they are
used, whereas functionalists do take into account this meaningfulness (in a broad
sense) of utterances in analysing their structure, thus trying to demonstrate how
the syntax of these utterances reflects their semantic and pragmatic properties.
So it seems that functionalists are doing more than formalists. And from a
psychological point of view, it indeed seems natural to take these functions into
account: given the nature of the study of psychological reality (see 1.), the
fact that the linguistic system is used for particular purposes is an important
support in the development of models of this system, since we have to accept that
its organization must be such as to allow the performance in this respect. That
is, we have to accept that the linguistic system is, at least minimally, a goal-
directed system (on this notion, see e.g. Nagel 1979), and therefore the use of
teleological explanations in analysing the syntax of utterances (as is done in
FG) seems perfectly sound.

However, this view is firmly denied by generative linguists: Chomsky has
transformed the functionalism/formalism distinction into a principled one, by
claiming that the purely formal TG-model is psychologically plausible, and by
developing a view on the psychology of language that is completely incompatible
with the functional view of language. Now, since Chomsky was the first to make
such strong claims with respect to the psychological reality of the TG-model,
this model has been in the focus of attention of psycholinguists. We may there-

fore, in the light of the conclusion of 1.2., consider the plausibility of
Chomsky's claims.

2.2. Competence and native-speaker intuitions

As is well-known, TG is according to Chomsky a model of the competence of the
native speaker/hearer, i.e. a completely autonomous system of syntactic rules
which is neutral as to the production and perception of utterances (the performance). Nevertheless it is central to both (i.e. the competence grammar forms a
central component of the performance systems (Chomsky 1965: 10ff)), and it is
reflected directly in the capacity to judge utterances. On this assumption, the
TG-model should be integrable into a performance model. But, given the outline
of TG, it is a priori difficult to imagine how this could happen, and Chomsky
himself has never given any hints on this matter.[5] And there indeed do appear to
be problems in this respect. As mentioned before, using language is obviously a
matter of linking together sounds and meanings, and psycholinguists seem to agree
that this happens through two systems, one for production, i.e. the linking of a
meaning to an observable utterance, and one for perception, i.e. the linking of
this observable sound pattern to a meaning. There are certainly links between
these systems, for there is no doubt that they make use of the same types of
concepts and representations, and moreover, one can expect feedback between them
for a number of reasons, but nevertheless, there is rather general agreement that
both systems have a considerable degree of independence (See e.g. Bever 1975,
Straight 1976, Des Tombe 1976, Schlesinger 1977, Clark and Clark 1977, Steinberg
1982, and many others). Now, various attempts at incorporating the TG-model in
one way or other into process models for these systems, particularly for the
perceptive aspect of the performance processes, have failed, and experimental
tests on its psychological adequacy have been negative in the majority of cases
(Reviews of the research in this respect are numerous: cf. Des Tombe 1976 and the
literature he mentions, but also Greene 1972, Levelt 1973, Cairns and Cairns
1976). This justifies the conclusion that 'the problems may be not that our experimental procedures fail to measure perceptual complexity, but rather that it
is a mistake to claim psychological reality for the operations whereby grammars
generate structural descriptions' (Fodor and Garrett 1966: 152).

Chomsky has defended his position by claiming that TG remains a plausible model
of the competence of the native speaker, but that the way this 'organ' is put
to use is still a complete mystery (e.g. Chomsky 1975a: 137ff and 1980: passim).

A simple way to deny psycholinguistics altogether. But there is little reason to
doubt that the psychological claim with respect to TG in itself is one big mys-
tification. For, what are Chomsky's arguments? In fact, there are none. He only
suggests that the adequacy of TG is warranted on the basis of the fact that it
takes into account the intuitions of the native speaker (this is in fact the
essence of the level of descriptive adequacy, on which TG is situated; cf. e.g.
Chomsky 1964: 923ff). When Chomsky (1975b: 36) says that 'the speaker-hearer's
judgements that the facts are as determined by the grammar are thus explained by
the linguistic theory', he clearly suggests that these intuitions open the way
to psychological reality. But obviously, this is not the case. Intuitions are no
better data than primary linguistic data, and Chomsky's statement is circular: a
native speaker does not judge an utterance to be grammatical (i.e. to be as is
stated by the grammar), he only judges it to be well-formed. 'Grammaticality' is
a theoretical notion, not an observational one, and the grammar (and thus 'grammaticality') is the linguist's interpretation of the judgments (see Levelt 1973,
Seuren 1977, Parret 1979). The question remains whether it is a good interpretation. In fact, for TG this is doubtful, since, first of all, the intuitions that
are treated are only a minimal subpart of the whole variety of linguistic intuitions (Nuyts 1983a); moreover, the way they are handled is completely counter to
their nature (Bever 1970, 1971, Levelt 1973). (Bever suggests that TG might be a
model of the mental mechanisms underlying the expression of intuitions; but this
would imply that these mechanisms are independent of the performance processes
themselves. Given the fact that intuitions are reflections on performances
(Levelt 1973), this view appears very implausible (Des Tombe 1976).)

2.3. Innatism

Generativists might reply that the descriptive adequacy of TG is warranted on
internal grounds (i.e. TG has internal descriptive adequacy; see 1.1.), on the
basis of the theory on language acquisition developed in UG (e.g. Chomsky 1965:
27). This UG is a hypothesis about the rich 'theory' of the form of possible
languages which forms part of the innate Language Acquisition Device (LAD),
together with a simplicity criterion.[5] It is, according to Chomsky, an empirical
question how the child acquires one specific TG for his native language (Chomsky
1965: 37ff). But in fact, there is nothing empirical in this theory, since it
has nothing to do with real study of language acquisition by the child. The system of UG is developed purely on the basis of TG descriptions of languages, from
which the concepts and principles that are considered to be universal are ab-

stracted.[6] So, LAD is nothing but an extension of the TG-model. In fact, the
various claims on which the fundamental idea of a LAD as an innate syntactic
system rests have been rejected on many occasions, and the empirical study of
child language and related disciplines strongly support a functional view of
language.

Not only is the way Chomsky uses the argument of innatism very unrevealing
from a methodological viewpoint, since it prevents one from really searching for
explanations in these matters (Schlesinger 1982), but also the whole idea is in
itself very implausible (for a review, see Levelt 1975). First of all, it is not
much of an argument to say that the child acquires its language in a minimally
short period, on the basis of very imperfect input-data. For this short period
(which nevertheless covers approximately 14 years) is in fact a critical period
for language acquisition, and is from the neuropsychological point of view to be
considered as a period of high sensitivity for linguistic inputs, enabling the
child to learn language with enormous ease (e.g. Lenneberg 1967, Lamendella
1977). And the imperfect input-data are not imperfect at all from the point of
view of the child: the language used by parents in interaction with children,
so-called 'baby-talk', is not random, but is optimally adapted to the capacities
of the child (Clark and Clark 1977); moreover, these input-data are strongly
situation-bound, and language acquisition relies heavily on situational factors
(e.g. Bruner 1974). In fact, the body of recent child language research takes it
for granted that the acquisition of syntax is dependent upon the global cognitive
development of the child, and strongly relies on earlier more primitive communicative (pragmatic) capacities (see e.g. Gillis 1983, 1984 for a general review).

This view fits in perfectly with what is generally expected to be the phylo-
genetic origin of language (on the relation between ontogeny and phylogeny, see
Lamendella 1976): although there is no doubt that a language with such a complex
syntactic system is inherent in man only, enough arguments and data on its evolution have been gathered to make the claim very plausible that this system indeed is a further development of communication systems that are inherent in
lower species, and that its development is due to an expansion in one way or
other of cognitive possibilities (see e.g. Lamendella 1976, 1977, Dingwall 1975,
1979).[7]

And finally, from the genetic point of view as well, there is very little
plausibility in the claim that there are very complex and specifically syntactic
innate structures like UG. There is rather general agreement on the view that
behavioral systems are only indirectly genetically determined: 'This point is
very well taken. It seems unlikely that genes actually transmit behaviour as we

observe it in the living animal because the course that an individual takes in
its peregrinations through life must necessarily depend on environmental contin-
gencies which could not have been 'programmed and prepared for' in advance'
(Lenneberg 1967: 22). Or, put differently, 'there is no need to assume 'genes
for language' (Lenneberg 1967: 265). In the case of the system of language, the
determination is most probably through an open genetic programme, i.e. a programme in which there is great scope for environmental influences (Mayr 1974,
Dingwall 1975): influences that are to be assimilated during the period critical
for learning (see above). In this way, 'we should no longer need to explain the
universal forms of linguistic behaviour as reflecting corresponding innate forms
in their underlying capacities and endowments. For universal forms might simply
reflect the universality of the 'objective functions' which language is every-
where used to perform' (Toulmin 1972: 465) (see also Whitaker 1973).

2.4. The domain of functionalism

In sum, then, there does not seem much room left for an autonomous syntactic
system like TG to be called a process model. As Watt (1974: 32) puts it, 'The
truth is that the 'mentalism' of most of us generativists is as irrelevant to
our linguistic practice as our taste in movies'. Moreover, the argumentation in
2.1. has not been refuted. We have not found any arguments to doubt the claim
that formalism in linguistics is in fact nothing but a restrictive way of analysing linguistic data, and that in order to develop process models for linguistic
behaviour, the functions language is used to perform are an important instrument.
On the contrary, the studies cited in 2.3. clearly reinforce this view, since
they stress the dependence of linguistic development on cognitive and situational
factors, factors that are indeed crucial in the functional view of language.

Of course, this does not mean that language must be considered to be an absolutely functional system. As Bossuyt (1983) states, one has to distinguish
clearly between the functionality of utterances, and the functionality of the
language system. Nevertheless, both are related to each other: the speaker/hearer
can use his language system in a more or less functional way, but this functionality is in any case restricted to the possibilities the language system offers;
and this system is most probably adapted more or less to the functions it is
used for, but this adaptation is restricted by the general possibilities the
human mind has, i.e. by the fundamental cognitive capacities of man (see 2.3.).
Functionality is dependent upon man's cognitive possibilities, in a positive
sense (they make functional systems possible), but at the same time in a negative

sense (they set a clear limit to the possibilities of developing functional systems) (see also Greenberg 1958: 78). Yet this fact obviously does not discredit
the use of teleological explanations in analysing the structure of language. In
this respect, functionalism is often misunderstood. Teleological explanation has
an important heuristic value, but it is not a dogmatic principle: it cannot be
forced against data (see also Dobzhansky et al. 1977: 497ff, from the biological
point of view). To make this point somewhat more concrete: the fact that,
according to the functional view of language, the syntactic organization of
utterances has to be treated in the light of semantic and pragmatic factors certainly does not imply that syntax could not have strictly independent principles
of organization (i.e. principles that are not reducible to semantic and pragmatic
aspects of utterances), and that from an epistemological viewpoint, these principles could not be considered without using semantic and pragmatic factors. It
only implies that, in an ontological way, syntax is used to express or retrieve
semantic and pragmatic aspects of linguistic utterances, and thus that its use is
determined by these aspects. Discovering to what extent syntax has particular
principles of organization will be a matter of proving to what extent such principles are necessary to account for the structure of utterances, and the discussion between Dik (1978) and De Schutter (1984) on this matter, for example,
can only be decided on the basis of data.

3. Functional Grammar and Functional Procedural Grammar

3.1. Functional Grammar and psycholinguistics

Unlike TG, FG has not (yet) been the object of research in psycholinguistics, so
that a direct comparison of FG with psycholinguistic evidence is not possible.
Nevertheless, its compatibility in principle with psycholinguistic theorizing is
obvious in three respects. First, section 2. has made clear that the fundamental
principles on which the model has been developed are psychologically plausible
(see also Bates and MacWhinney 1982). Second, it is not difficult to see that the
model of FG must be integrable into a complete process model for the productive
mode, along the lines stated in 2.2. (that this is indeed possible is demonstrated
in De Schutter and Nuyts 1983). Undoubtedly, a number of psycholinguists will
doubt the relevance of incorporating a 'syntactic' model like FG (or any other
linguistic model treating syntax) into a process model (probably due to their bad
experiences with TG in this respect): in psycholinguistics, there has been over
the years a clear move away from primarily syntactic parsing systems to models of
the perceptive capacity that are more and more semantically and pragmatically

oriented, and in which the role of syntax has become more and more subsidiary
(see e.g. Miller and Johnson-Laird 1976, Clark and Clark 1977, Schlesinger 1977,
Hörmann 1978, etc.). And although until now psycholinguistic research on the
productive processes has been minimal (e.g. Schlesinger 1977, Clark and Clark
1977), there is a clear tendency to take the same position in this respect. For
perception, this move is no doubt adequate, in order to understand how a speaker/
hearer runs through his performance systems in decoding utterances; probably it
is less adequate in the case of production, for this certainly is a much stricter
and more formal procedure, in which syntax remains more important (see Levelt
1973). But anyhow, these are no arguments against an incorporation of linguistic
syntax-models into process-models, for since these syntactic principles can be
noted in real utterances, they must be producible and interpretable, and thus,
no matter how important they are, they must be present in the performance processes. (On these problems concerning the relation between linguistic and psycholinguistic models, see Levelt 1973).

Third, the relevance of many of the principles and concepts used in FG is confirmed in psycholinguistics. To mention only some crucial aspects: syntactic,
and certainly semantic and pragmatic functions are used in nearly every proposal
concerning both adult language processing and child language development (cf.
Clark and Clark 1977, Bates and MacWhinney 1982) (which demonstrates that
accusing FG of eclecticism (Hoekstra 1978) is beside the point (Nuyts 1983b)).
The superiority of the dependency-like treatment of the syntactic organization
of utterances over the strongly hierarchical constituent analysis in TG is demonstrated by Levelt (1973, vol. 3: 25ff), on the basis of experiments on
speakers' intuitions with respect to syntactic coherence in utterances. Other
arguments in this respect can be found in Kempen (1978). The use of essentially
unordered underlying representations and of placement rules, rather than re-
placement rules (i.e. transformations) is comparable to the options taken, for
example, in Schlesinger (1977). On the fundamental plausibility of this choice,
given an underlying cognitive structure as input for production, see Levelt
(1973, vol. 3: 166ff).

3.2. Shortcomings of Functional Grammar as a psychologically real model

These positive signs notwithstanding, there are a number of reasons to hesitate
in calling FG as it now stands a psychologically real model. Firstly, there is
the matter of the observational adequacy of the model. Just like the majority of
linguistic models, FG focusses almost exclusively on an idealized corpus of data,

viz. short, simple and complete sentences that are considered to be acceptable on an intuitive basis, and not on real, natural performances (there are only first attempts in this direction by e.g. Lalleman 1983). Although this restriction is, on practical grounds, completely legitimate, expansion of the data base in that direction will lead without doubt to a number of essential modifications, at least in the type and character of the rules that are being formulated.

Secondly, there are more fundamental considerations concerning the 'internal descriptive adequacy' of FG. Again, just like any other syntactic model in linguistics, FG treats only particular (syntactic) aspects of the whole variety of aspects we can expect to be involved in the performance processes (see 1.2.). And again, there is, of course, no principled argument against this practical restriction. But we should be aware of the fact that this restriction can be dangerous, in that it can be misleading in a number of respects. Consider, first, the restriction to the treatment of sentence structure. Undoubtedly, the inclusion of text or discourse organization will lead to considerable changes in the treatment of the pragmatic functions in FG (cf. e.g. Bolkestein this vol., Hannay this vol.), and consequently in the whole system of expression rules. Moreover this would make it abundantly clear that these pragmatic functions are in the wrong place in the present outline of the model (Nuyts 1983a, De Schutter and Nuyts 1983). Another matter is the absence of a cognitive or knowledge system (the conceptual networks, in the sense used in AI). Integration of such a system will lead to a redefinition of the role of the lexicon, and to the formulation of a number of relations between the lexicon and this system which will cause modifications in the representation of lexical entries. Thus, semantic selection restrictions might become superfluous (e.g. Levelt 1973, Miller and Johnson-Laird 1976, Schlesinger 1977); and probably, the number of semantic functions now accepted in FG might be reduced, for several among them might in fact be cognitive roles, but not grammatically relevant semantic functions.

3.3. Towards a Functional Procedural Grammar

Until now, the bulk of work in FG has been directed towards treating as much data as possible within its framework, and the accent has been on its 'practical applicability' in typological research, on detecting 'surface structure' universals. In fact, the prime interest lies in the data, not in the model. Of course, universals are important, and the data are crucial. But nevertheless, we may not forget that the model will not take care of itself and eventually fall in line merely through the analysis of data. Indeed, the interpretation of the

data, of the universals detected, crucially depends on the possibilities inherent
in the model that is used, and there is every reason to look for a model that is
rich enough to cope with as many aspects as possible of the data. Induction and
deduction are equally important, and probably, deduction comes first.

It is here that the motivation can be found for setting up the project of an
integrated model of FG (an FPG), as sketched in De Schutter and Nuyts (1983).
This model is a first, and doubtless very tentative attempt to incorporate all
aspects of language that can be expected to be of any relevance for understanding
the use of language, into one strong deductive system that is conceived in the
productive mode, i.e. as a device transforming conceptual structures into acoustic strings (of course it will have to be completed with a model for the perceptive mode). It is hoped that in such a model a number of the problems of linguistic analysis in FG mentioned in 3.2. can be avoided.

But there is another hope underlying the model as well. As I said in 1.2.,
there is every reason to strive for a stronger integration of linguistics and
psycholinguistics, for both 'disciplines', having the same goals, appear to be
complementary in a number of respects. Since the failure of the intense collabo-
ration between them on the basis of TG, a new distance has grown. Certainly, one
of the reasons for this is that many psycholinguists, while they do not believe
any longer in the relevance of TG for their theory-building, still do believe
that the fundamental options of TG are inherent in linguistics in general (as
can be seen from the fact that they still pay lip service to TG, without in fact
taking notice of it; see e.g. Schlesinger 1977: 2ff, McNeill 1979: 281ff).
Therefore, the time has come to make psycholinguists aware of the fact that there
are indeed linguists working in the same vein as they are, and that an integration on the basis of the functional paradigm in linguistics is perfectly con-
ceivable. FPG might well be a point from which to start this new dialogue.

4. Conclusion

In this paper, I have argued for a new integration of linguistics and psycholinguistics, on the basis of the functional paradigm in the study of language.
An analysis of the problems inherent in studying the mental systems underlying
linguistic behaviour clearly demonstrates the methodological importance of the
functions of language for this study. Moreover, a scrutiny of the claims advanced
in TG and the formal paradigm connected with it and their relation to insights
generally accepted in both developmental and procedural psycholinguistics

unavoidably leads to a rejection of this paradigm (and of TG in particular) and to a reinforcement of the functional paradigm in linguistics. It should, therefore, be possible to start working on this new integration on the basis of an FPG, a model in which a somewhat modified version of FG is integrated.

NOTES

[1] I am grateful to G. de Schutter, S. Gillis and T. de Rycker for discussing with me some of the topics presented in this paper. A more elaborate version of it is to appear as Nuyts (forthcoming). See also Nuyts (in preparation).

[2] For reviews, see e.g. Marin (1976) and Dingwall (1979). On the relation between linguistics and the study of aphasia, see also Nuyts (1982a, 1982b). An argument in favour of a bifurcated model for linguistic performance (see 2.2.) as used for example by Straight (1976), on the basis of the existence of distinct regions in the brain for the production and perception of language (Broca's and Wernicke's area respectively), cannot be conclusive, for it is not clear to what extent these regions are involved in language for more than only speech and hearing. At most one can say that this fact does not exclude the bifurcation idea.

[3] As Chomsky (1959: 27) puts it: 'the only hope of predicting behaviour even in a gross way will be through a very indirect program of research that begins by studying the detailed character of the behaviour itself, and the particular capacities of the organism involved'.

[4] Formally speaking, TG is an algorithmic system, i.e. a productive device generating theorems. Or, put differently, TG produces structural descriptions for grammatical sentences. (On the formal properties of TG, and the problems with respect to its generative capacity, see Levelt 1973; see also Schank and Wilks 1974). Thus, we might wonder what it means to say that TG is neutral as to production and perception. In fact, it appears that TG was initially intended as a simple formal device; as Steinberg (1975, 1982) demonstrates, the mentalistic claims with respect to the model were only introduced from Chomsky (1959) on. And the psychological sense of 'generating' is therefore certainly a very disputable post hoc (and ad hoc) interpretation.

[5] This way of stating the problem has often lead to the assertion that the knowledge of language that is claimed in TG is 'knowledge that' instead of the 'knowledge how' that we could expect the performance processes to be. (See e.g. a number of contributions in Hook ed. 1969). Chomsky himself denies the validity of this distinction (which is borrowed from Ryle 1949), for classifying the 'tacit knowledge' of the competence of the language user. But, from a psychological viewpoint, there is little reason to doubt this distinction. See Nuyts (in preparation).

[6] The actual way of proceeding has little to do with detecting universals on the basis of the study of a wide range of languages, as might be expected. This is due to the fact that TG-descriptions are available for only a few languages. Actually, the universals are abstracted on the basis of a (more or less vague) criterion of 'learnability'. See Chomsky (1981).

7   Chomsky has always denied the relevance of a comparison of language with more
     primitive 'symbol systems', both in ontogeny and phylogeny (e.g. Chomsky
     1972: 175, 1975a: 41). But, as Goodman (1969: 139f) states: 'Chomsky argues
     that if the symbol systems we acquire prior to the acquisition of a full-
     fledged language have the characteristics he finds to be essential for a lan-
     guage, then acquisition of the prior systems would be equally remarkable and
     in need of explanation, while if the prior systems do not have these features,
     they can be of little help in acquiring a language. The latter part of this
     argument seems to me quite specious. If a man has made a clock by hand, that
     is a remarkable accomplishment. I understand it better if he tells me how he
     first fashioned crude tools, used these to make more refined ones, and even-
     tually made the clock. I do not protest that he could not have made the clock
     without first having made a timekeeping instrument. The tools used in making
     the clock are not timekeepers, and from the clock alone we cannot infer back
     to any specific characterization of the tools made and used at any stage
     along the way'. Or, as Greenberg (1958: 65) has put it, 'language evolves
     by begetting that which is not language but transcends it, even while it is
     dependent upon it'.

Chapter 8

The discourse function of the passive

Harm Pinkster
Department of Latin, University of Amsterdam

0. Introduction

The number of studies on the use and function of the passive - both studies on
individual modern languages and typological ones - is rapidly increasing. Within
the framework of Functional Grammar Dik's initial ideas on the passive construction have been elaborated by Bubenik (1983) and De Vries (1983). In this
article I will describe certain aspects of the so-called personal passive by
using the notion of perspective that figures in Dik's definition of the function
Subject (for example 1978: 92). I will use as an illustration examples from
classical Latin. My article is organized in the following way: I start with some
statistics in order to show that the frequency of the passive is higher than
most studies would suggest. Next I make a few observations on the presence, or
rather absence, of Agent expressions in passive sentences. I will argue that
Svartvik's (1966) distinction of agentive and non-agentive passive sentences is
useful, as can be shown on the basis of certain properties of the sentences involved. I then proceed to a discussion of the function of the passive in discourse and reject two current views, viz. the view of the passive as a device
for either discontinuity (for example in Givón (ed. 1983)) or continuity
(already to be found in Ernout 1908).

1. Statistics

In Latin the number of passive verb forms (both finite and non-finite) has been
computed at ca. 16% of all verb forms (Flobert 1975). The percentage does not
differ markedly from the figures given for modern languages such as German and
English. There is considerable variation between various authors and types of
text. I will come back to this later on. I see no reason to doubt the value of
the calculations one finds in the literature. However, in my opinion it is not
sufficiently clear what criterion has been used in establishing the frequency
of the passive. With one exception (Kilby 1984: 58) all studies I have seen
compute the frequency of the passive verb forms on the basis of the total number
of verb forms in a certain corpus, which, in my view, is not very fair: there is
not much sense in comparing passive verb forms with, for example, the forms of

the verb *to be* or Latin *esse* which, formally speaking, have active endings. A
verb like *esse* simply does not allow passive forms, so there is no sense in
calling *est* ('(he) is') an active form. The real frequency of the passive can
only be established by comparing the passive forms of verbal lexemes which allow
both an active and a passive form (that is to say two- or three-place predicates)
with the active forms of the same class of verbal lexemes. I will give an impression of the frequency of passive verb forms in two Latin texts,[1] comparing
the actual number of finite passive verb forms which might be transformed into
active verb forms with active verb forms which might reasonably be transformed
into passive verb forms. By 'reasonably' I mean, among other things, that I have
left out of account imperative and second person so-called adhortative subjunc-
tive forms which cannot be transformed into passive verb forms (a passive imperative does not exist in Latin). Participial phrases have also been left out of
account because the Latin verb system is quite defective in this respect. The
procedure of course implies decisions about which verbs may occur in the active
and the passive and about the notion of 'passive' itself: for example, are gerund
forms to be regarded as passive forms? I have decided to leave these out of
account, because they are not *simple* passive forms, to say the least. An examination of ca. 100 finite clauses in a comedy by Plautus (*Mostellaria*, with some
additional cases from the *Miles Gloriosus*) and in Book I of Cicero's philoso-
phical treatise *De Republica* yielded rather interesting results: whereas the
overall percentage of passive verb forms is about 10% of all verb forms in
Plautus (Flobert 1975), the result of my approach is that lexemes that allow
both passive and active forms do in fact occur as passive verb forms in 18% of
the cases concerned. The figure is even remarkably higher in the case of Cicero.
According to Flobert the frequency of passive verb forms in Cicero's philoso-
phical works is ca. 30%. I computed that no fewer than 43% of the finite verb
forms of those lexemes that do allow both active and passive are in the passive
voice. Now, although the frequency of passive verb forms in Cicero's *De Republica*
may be, and in fact is, higher than in other types of text, it is nonetheless
obvious that in certain circumstances the selection of the passive is not particularly marginal.

The percentages given above illustrate a fact that is mentioned in several
studies on the variation in frequency in various authors and various texts. For
Latin Ernout (1908) observed a considerable increase of the use of the passive
from archaic Latin (including *Plautus*) onwards, a phenomenon for which he suggested a diachronic explanation (see below). In modern languages the passive
construction occurs much less frequently in everyday speech than in scholarly

texts, for example. To my knowledge, Granger (1983) is the only study that tries
to explain why differences in frequency are found. According to her, colloquial
conversation as opposed to non-colloquial text types like 'discussion' and
'oration' contains relatively few activity verbs as opposed to mental process
verbs which in many languages do not passivize easily (1983: 318). Hence there
is a low number of passive verb forms. In other words, the subject matter of
the discourse influences the probability of occurrence of passive verb forms in
certain types of text. I have not been able to establish this for Latin (as yet).

   Another fact, which has recently been noted for English, concerns the uneven
distribution of passive verb forms within a specific text. Weiner and Labov
(1983) have argued on the basis of an extensive corpus study that the chance of
a passive verb form occurring does not so much depend on factors such as Subject
continuity but rather on the voice of the preceding verb form: if a passive verb
form precedes, the chance of a following verb form being passive is remarkably
higher than if an active verb form precedes. In other words, passives seem to
form clusters. A first impression is that, in Latin too, the distribution of
passive and active verb forms is quite uneven. This might suggest that not only
subject matter and text type are involved, but also the way of presenting the
subject matter. I will come back to this later.

2. Agent expressions

In Latin, as in English and German, the Agent - where Agent is used a in broad
sense for the first argument of a two- or three-place predicate - of an action
or process may be expressed in passive sentences, but normally this does not
actually happen. Conversely, if the Agent is explicit it may be omitted without
causing the remaining expression to be ungrammatical. In fact, the number of
instances of obligatory Agents in passive sentences given in the literature[2] is
very limited and these are open to other explanations. Examples like German

(1) a.   Das Dach wurde von vier Säulen getragen
         the roof was   by four columns carried
         'The roof was supported by four columns'

    b. *Das Dach wurde getragen

and

(2)   Das Tal   wird von einem Fluss durchzogen
        the valley was by a   river traversed
        'The valley was traversed by a river'

    b. *Das Tal wird durchzogen

are mentioned without any context, which may explain their oddity. The option-
ality of Agent expressions may be seen in various ways with respect to the
relationship between active sentences and their passive counterparts. For example,
one might hold that passives are derived predicates with certain characteristics
of their own to which optionally an Agent satellite may be added (for arguments
in favour of assuming a difference in meaning between active and passive sentences see Keenan 1981 and Pinkster 1984). Flobert (1975: 564) and others regard
the passive as an intransitivization device.[3] In my view the overwhelming absence
of Agent constituents should neither be neglected nor used as an argument too
rashly. One ought to distinguish at least two types of absence of Agents: the
first type is constituted by those cases in which no specific Agent is involved;
the other by those cases in which a specific Agent is involved which may be
identified on the basis of the information presented by the context and/or situation but need not be mentioned explicitly. I follow Svartvik's (1966) terminology in distinguishing 'non-agentive' and 'agentive' passive sentences, the
latter category being divided into 'agentful' and 'agentless' sentences. These
distinctions may be exemplified by the following sentences:

(3)   siquidem   quid   *agatur*   in caelo   quaerimus
        if at least what$_{nom}$ act$_{3sg\ pass}$ in heaven$_{abl}$ seek$_{1pl\ act}$
        ('Since we are now seeking what is going on in the heavens',
        Cic. *Rep.* 1, 19) - Non-Agentive: compare *fiat* ('is happening')

(4)   haec pluribus a *me* verbis   *dicta sunt*
        these more$_{abl}$ by me$_{abl}$ words$_{abl}$ say$_{3pl\ pass}$
        ('I have treated this matter at considerable length',
        Cic. *Rep.* 1, 12) - Agentive-agentful: compare the active trans-
        lation in the Loeb-edition

(5)   commemorare   eos   desino,   ne   quis
        mention$_{pres\ inf\ act}$ they$_{acc}$ stop$_{1sg\ act}$ lest someone$_{nom}$

        se   aut suorum   aliquem   *praetermissum*   queratur
        self$_{acc}$ or his (own)$_{gen}$ someone$_{acc}$ omit$_{perf\ inf\ pass}$ complain$_{3sg\ act}$[4]
        ('I will refrain from mentioning their names, lest someone complain
        of the omission of himself or some member of his family',
        Cic. *Rep.* 1, 1) - Agentive-agentless: the Agent ('by me') can be
        inferred from the main clause)

It is not always easy to decide whether a passive sentence is non-agentive or
agentless. However, a decision can be arrived at by examining first whether the
predicate involved may occur in the active voice at all with the same meaning -
which is not always easy either -, and, second, whether it is possible to identify
the Agent on the basis of the information contained in the context and/or sit-

uation. Latin has a marginal alternative for non-agentive passive sentences in
sentences with an active third person plural construction, exemplified by (6),
but (3) and (6) differ at least in one respect: in (6), just as in the case of
English *they*, the unspecified Agent is always human. This need not be the case
in the third person singular passive construction (example (3)).

(6)   Xenocratem   ferunt   respondisse
          Xenocrates$_{acc}$ say$_{3pl\ act}$ answer$_{perf\ inf\ act}$
          ('Xenocrates is said to have replied', Cic. *Rep.* 1, 3)

The non-agentive passive sentences, therefore, cannot simply be regarded as an
alternative for active sentences. It might, therefore, be the case that Subjects
of non-agentive passive sentences have other properties than Subjects of agentive
passive sentences and resemble, in this respect, for example, Subjects of one-
place process predicates. I will come back to this later. On the other hand, the
absence of Agent constituents in agentive passive sentences need not surprise us
at all. In active sentences in Latin, too, the Agent is quite frequently not
expressed if its identity is obvious on the basis of the information contained in
the context and/or situation. Anyway, the Agents might have the same properties
in both agentful and agentless sentences. They might even have the same properties as Agents of active sentences.

An application of the distinction between agentive and non-agentive passive
sentences to the texts of Plautus and Cicero shows that these texts do not differ
very much as to the number of non-agentive passive sentences - in both about half
of the number of passive sentences. They do differ, however, and very markedly
so, as to the presence of the Agent in agentive passive sentences. Whereas in
Cicero the Agent is expressed in 39 out of 46 sentences, the proportion in
Plautus is just the other way around: 7 out of 49 sentences (Table 7):

(7)   Explicitness of Agents

	Agentful	Agentless
Cic.	39	7
Plt.	7	42

The difference in frequency of expression of the Agent between Plautus (and other
archaic Latin texts) and Cicero (and his contemporaries) has been used as evidence

for a diachronic development by Ernout (1908) and Calboli (1962). Ernout suggests, in fact, that in prehistoric times the passive was a means of impersonalisation which did not allow the expression of an Agent, that is as some sort of basic passive in the sense of Keenan (1981). However, it is very unlikely that the difference in frequency is due to a diachronic development. The explanation must be sought in the difference between the types of text involved. Whereas Plautus deals primarily with interhuman activities between Agents and Goals ('Goal' also used in a broad sense) present on the stage, Cicero's *De Republica* contains a discussion, and Cicero's introduction to it, about heavenly bodies and principles of government, the 'presence' of which depends entirely on the discussion partners mentioning them. This is confirmed by the fact that both in active and in passive sentences the percentage of inanimate Agents is higher in Cicero than in Plautus (Table 8):

(8)   Percentages of inanimate Agents

	Pass.	Act.
Cic.	32%	13%
Plt.	9%	8%

3. The function of the passive

Functional explanations of the use of the passive can be found from antiquity onwards. One such explanation is that the passive expression, especially the so-called impersonal one, is used in order to avoid mentioning the Agent, i.e. the 'demotion' function of the passive or the function of 'deperspectivization' of the Agent (De Vries 1983). Another explanation is that the passive is used in order to avoid ambiguity (Ernout 1908). As a matter of fact, the material I have used shows a remarkably higher number of passive Accusative and Infinitive constructions than active ones. This might result from a desire to disambiguate formally identical accusative Subjects and Objects in this construction. Furthermore, there are several explanations which all have in common that they refer to certain properties of the Subject Goals of passive sentences. Ernout (1908) suggests that the passive is used in order to continue the Subject of the preceding sentence or clause (compare Svartvik 1966). In several studies on the German passive it has been shown that Subject Goals of passive sentences usually contain old information (are 'thematic') whereas Agents in passive sentences contain new

information (are 'rhematic') (compare Pape-Müller 1980: 124; Schoenthal 1976: 115).
A more or less opposite view about the Subject Goals of passive sentences can be
found in studies in Givón (ed. 1983). My data, as I will now explain, point in a
different direction.

In order to answer the question whether the passive may be viewed as a device
for either establishing continuity or interrupting continuity, I have compared
two properties of Subject Goals in passive sentences with those of Object Goals
and Subject Agents in the active sentences studied in the Cicero text while
limiting myself to passive and active sentences as defined in section 1.[5] The
properties involved are 'identifiability' in the preceding context, or in the
situation (one might also speak of 'givenness') and - in cases where the Subject
Goal is co-referential with a constituent in an immediately preceding clause or
sentence - the syntactic function of this constituent. From this comparison it
becomes clear whether Subject Goals are primarily Goals (and therefore resemble
Object Goals in active sentences), or primarily Subjects (and therefore resemble
Subject Agents in active sentences). The results can be found in (9):

(9)   Givenness and syntactic function (i)

	Passive (92 sentences)	Active (100 sentences)	
	Subject Goal	Subject Agent	Object Goal
Known from context or situation	53%	77%	48%
Subject in preceding clause or sentence	23%	39%	12%

The table shows, among other things, that the Subject Goal in passive sentences
is known from the preceding context or situation in 53% of the sentences involved
and fulfils the function of Subject in the preceding clause or sentence in 23% of
the sentences involved. On the basis of these data it might be inferred that - at
least in this text - the Subject Goal occupies a position in between Subject
Agent and Object Goal. Passivization, therefore, might seem to produce, or at
least to correlate with, discontinuity of givenness and particularly of Subject.

This conclusion would fit in with the result of the examination of a variety of other texts, where, however, my students and I did not limit ourselves to passive and active sentences in a narrow sense, as defined above. However, if one rearranges the material and compares only the agentive passive sentences with the agentive active sentences the result is quite different, witness Table (10):

(10)   Givenness and syntactic function (ii)

	Agentive passive (47 sentences)	Agentive[6] active (98 sentences)	
	Subject Goal	Subject Agent	Object Goal
Known from context or situation	62%	79%	48%
Subject in preceding clause or sentence	38%	40%	12%

In agentive passive sentences the Subject Goal is much more like the Subject Agent as far as continuity is concerned than like the Object Goal. The 'bad' result of Table (9) on the other hand derives from the fact that Subject Goals in non-agentive sentences are highly discontinuous. So the answer to the question whether passivization is a continuity or a discontinuity device must be that it is both. I will elaborate on this further on.

Which then are the Goals that 'profit', so to speak, most from the fact that they appear as Subjects instead of as Objects? Table (11) shows the frequency of combination of Agents and Goals with the features animate/inanimate in the agentive active and agentive passive sentences:

(11)   Animate/inanimate combinations

Agentive active

Goal	animate	inanimate
Agent animate	15%	72%
inanimate	2%	11%

Agentive passive

Goal	animate	inanimate
Agent animate	11%	55%
inanimate	21%	13%

Table (11) shows, among other things, that in 72% of the active sentences involved the Agent is animate and the Goal inanimate. In the passive sentences the percentage of this combination is lower (55%). On the other hand, the combination of inanimate Agents and animate Goals is more frequent in passive than in active sentences. This proves that a major effect of passivization is the presentation of animate Goals as Subjects of their sentences. This seems to confirm the idea found in the literature that there is a relationship between animacy and Subjecthood. However, in the material used for this paper the majority of Subjects of passive sentences are inanimate entities, especially in the case of the non-agentive passive sentences. So passivization cannot simply be regarded as some sort of animacy promotion device either.

So far we have seen that the passive is used both when continuity and when discontinuity of the Subject is at stake. How can we account for this? The most natural answer to this question seems to be that passivization is not at all a device relevant to continuity of givenness and Subject. Adopting Dik's definition of Subject, the function of the passive is to present an action or process from a perspective in which the Goal is taken as the point of departure as opposed to active expressions in which roughly the same action or process is presented from the perspective of the Agent. The reason why a speaker or writer should want to present a state of affairs from the perspective of the Goal or from that of the Agent in those cases in which both an Agent and a Goal are involved is probably a matter for psychological research. Yet, the linguistic material may suggest a few answers.[7]

A first reason for, or perhaps even a condition on, the selection of a particular perspective is that the speaker or author considers the facts to be reported interesting enough to present them from the perspective of the Subject chosen. This may be because he identifies himself in some respect with the Subject (compare Allerton 1980 on the notion of 'empathy') or because he deems it worthwhile for the listener (reader) (or sometimes even profitable for himself) to have the information presented in that way. This principle, to my mind, explains several of the sentences that have been adduced to illustrate the supposed difference in meaning between active and passive sentences, for example (12) and (13):

(12) a. John supports the Democratic Party

     b. The Democratic Party is supported by John

(13) a.?The army was deserted by the private

     b. The army was deserted by Simon Bolivar

(12) is cited by Keenan (1981: 22) as an illustration of a difference in
'affectedness' between active and passive sentences. In (12b) the Democratic
Party seems to be more dependent upon John's support than in (12a). (13) is
given by Longacre (1983: 229ff) for more or less the same reasons.[8] I would
like to maintain that in both examples the difference, which I accept, is precisely the difference which arises when the perspective for the presentation of
a State of Affairs is changed.

A second reason for selecting a particular constituent to fulfill the function
of Subject may be that the speaker (or writer) wants to continue the perspective
from which the State of Affairs in the preceding sentence or clause is presented.
If the constituent which is taken as the point of departure is an Agent, the
State of Affairs must be expressed in the active voice. Conversely, if the constituent involved is associated as a Goal with a two- or three-place predicate
the State of Affairs must be expressed in the passive voice. An example of the
latter is (14):

(14)   si qui   sunt, qui   philosophorum   auctoritate   *moveantur*
        if any$_{nom}$ be$_{3pl}$ who$_{nom}$ philosophers$_{gen}$ authority$_{abl}$ move$_{3pl\ pass}$

        ('If there be any who are influenced by the authority of
        philosophers', Cic. *Rep.* 1, 12)

However, a speaker (or writer) may want to change the perspective – a third
reason for selecting a particular constituent as Subject of the sentence –,
either for a special purpose, or quite simply because one cannot go on presenting
States of Affairs from the perspective of the same entity. A special purpose may
be, as in (15), rapid action in the report of a battle:

(15)   invadunt   urbem   somno   vinoque   sepultam.
        invade$_{3pl\ act}$ city$_{acc}$ sleep$_{abl}$ wine$_{abl}$ – and buried$_{pass\ part\ acc}$

        caeduntur   vigiles   portisque   patentibus omnes
        kill$_{3pl\ pass}$ watchmen$_{nom}$ gates$_{abl}$ – and open$_{abl}$ all$_{acc}$

        accipiunt   socios
        welcome$_{3pl\ act}$ comrades$_{acc}$
        ('They storm the city, buried in sleep and wine; slay the watch,
        and at the open gates welcome all their comrades', Verg. *A.* 2, 265-7).

In (15) the Greeks are the Subject Agent of *invadunt* (active). They are also the implied Agent of *caeduntur* (passive). However, their victims (the Trojans) occur as Subject Goal of the clause. In the following coordinate clause the Greeks return as Subject Agent of *accipiunt* (active). So both continuity of perspective and discontinuity of perspective may determine the selection of a particular entity as the Subject of its sentence or clause. Subject selection, in other words, is a consequence of perspective selection, which in turn is related to, but not entirely dependent upon, suprasentential factors such as narrative structure, text type, and so on. There may even be some sort of continuity of perspective in combination with discontinuity of Subject. Examples are (16) and (17):

(16)   itur   in antiquam silvam, stabula   alta   ferarum;
       $go_{3sg\ pass}$ in old_{acc} $wood_{acc}$ $stables_{acc}$ $high_{acc}$ $beasts_{gen}$

       procumbunt piceae,   sonat   icta   securibus ilex
       $fall_{3pl}$ $pines_{nom}$ $sound_{3sg}$ $strike_{pass\ part\ nom}$ $axes_{abl}$ $ilex_{nom}$

       fraxineaeque   trabes cuneis   et fissile   robur scinditur
       $ashen_{nom}$ - and $logs_{nom}$ $wedges_{abl}$ and $splintering_{nom}$ oak_{nom} $cleave_{3sg\ pass}$

       ('They pass into the forest primeval, the deep lairs of beasts; down
       drop the pitch pines, and the ilex rings to the stroke of the axe;
       ashen logs and splintering oak are cleft with wedges', Verg. A. 6, 179-82).

(17)   tum emplastrum hoc   modo   fit: arida medicamenta   per
       then $plaster_{nom}$ $this_{abl}$ way_{abl} $become_{3sg}$ dry_{nom} $medicaments_{nom}$ by

       se   teruntur,   deinde mixtis   iis   instillatur
       $self_{acc}$ $rub_{3pl\ pass}$ then $mix_{pass\ part\ dat}$ $these_{dat}$ $drop_{3sg\ pass}$

       aut   acetum   aut si quis   alius   non pinguis umor
       either $vinegar_{nom}$ or if $some_{nom}$ $other_{nom}$ not fat_{nom} $liquid_{nom}$

       accessurus est et ea   rursus teruntur
       $come_{3sg\ fut}$ and $these_{nom}$ again $rub_{3pl\ pass}$
       ('Then a plaster is made in this way: dry medicaments are rubbed down
       separately, then when they have been mixed, either vinegar is dropped
       in or any other liquor free from fat that is at hand, and these in-
       gredients are rubbed together again', Cels. 5, 17, 2B).

In (16) Aeneas' men have gone into a wood and are gathering wood. The action of cutting the trees is presented from the perspective of the trees. *procumbunt* and *sonat* are one-place predicates with which the trees can only be presented as Subject. *scinditur*, however, is the passive form of a two-place predicate, chosen here to continue the perspective. From the grammatical point of view the Goal *robur* might just as well have been presented as the Object.[9] Similarly, in (17) a series of States of Affairs in which different entities are involved is presented from the same perspective: that of the components of a plaster.[10]

4. Conclusion

The passive appears to be a device which the speaker (or writer) may use at his will, according to his individual wish with respect to the presentation of one or a series of States of Affairs. He may, but need not, choose to continue a certain perspective and as a consequence he may, but again need not, choose either the active or the passive expression for a certain State of Affairs. This means that rules for the use of the passive in discourse cannot be given, only indications of the probability of its use, or 'tendencies' (Bolkestein, this volume) in certain contexts or situations. It appears that different tendencies can be established for different types of passive sentences, viz. agentive and non-agentive passive sentences.*

NOTES

*   I thank Machtelt Bolkestein, Caroline Kroon and Hotze Mulder for their comments on content and style of an earlier version of this paper.

[1]   The choice of these texts is, of course, quite arbitrary. However, the overall conclusions presented below are also valid for other types of Latin texts (compare Pinkster 1984).

[2]   Stein (1979: 126-129) gives English examples. The sentences in (1) and (2) are from Höhle (1978: 140).

[3]   Mackenzie (to appear) deals with a problem which in certain respect resembles the one discussed here.

[4]   queratur is a so-called deponent verb form ('passive form: active meaning').

[5]   My approach differs from both Givón (ed. 1983) and Weiner-Labov (1983). In these studies subject constituents of all sentences are taken into account.

[6]   By 'agentive' active sentences I mean active sentences with the exception of sentences like (6) above ('they').

[7]   Compare, among others, Granger (1983), Kilby (1984), Pape-Müller (1980).

[8]   Both examples seem to be Bolinger's, in an article which I have not been able to read.

[9]   Hahn (1930: 19) comments upon the 'choppy' style in these lines which 'is well-suited to the subject-matter, and may have been deliberately retained by Vergil for this very reason' (Vergil is imitating Ennius).

[10]   This type of 'perspective' is comparable with the phenomena discussed by Hannay (this volume) and Bolkestein (this volume).

Chapter 9

Semantic and syntactic functions in Toba Batak: some implications for functional grammar

Paul Schachter
Department of Linguistics, University of California

1. Introduction

An apparently unique property of the model of Functional Grammar (hereafter, FG) proposed in Dik (1978) is the capacity of the so-called expression rules of the grammar - the rules responsible for case marking, word order, and other aspects of surface morphosyntax - to refer to information about three distinct types of argument functions: semantic functions such as Agent, syntactic functions such as Subject, and pragmatic functions such as Topic. If this capacity is indeed unique to the FG model, then any evidence that the capacity is required in order for the grammar of some language to achieve descriptive adequacy must count as prima facie support for FG as opposed to other grammatical theories.

In this paper I propose to offer this kind of support for FG in the form of evidence that the morphosyntactic rules of the Toba dialect of Batak, an Austronesian language of Sumatra, must in fact refer to the three types of functions that are recognized in FG. I also propose to show, however, that, with respect to two of these three types of functions, semantic and syntactic, Batak points to certain inadequacies in existing versions of FG. In particular, I shall argue that, if FG is to give a descriptively adequate account of Batak morphosyntax, then the inventory of functions recognized in the theory must be expanded so as to include one new semantic function, the Actor, and two new syntactic functions, the Adjunct and the Trigger. But since, in the course of justifying the need for these new functions, I also call attention to various rules of Batak morphosyntax that are sensitive to information about semantic and syntactic functions (and, to a lesser extent, pragmatic functions), I provide general support for the FG account of functions in relation to grammar at the same time that I propose specific revisions of this account.

Before attempting to justify the proposed revisions of FG, I shall first need to provide some background information about the structure of the Batak transitive clause. Batak, then, is a verb-initial (or, more generally, predicate-initial) language. In a simple transitive clause, a verb is followed by two nominal arguments, the first of which has the syntactic function I refer to as Adjunct, the second the syntactic function I refer to as Trigger. (These terms,

and the properties associated with them, are explained in section 3, below.) The
verb is marked with an affix that belongs to one of two classes that I shall
call Actor-Adjunct (AA) affixes and Actor-Trigger (AT) affixes. These two classes
of affixes are correlated with the semantic functions of the associated nominals.
Specifically, when the verb carries an AA affix, the first, or Adjunct, nominal
must have the semantic function Actor (see the explanation of this term in section 2.), and the second, or Trigger, nominal must have some other semantic
function. The structure and the relevant function assignments of the two basic
types of transitive clauses may be represented schematically as follows:

(1) a. *Actor-Adjunct (AA) Clause*

AA-V	NP$_1$	NP$_2$
	Actor	non-Actor
	Adjunct	Trigger

   b. *Actor-Trigger (AT) Clause*

AT-V	NP$_1$	NP$_2$
	non-Actor	Actor
	Adjunct	Trigger

As shown in (1a), an AA clause consists of a verb with an AA affix followed by
an Actor Adjunct noun phrase and a non-Actor Trigger noun phrase, and, as shown
in (1b), an AT clause consists of a verb with an AT affix followed by a non-Actor
Adjunct and an Actor Trigger.

   Illustrations of these two types of clauses are given in (2), where (2a) is an
AA clause, (2b) the corresponding AT clause:

(2) a. Diallang si John dengke i
       AA-eat   PM John fish   the
       'John ate the fish'

       (PM = personal-name marker)

   b. Mangallang dengke si John
      AT-eat   fish   PM John
      'John is eating fish'

The verb of (2a), *diallang*, is marked with the most common AA affix, the prefix
di- (pronounced [i]). The verb of (2b), *mangallang*, is marked with the most common AT affix, the prefix *mang-*. (All of the verbs to be cited in this paper carry
these same affixes, with *mang-* occurring in several morphophonemically-conditioned

alternate shapes that will not be further commented on.)

To judge just from the English translations of (2a-b), one might assume that
the AA/AT distinction is basically one of tense or aspect, with AA clauses being
past and perfective, AT clauses present and imperfective, but this is in fact
not the case. Although it is true that, in the absence of any context, AA and AT
clauses are generally translated into English as indicated, in an appropriate
context - e.g., when the tense and/or aspect are indicated adverbially - either
type of clause may be interpreted as past or present, perfective or imperfective.
Rather than tense or aspect, the most consistent semantic-syntactic correlate of
the AA/AT distinction turns out to be what Wouk (1984), in a detailed study of
this matter based on an analysis of a set of spoken texts, has called 'the individuation of the Patient'.[1] An individuated Patient, in Wouk's usage (which differs somewhat from that of her source for the notion of individuation, Hopper
and Thompson 1980), may be identified as such on semantic grounds, on syntactic
grounds, or both. A semantically individuated Patient is one with an established
referent; a syntactically individuated Patient is one that is expressed by a
nominal that includes one or more modifiers of the head noun. What Wouk finds in
her examination of the Batak texts is that, in a substantial majority of cases,
if the Patient is individuated, an AA clause is preferred, while if the Patient
is not individuated, an AT clause is preferred. This generalization, together
with certain subsidiary hypotheses is in fact able to account for some 90% of the
relevant textual data - far more than any of the other hypothesized explanations
of the AA/AT distinction that Wouk considers.

2. The Actor

With the above background, we are now in a position to examine the evidence for
recognizing certain new semantic and syntactic functions in an FG of Batak. Let
us begin with the proposed new semantic function, the Actor. The term Actor is
common in Austronesian - particularly, Philippine - linguistics (e.g., Schachter
1976) for the participant in an event that is presented as central to that event
- the protagonist, as it were. The Actor generally corresponds to the active
Subject in English, and like the English Subject, is typically an Agent if the
verb is what Dik would identify as an Action verb (e.g. *eat*), but may have one
of several others of the semantic functions that Dik recognizes if the verb is a
non-Action verb, such as *hold, receive,* or *see.*

Now a sufficient reason for recognizing the Actor in an FG of Batak (though,
as we shall see, not the only one) is that we should otherwise not be able to

formulate descriptively adequate expression rules for transitive-verb morphology.
That is, we want the grammar to say, in the most general possible way, in what
contexts affixes like *di-* are used, as in (2a), and in what contexts affixes
like *mang-* are used, as in (2b). To judge just from *these* examples, we might
think that it would be possible to state the generalization on the basis of the
already-recognized semantic function Agent: i.e., to say that when the first argument after the verb is the Agent, *di-* is used, and when the second argument is
the Agent, *mang-* is used. However, examples like the following show that this
cannot be the case:

(3) a. Ditiop   si John buku i
        AA-hold PM John book the
        'John held the book'

    b. Maniop   buku si John
        AT-hold book PM John
        'John is holding a book'

(4) a. Dijalo   si John hepeng i
        AA-receive PM John money   the
        'John received the money'

    b. Manjalo   hepeng si John
        AT-receive money PM John
        'John is receiving money'

(5) a. Diida si John horbo   i
        AA-see PM John water-buffalo the
        'John saw the water buffalo'

    b. Mangida horbo   si John
        AT-see water-buffalo PM John
        'John sees a water buffalo'

Given Dik's typology of states of affairs, in terms of which the semantic functions of FG are defined, none of the examples of (3)-(5) presumably contains an
Agent. Dik distinguishes four states of affairs - Actions, Positions, Processes,
and States - and it is only in the first of these, Actions, that the semantic
function Agent is assignable. Thus the examples of (2), having Action predicates,
may contain Agents. But the examples of (3), (4), and (5) presumably have,
respectively, Position, Process, and State predicates, and thus cannot contain
Agents. Indeed, since these are all different types of states of affairs, the
argument *si John* 'John' may well have a different semantic function in each of
these pairs of examples. In the examples of (3) *si John* has the semantic function
Dik calls Positioner. In (4) and (5), it is not clear to me just what semantic
function Dik would assign to *si John*. (Indeed, I am not altogether sure that (4)
is a Process and (5) a State, although with respect to the latter, at least,

there is a similar example that Dik 1978: 34 does identify as a State.) But it
seems that in any case it could not be the function Agent.

I propose that in all of the examples of (2)-(5), *si John* does indeed have
the same semantic function, namely the Actor function. This is, to be sure, a
function of a somewhat different kind from the semantic functions that are currently recognized in FG. Whereas the latter all have to do with the *kind* of role
played by a participant in a certain state of affairs, the Actor function has to
do with the perceived *centrality* of this role to the state of affairs. Moreover,
the Actor function may be predictable, at least in the unmarked case, on the
basis of the already-recognized semantic functions. For example, it seems to be
true that if there is an Agent, as in (2), then the Agent is regularly the Actor.
Similarly, if there is a Positioner, as in (3), then *this* is regularly the Actor.
In fact, the Actor seems to correspond closely to what De Groot (1981b) refers
to as *the first argument of the Semantic Function Hierarchy* (SFH).[2] But even if
the Actor function is predictable in this way, it is still necessary to give it
formal recognition in the grammar, at least if the expression rules for verb
morphology are to be stated in a fully general way. Thus one would wish (begging
the question for the moment of the justification for the Adjunct and Trigger
functions) to have expression rules like:

(6) a. $V_{ActorAdjunct}$ ---> *di-* + V

    b. $V_{ActorTrigger}$ ---> *mang-* + V

(The rules of (6) presuppose the registration on the verb, by means of general
conventions, of information about the semantic and syntactic functions that have
been assigned to certain arguments - cf. Dik 1978: 84.) And such rules are, I
claim, statable only if the Actor function is recognized.

In order for this claim to be valid, however, it is still necessary to justify
a certain choice that appears to have been made in the formulation of the rules
of (6). These rules are stated in terms of the argument to which the *Actor* function is assigned. But might it not have been equally possible to state the relevant rules in terms of the argument to which, say the *Patient* function is
assigned instead? On the basis of the examples presented so far, at least, this
would certainly appear to be the case. That is, if we assume that the non-Actor
argument in examples (2)-(5) can in all cases be identified as the Patient,
could we not generalize the Batak verb morphology we are concerned with just as
well by means of the rules in (7) as by means of those in (6)?

(7) a. V$_{PatientTrigger}$ ---> *di-* + V

      V$_{PatientAdjunct}$ ---> *mang-* + V

Indeed, if the rules of (7) are equal to those of (6) in descriptive adequacy, they should, from the point of view of current FG, be preferred. For, while the rules of (6) require that the inventory of semantic functions recognized in FG be revised so as to include a new kind of function, the Actor, the rules of (7) require no such revision (at least if we assume that Patient is simply a different *name* for the already-recognized function that Dik has called Goal).

But as it happens, the rules of (7) are in fact *not* equal to those of (6) in descriptive adequacy. This becomes clear when we bring into consideration certain clauses with *di*transitive verbs such as those in (8):

(8) a. Dilean si John si Bill buku i
      AA-give PM John PM Bill book the
      'John gave Bill the book'

    b. Mangalean si Bill si John buku
      AT-give   PM Bill PM John book
      'John is giving Bill a book'

In the sentences of (8), the verb is followed by *three* nominal arguments, rather than the *two* of previous examples. Again, however, on the basis of the distinctive syntactic properties of the Adjunct and the Trigger that we shall be examining below, it is the first argument after the verb that is the Adjunct and the second that is the Trigger. (The third argument of (8) is neither the Adjunct nor the Trigger - cf. the English translations, where the third argument is neither the Subject nor the Object, but what is referred to in Relational Grammar - cf. Perlmutter 1980 - as a Chômeur Thus in the examples of (8) neither the Adjunct nor the Trigger has the semantic function of Patient. Rather, the Trigger in (8a) and the Adjunct in (8b) have the *Recipient* function (while the Adjunct in (8a) and the Trigger in (8b) of course have the *Actor* function). But this means that the rules given in (7) are irrelevant to the examples of (8). The rules given in (6), on the other hand, apply just as well to these examples as to those previously cited. It thus seems that we do indeed need to recognize the Actor function in order to be able to express generalizations about Batak verb morphology.

Moreover, there are certain other kinds of generalizations, including, I believe, some *universal* generalizations, that require recognition of the Actor function. In Schachter (1984), I propose that, in all languages that have clause-bound reflexive pronouns (i.e., reflexive pronouns whose reference must be controlled by an argument in the same clause), the reference of such pronouns is subject to the following condition:

(9)   Control of clause-bound reflexive reference is subject to the
        condition: Actor > non-Actor

What (9) is meant to say is that an Actor may control the (clause-bound) reference of a non-Actor reflexive pronoun but may never itself *be* a reflexive pronoun.

The condition in (9) is proposed as an alternative to certain purely *syntactic* conditions on reflexive reference that have been proposed in the literature (such as clause (A) of the Binding Theory of Chomsky 1981: 188). Batak happens to provide very clear evidence against any such syntactic condition and in favor of the semantic-function-based condition (9). (For a fuller account of Batak reflexivization, see Sugamoto 1984   Consider the following examples:

(10) a. Disukkur si John dirina
        AA-shave PM John himself
        'John shaved himself'

     b. Manukkur dirina si John
        AT-shave himself PM John
        'John is shaving himself'

     c.*Disukkur   dirina si John
        AA-shave   himself PM John
        '*Himself shaved John'

     d.*Manukkur si John dirina
        AT-shave PM John himself
        '*Himself is shaving John'

As these examples show, in both AA clauses like (10a) and AT clauses like (10b), an Actor can control the reference of a non-Actor reflexive pronoun, while in neither type of clause (cf. 10c-d) can a non-Actor control the reference of an Actor reflexive pronoun. It is obvious, moreover, that the *syntactic* functions of the arguments are entirely irrelevant. Thus in one of the two grammatical examples of (10) the controller is the Adjunct and the reflexive pronoun is the Trigger while in the other the controller is the Trigger and the reflexive pronoun is the Adjunct. And the same is true of the two ungrammatical examples. (I am still begging the question, admittedly, of the justification for these syntactic-function assignments, but this justification will soon be provided.)

In this connection, it may be noted that Batak presents much clearer evidence than does English of the fact that reflexive reference is semantically, rather than syntactically, conditioned. For example, if we were to consider just the English equivalents of the above Batak examples (see the English translations in (10)), while the facts can certainly be accounted for on the basis of the semantic condition of (10), they can also be accounted for on a syntactic basis (such as, for instance, that a Subject can control the reference of a reflexive non-Subject, but not vice versa). But if there is to be a *universal* account of the control of reflexive reference, which will hold not only for English but for Batak and other languages as well, then this account must be semantically based - and the account must, moreover, make reference to the semantic function Actor.

With regard to this last point, I have not yet shown that it is indeed Actor - and not, say, Agent - that is the relevant semantic function for stating the condition on reflexivization. To satisfy ourselves that this is the case, however, we need only consider some additional examples involving non-Action predicates, e.g.:

(11) a. Diida   si John dirina   di hassa
        AA-see PM John himself in mirror
        'John saw himself in the mirror'

     b. Mangida dirina   si John di hassa
        AT-see   himself PM John in mirror
        'John sees himself in the mirror'

     c.*Diida   dirina   si John di hassa
        AA-see himself PM John in mirror
        '*Himself saw John in the mirror'

     d.*Mangida si John dirina   di hassa
        AT-see   PM John himself in mirror
        '*Himself sees John in the mirror'

In the grammatical examples (11a-b), the controller of the reference of the reflexive pronoun is an Actor but presumably *not* an Agent. And similarly, in the ungrammatical examples (11c-d) the reflexive pronoun is an Actor but not an Agent. So clearly it is the 'new' semantic function Actor that is relevant for expressing generalizations about reflexive-pronoun distribution (both in Batak and universally, I would claim), just as it was the new semantic function that was relevant for expressing generalizations about Batak verb morphology. (See Schachter 1984 for some additional grammatical phenomena, both Batak-specific and putatively universal, to which the Actor function appears to be relevant.)

3. The Adjunct and the Trigger

Let us move on now to the new *syntactic* functions, Adjunct and Trigger, that I claim
are needed in order to express certain additional generalizations about the grammar
of Batak. With respect to these syntactic functions, I shall address the following two questions in turn: first, the question of the distinctive properties
that are associated with each of the proposed functions, distinctive properties
that justify assigning the same function label, Adjunct, to the first argument
of both AA and AT clauses, and the same function label, Trigger, to the second
argument of both types of clauses; and second, the question of why these functions cannot be identified with the syntactic functions that are already recognized in FG, Subject and Object.

The most salient syntactic characteristic of the Adjunct is that it is always
adjoined to the preceding verb (hence the name Adjunct), with which it forms a
highly cohesive unit. One kind of evidence of this cohesiveness is the fact that
nothing can ever come between the verb and the adjunct. For instance, time adverbs in Batak, as in many other languages, may occur initially, medially, or
finally, but they may never intervene between the verb and the Adjunct, as is
illustrated by the following examples (in which the time adverb *nantoari* 'yesterday' is italicized):

(12) a. *Nantoari* diantuk si Bill si John
          yesterday AA-hit PM Bill PM John

         *Diantuk *nantoari* si Bill si John

         Diantuk si Bill *nantoari* si John

         Diantuk si Bill si John *nantoari*
         'Bill hit John yesterday'

     b. *Nantoari* mangantuk si John si Bill
          yesterday AT-hit   PM John PM Bill

         *Mangantuk *nantoari* si John si Bill

         Mangantuk si John *nantoari* si Bill

         Mangantuk si John si Bill *nantoari*
         'Bill hit John yesterday'

(Note, incidentally, that both the AA clauses of (12a) and the AT clauses of
(12b) are translated as past perfective, evidence of the point made above that
the AA/AT distinction is not basically one of tense or aspect.)

Another kind of evidence of the cohesiveness of the verb-Adjunct unit is that
the Adjunct, unlike the Trigger, which may be placed in pre-verb position by
certain rules that are sensitive to pragmatic function, is never placed in pre-

verb position. One relevant rule is the rule that optionally places a questioned
constituent (with the pragmatic function Focus) at the beginning of the clause.
Such a clause-initial questioned constituent never corresponds to an Adjunct,
but may correspond to a Trigger. Note, for example, the allowed and disallowed
interpretations of the following sentences:

(13) a. Ise diantuk si Bill?
        who AA-hit   PM Bill
        'Who did Bill hit?'
        ('*Who hit Bill?')

     b. Ise mangantuk si John?
        who AT-hit   PM John
        'Who is hitting John?'
        ('*Who is John hitting?')

In (13a), which has an AA verb, the pre-verbal question word *ise* 'who' cannot be
interpreted as the Actor, while in (13b), which has an AT verb, the pre-verbal
question word can *only* be interpreted as the Actor. Thus in both cases the
clause-initial argument is taken to be the Trigger and the argument that immediately follows the verb is taken to be the Adjunct: i.e., the Actor Adjunct
with the AA verb of (13a), the non-Actor Adjunct with the AT verb of (13b).

    It is clear, incidentally, that it is the *positioning* of the Adjunct in some-
thing other than immediately-post-verb position, rather than the *questioning*
of the Adjunct, that is disallowed. Thus questioned Adjuncts are perfectly grammatical, provided they occur in immediately-post-verb position, e.g.:

(14) a. Diantuk ise si Bill?
        AA-hit   who PM Bill
        'Who hit Bill?'

     b. Mangantuk ise si John?
        AT-hit   who PM John
        'Who is John hitting?'

(As indicated above, the rule that permits a questioned *Trigger* to occur clause-
initially is optional, so the following are also grammatical:

(15) a. Diantuk si Bill ise?
        AA-hit   PM Bill who
        'Who did Bill hit?'

     b. Mangantuk si John ise?
        AT-hit   PM John who
        'Who is hitting John?')

By contrast with the Adjunct, which must always occur in immediately-post-verb
position, the Trigger shows considerably greater syntactic versatility. (The
term Trigger was coined by Barbara Fox (p.c.) for the argument in *Philippine*
languages whose semantic function triggers a certain choice among the verbal affixes. In these languages there are distinctive verbal affixes to indicate not
only that the Trigger has the semantic function Actor, but also that it has the
semantic functions Patient, Recipient, Beneficiary, Instrument, etc. Although
the term Trigger is somewhat less appropriate to Batak, it has the virtue of
being a neologism, and of thus not having any inappropriate connotations.) As
already indicated, the Trigger in Batak, unlike the Adjunct, may occur in pre-
verbal, clause-initial position under certain pragmatically conditioned circumstances. The Trigger, but not the Adjunct, may also be relativized, as is clear
from the allowed and disallowed interpretations of the following relative constructions:

(16) a. halak na diantuk si Bill i
        man   Li AA-hit PM Bill the   (Li = Linker)
        'the man who Bill hit'
        ('*the man who hit Bill')

     b. halak na mangantuk si John i
        man   Li AT-hit   PM John the
        'the man who is hitting John'
        ('*the man who John is hitting')

As these examples illustrate, the basic relativization strategy employed in Batak
is a so-called deletion strategy. The antecedent is followed by a clause (introduced by the linker *na*) from which one of the arguments that would be found in a
complete independent clause is absent, and this absent argument is interpreted
as referentially bound by the antecedent. Although the absent argument may be
(and in most cases *must* be) the Trigger, it can never be the Adjunct. Thus in
(16a), in which the relative clause contains an AA verb, the absent argument is
the Patient Trigger, while in (16b), in which the relative clause contains an AT
verb, the absent argument is the Actor Trigger.

It is clear, then, that the Adjunct - the first argument that follows the verb
in a basic transitive clause - and the Trigger - the second argument in such a
clause - have quite distinct syntactic properties to which the rules of Batak
grammar are sensitive. One such rule is, of course, the basic word-order rule
itself, which may be stated in some such form as:

(17)   Verb, Adjunct, Trigger, X ---> Verb Adjunct Trigger X

(where the constituents to the left of the arrow are unordered, those to the right of the arrow ordered as indicated). Other relevant rules (which I shall not try to formulate here) are those for clause-initial question words and for relative-clause formation, which must obviously reflect the fact that, while the Trigger has considerable freedom to be repositioned or deleted, the Adjunct has none. (For some further distinguishing properties of the Adjunct and the Trigger, including some further cases in which the Trigger, but not the Adjunct, is subject to pragmatically conditioned repositioning, see Schachter 1984). But, granting that these two syntactic functions must indeed be distinguished, need we also grant that they must be designated by such neologisms as Adjunct and Trigger? Might not the familiar syntactic-function labels Subject and Object be used instead?

There are, in fact, several good reasons why, at least within the framework of FG, the Batak syntactic functions should not be identified as Subject and Object. In the first place, it is by no means obvious which of these labels to assign to which of the Batak functions. Let us suppose, first, that we were to identify the first argument after a transitive verb as the Subject, the second as the Object - an identification that at least has the virtue of classifying Batak as a VSO language, certainly a more common language type than VOS, and a type, moreover, that, unlike VOS, conforms to the FG Functional Pattern Schema of Dik (1978: 175). Given this identification, then for the type of clause I have been calling Actor-Adjunct (e.g. the clauses in (2-5a)), we have an Actor Subject and, typically, a Patient Object - certainly a very reasonable situation. But what is to be made of the type of clause I have been calling Actor-Trigger (e.g., the clauses in (2-5b))? Here we would have to say that we have a Patient *Subject* and an Actor *Object*. But while a Patient Subject - in Dik's terms, a Goal Subject - is permissible in FG (for example, in passive clauses), an Actor Object would, at least in some cases, violate a proposed *universal* of the theory.

The cases in question are those like (2b), in which the Actor is an Agent, and the proposed universal that would be violated is evident from the following chart (adapted from Dik 1978: 76):

(18)   Ag > Go > Rec ...
        Subj x > x > x   ...
        Obj   > x > x   ...

This chart is supposed to represent certain universal conditions on the choice of Subject and Object on the basis of semantic functions. The semantic functions that are relevant to Actions - Agent, Goal, Recipient, etc. - are arranged on the chart in conformity with a proposed universal Semantic Function Hierarchy, and it is proposed that Subject and Object assignment are universally sensitive to this hierarchy in the way indicated. Of particular relevance here is the claim that Agents, while universally preferred as Subjects (in the sense that, if a language has Subjects at all, it will have Agent Subjects), are universally disallowed as Objects. This restriction on Agent Objects is, as a matter of fact, quite unsurprising, and is in conformity with linguistic tradition; but it would obviously preclude an analysis of the Batak syntactic functions in Subject-Object terms.

Another reason for rejecting the identification of the first argument after a transitive verb as the Subject and the second as the Object has to do with semantics. Dik - quite properly, in my view - attributes a certain kind of semantic significance to the assignment of Subject and Object functions. These functions, he claims have to do with the 'perspective' or 'point of view' from which a state of affairs is presented. Thus, 'Subj assignment determines the perspective from which the state of affairs is described' (Dik 1978: 71), and 'Obj assignment ... [determines] a perspective on the terms remaining after Subj assignment has taken place' (1978: 73). (A similar account of the semantics of Subject and Object assignment is to be found in Fillmore 1977.) But if these claims about the semantic properties of Subjects and Objects are correct, then it can hardly be the case that the first post-verbal argument of a simple trans- itive clause in Batak is the Subject and the second the Object. For if this were so, then the difference between the two clause types I have been calling AA and AT should involve a difference in the 'perspective' that is taken on a state of affairs, and there is no evidence that this is the case. Corresponding AA and AT clauses both appear to describe a given state of affairs from the same perspec- tive, that of the Actor. Rather than perspective, the main determinant of the choice between the two clause types seems, as noted earlier, to be the individu- ation of the Patient: if the Patient is individuated, an AA clause is generally preferred; if the Patient is non-individuated, an AT clause is generally pre- ferred.[3] And, while it might be true that an individuated Patient is, in some sense, more 'in perspective' than a non-individuated Patient, this should pre- sumably be irrelevant to Subject and Object assignment if, as seems to be the case, the primary perspective from which the state of affairs is described re- mains that of the Actor in both AA and AT clauses.

The above arguments against an analysis in which the first argument after a transitive verb is identified as the Subject and the second as the Object also hold, mutatis mutandis, for an alternative analysis in which the *second* argument after a transitive verb is identified as the Subject and the *first* as the Object; for this analysis too would require the recognition of Agent Objects, contrary to the universal claim expressed in (18), and would entail that Subject and Object selection in Batak lacks its usual semantic (perspectival) correlates. There are, however, two other analyses making use of the standard syntactic functions recognized in FG that warrant further consideration. These two analyses agree with the analysis just rejected in identifying the second argument after the verb as the Subject, but they differ from this analysis (and from one another) in their treatment of the first argument. According to one of these analyses, AT clauses are active and AA clauses passive, with the result in FG that the first argument of an AT clause is assigned Object function but the first argument of an AA clause is assigned no syntactic function. According to the second analysis, Batak is what Dik (1980a) calls a VXS language, and the first argument has no syntactic function in either type of clause. Let us consider these two analyses in turn.

The active-passive analysis is in fact the kind of analysis provided by traditional descriptions of Batak, such as Van der Tuuk (1867). There are, however, some serious objections that can be raised to it, on the basis of what is known about genuine active-passive systems in other languages. First, as Wouk (1984) points out, AA clauses are considerably more common in texts than AT clauses (about twice as common in the texts examined by Wouk), which would certainly be surprising if AA clauses are indeed passive and AT clauses active. Also, as observed in Schachter (1984), if AA clauses are passives, then the first nominal in an AA clause must be the passive Agent, yet, unlike Passive Agents in languages in general, it is not marked as an oblique, but, rather, is syntactically indistinguishable from the presumed active *Object*. Moreover, the presumed passive Agent is never deletable, while the presumed passive Subject *is* deletable, which is again contrary to expectations based on passives in other languages. Taken together, these observations should suffice to rule out the active-passive analysis (though in fact other arguments against this analysis, analogous to those about to be presented against the VXS analysis, are also available).

What, then, of the VXS analysis, according to which the second argument of either an AT or an AA clause is the Subject while the first argument has no syntactic function? Leaving aside the fact that Subject selection under this analy-

sis, as under all the previously rejected analyses, lacks its usual semantic
effects, we can find some more pointed reasons to reject the VXS analysis. These
reasons have to do with the fact that under this analysis there is no uniform
way of identifying the argument that I have called the Adjunct, which makes it
impossible to express generalizations that involve this argument. One such generalization is the rule for the basic word-order of transitive clauses, which
must be able to distinguish the Adjunct not only from the Trigger but from other
arguments as well, as in the following ditransitive clauses:

(19) a. Ditongos si John si Bill surat i
        AA-send PM John PM Bill letter the
        'John sent Bill the letter'

     b. Manongos si Bill si John surat
        AT-send PM Bill PM John letter
        'John is sending Bill a letter'

Under the analysis that I have proposed above, the expression rule (17) assigns
the correct word-order in these clauses. But under the VXS analysis, there seems
to be no non-ad-hoc way to distinguish the 'X' that must come between the V and
the S from the 'X' that must follow the S.

  Another generalization that appears to be unstatable under the VXS analysis
is that ditransitive verbs may take as their first argument not only an Actor,
as in (19a), or a Recipient, as in (19b), but also a Patient, as in (20):

(20)   Manongos surat si John tu si Bill
        AT-send letter PM John to PM Bill
        'John is sending a letter to Bill'

(As this example illustrates, when the Recipient is neither the first nor the
second argument - i.e., neither the Adjunct nor the Trigger - it is expressed as
a prepositional phrase.) Under the analysis that I have proposed, one could
simply state a rule that allows the Adjunct function to be assigned to any argument of a ditransitive verb.[4] But under the VXS analysis there again seems to
be no way to state the rule.

  It seems, then, that there is in fact no satisfactory way to fit the Batak
syntactic functions into the established FG Subject-Object mold, and that there
is a need to expand the inventory of syntactic functions recognized in FG to
include functions like those I have been calling the Adjunct and the Trigger.[5]

4. *Conclusion*

I have argued in this paper that the inventory of semantic and syntactic functions proposed in Dik (1978) must be modified in certain ways if FG is to become capable of expressing certain generalizations about the grammar of Toba Batak. In particular, I have argued for the recognition of a new semantic Function, Actor (which appears to have a certain universal utility beyond its relevance to Batak), and two new syntactic functions, Adjunct and Trigger. These new functions, I have argued, are needed for a descriptively adequate formulation of certain Batak expression rules, such as (6) and (17) above. Implicit in my arguments throughout the paper, however, has been a strong general endorsement of a basic claim - indeed *th* basic claim - of FG: the claim that morphosyntactic rules must have access to information about semantic and/or syntactic and/or pragmatic functions.

NOTES

[1]   Wouk uses the label Patient for a semantic function that corresponds, in general, to Dik's Goal function. I shall follow Wouk's practice here, on the practical grounds that Patient is a less ambiguous term than Goal, which certain other linguists, such as Jackendoff (1972), have used for a different semantic function altogether: namely, the function that Dik calls Recipient.

[2]   De Groot's SFH differs somewhat from the one originally proposed in Dik (1978) both in its scope and in its range of uses. Dik's SFH included only those semantic functions that occur in Actions, and was used to make certain generalizations about Subject and Object selection: e.g., Agent, which is at the top of the hierarchy, is identified as the universally preferred Subject of an Action, and Goal (= what I call Patient), which is next on the hierarchy, is the universally preferred Object: cf. the discussion in section 3., below. De Groot's SFH, on the other hand, covers all four types of states of affairs, and is used to generalize the verb agreement facts of Hungarian, which, according to De Groot, require that the verb agree with the first argument of the SFH: Agent for Actions, Positioner for Positions, etc.

[3]   Other factors may, however, overrule this general preference. If, for example, the antecedent of a relative clause corresponds to an Actor within the clause, then, as indicated above, the clause must be AT, and this will be so whether or not the clause contains an individuated Patient.

[4]   Trigger can also be assigned to any argument, as is clear from comparing (19a-b) with (i):

(i) Ditongos si John surat i   tu si Bill
    AA-send PM John letter the to PM Bill
    'John sent the letter to Bill'

However, the rules for Trigger and Adjunct assignment must be stated in such a way that the Actor is always assigned one or the other of these syntactic functions.

[5]   Another possibility is that the set of syntactic functions found in Batak and the familiar Subject-Object set are simply different realizations of some more abstract set of syntactic functions. Such an analysis would presumably predict that the Batak-type syntactic functions could never occur in the same languages as the Subject-Object type. I have no idea whether this prediction is correct, and in any event will not pursue the matter further here.

Chapter 10

Pragmatic and syntactic aspects of word order in Dutch

Georges de Schutter
Department of Germanic Philology, University of Antwerp

0. Introduction

In this paper it will be argued (a) that the number of pragmatic positions in FG has to be extended to four (Dik 1978 gives only three, recognizing positions for 'theme, topic/focus and tail') and (b) that it is not appropriate to associate these positions with the notions just mentioned: the function of the pragmatic positions appears to be to strengthen pragmatic relations between parts of sentences. Therefore I will not give them any suggestive names, but stick to neutral characterisations (P$\emptyset$, P1, P2, P3). Evidence for these points will be taken from word-order characteristics of Dutch. I will work within the framework sketched in De Schutter and Nuyts (1983).

1. Dutch as an SOV-language

Dutch word order has recently been given considerable attention, and different analyses have been proposed concerning its fundamental nature.[1] Dutch can most convincingly be shown to display fundamentally an SOV-structure, not only in subclauses, where this can hardly be doubted, but also in main clauses, though the latter at first sight display a structure that might be labelled $[X \ V_1 \ S \ O \ (V_{2...n})]$, in which X is a random constituent, V_1 the finite verb and $V_{2...n}$ any sequence of verbs formally depending on V_1 (cf. Dik 1981: 173, who posits a fundamental structure SV_fOV_i):

(1)　　(Omdat)　Wouter gisteren　een paar vrienden terugbracht
　　　　(Because) Walter yesterday a　few　friends　back brought
　　　　'(Because) Walter brought back a few friends yesterday'

(2)　　Blijkbaar　bracht　Wouter gisteren　een paar vrienden terug
　　　　Apparently brought Walter yesterday a　few　friends　back
　　　　'Apparently Walter brought back a few friends yesterday'

(3)　　Blijkbaar　heeft Wouter gisteren　een paar vrienden teruggebracht
　　　　Apparently has　Walter yesterday a　few　friends　back brought
　　　　'Apparently Walter brought back a few friends yesterday'

That the typological status of (2) and (3) cannot be said to be either VSO or SVO may be concluded from

- the constant place of the verb particle *terug* (back) at the end of the clause
  (cf. Koster 1975, Abraham and Scherpenisse 1983)
- the order of the time-satellite before the object.

The importance of both facts comes to the fore when sentences like (2) and (3) are compared to their English counterpart, English being a fairly good example of an SVO-language:

(2'-3') Apparently Walter brought *back* a *few friends yesterday*

Hypothesizing an SOV-structure for (2) implies, as a matter of course, that we have to account for an empty V-place at the end of the clause, in other words for a null-realisation of that slot. This can be accounted for fairly easily within the TGG framework, if we assume that sentences such as (2) and (3) have a so-called root transformation applied to them, transferring the tensed verb to the first (second) place in the clause, but of course leaving a (verbal) trace behind. Being a root transformation, it would not apply to embedded clauses such as (1).

   The problem that interests us now is whether the dubious notion of transformations can be avoided, without however denying the fundamentally equal status of the structures in the main clause and in the subordinate clause. I assume it can be, but in order to be in keeping with the thesis of language functionality, we shall have to investigate the principle(s) underlying the language system. As far as constituent ordering is concerned this (these) principle(s) appear(s) to boil down to the existence of an abstract scheme that can be represented as:

(4)   P1 [...S...O...V] P∅

where P indicates a position. The dots stand for possible places that may be filled with non-argument constituents; consider:

(5)   Natuurlijk heeft [gisteren dat gruwelijke ongeluk door zijn wreedheid
        of-course has   yesterday that awful   accident by   its cruelty

        heel wat opschudding onder de omwonenden teweeggebracht]
        quite some emotion   among the inhabitants caused

        (= Sat_1-S-Sat_2-O-Sat_3-Part-V)

        'Of course the grimness of that awful accident yesterday threw those
        living nearby into considerable commotion'

Scheme (4) of course implies that Dutch is not a pure SOV-language. What the
SOV-principle stands for is a purely and exclusively syntactic device that is
itself incorporated in an encompassing pragmatic scheme. In other words: the
nature of P1 and PØ is pragmatic, a thesis that cannot amaze anybody acquainted
with the work of Dik, although it may seem odd that the sentence-initial V_1 of
our original scheme should be seen as part of P1.

2. Filling P1

2.1. P1 left open or filled by V

As has been seen, Dutch subordinate clauses manifest a constituent order that
seems essentially different from that in main clauses. In fact it is not: if we
assume for the moment that P1 is a possible indicator of the pragmatic value of
clauses (declarative, interrogative, imperative, hypothetical, ...), it stands
to reason that in subclauses the subordinating word (or wordgroup) has to be
taken as P1: it is always in the first place (thus meeting the first condition
for any part to be used as P1), and its lexical content is always sufficient to
indicate the clause's pragmatic function conclusively, cf. *dat - of* (that - if/
whether), interrogative words as subordinators, etc. (cf. De Schutter and Nuyts
1983: 395). Contrary to the situation in subclauses, the pragmatic functionality
of main clauses is primarily indicated by intonational contours. As a consequence,
Dutch (as well as other SAE languages) does not contain any special words to indicate the speech-act character of sentences, and thus P1 in the abstract ordering scheme is left open.

Such a P1-less sentence is perfectly possible in Dutch, especially in the
spoken language, and in contexts in which such sentences are directly incorporated into a narration, a vivid description, etc.; consider:

(6)   (En) wij dus maar heel de   tijd verhaaltjes vertellen ...
        (and) we   thus but   whole the time stories   tell(ing) ...
        'So there we were, telling stories all the time, ...'

(7)   (En) wij heel de tijd op je wachten   zeker? (Nee, dank je lekker)
        (and) we   whole the time for you wait(ing) surely (no, thank you well)
        'So we're supposed to wait for you all that time? No, thanks'

(8)   Jullie eerst alle rommel opruimen!   (Dan zien we wel   weer verder)
        you   first all mess   up-clean(ing) (then see we indeed again further)
        'You just clean up all the mess first! Then we'll see'

These sentences show that all major kinds of speech acts can be formed this way;
what they also show is that this type of sentence formation leads to so-called

'context-sentences': sentences that are interpretable in certain contexts only.

In order to go beyond this limitation, it appears to be necessary for the speaker/writer to indicate the relative place of the SoA (State of Affairs) within his/her UoI (Universe of Interpretation); an essential means to achieve this is the indication of tense (cf. De Schutter 1981a, 1981b), which in Dutch is assigned to the pragmatically principal verb (the verb that is highest in the pragmatic hierarchy). It is exactly this verb that is going to be the core of P1 in all unmarked main clauses. In fact it is not put in its 'normal' clause-final place, but in front of S and O; consider:

(9) a. Neem je je   vriendje mee   naar die fuif, en er   komt weer
       take you your friend   along to that party, and there comes again

       niets   dan narigheid
       nothing but misery
       'If you take your friend along to that party, there'll be nothing but
       misery again'

    b. Neem je je   vriendje mee   naar die fuif?
       take you your friend   along to that party
       'Are you taking your friend along to that party?'

    c. Neem (jij) je   vriendje maar eens mee   naar die fuif!
       take (you) your friend   but once along to that party
       'Why not take your friend along to that party!'

(10)a. Had je je   vriendje meegenomen naar die fuif, dan ...
       had you your friend   along-taken to that party, then ...
       'If you had taken your friend along to that party, ...'

    b. Had jij je   vriendje meegenomen naar die fuif?
       had you your friend   along-taken to that party
       'Had you taken your friend along to that party?'

    c. Had (jij) je   vriendje maar eens meegenomen naar die fuif!
       had (you) your friend   but once along-taken to that party
       'If only you had taken your friend along to that party!'

We thus see that the tensed verb *has* to occupy P1 in main clauses. Sentences with the speech-act character of interrogatives or imperatives are then 'complete' (though P1 can be further extended in both of them), but those with declarative function are still just as marked as sentences without any 'filling' of P1: they are context-sentences as well, requiring some sequel or result-phrase as a consequence (see (9a) and (10a) respectively). It will also be clear that, with the only verb in P1-position, the V-slot in the [SOV]-part of the scheme can be filled at most by the inherent verb-particle (in (9) *mee*). If there is no such particle, that slot will of course be empty.

The difference in markedness between the a-sentences (marked) and the b- and

c-sentences (unmarked) appears to be in agreement with the difference in functionality between declarative sentences (giving a comment on a given topic), and
interrogative or imperative ones (basically bringing in a whole SoA, without the
theme-rheme-structure getting any prominence).

2.2. P1 filled by an element other than V

In all speech-act types, then, it is possible for the tensed verb to be preceded
by one constituent or term. There are basically two cases:

2.2.1. Tensed verb preceded by a sentence modifier

By sentence modifiers we mean modal particles (adverbs), clause-connecting words,
and other particles indicating the SoA's place and status within the UoI (cf.
De Schutter 1983: 278-286). Examples are:

(11) a. Misschien neemt-ie (dus) zijn vriendje mee
        Maybe   takes-he (thus) his friend   along
        '(So) maybe he'll take his friend along'

     b. Misschien (wie weet)   neemt-ie zijn vriendje mee?
        Maybe   (who knows) takes-he his friend   along
        'Maybe (who knows?) he'll take his friend along'

     c. Misschien neem je je   vriendje mee!
        Maybe   take you your friend   along!
        'Maybe you could take your friend along!'

By putting this type of term in P1, the utterance's speech-act character is
slightly altered: a. is turned into a hypothesis, b. into a careful supposition,
and c. into a suggestion to do what is expressed in the clause. As for the last
sentence, it should be noted that the possibility of using the imperative does
not hold any more when the verb is preceded by a sentence modifier (or by any
other term or constituent for that matter).

2.2.2. Tensed verb preceded by any constituent

No specific semantic or syntactic functional type is preferred for incorporation
into P1, and if the factual distribution of certain types over P1 and other
positions may be interpreted as indicating the contrary, this can only be attributed to partial parallels between syntactic and pragmatic functions.[2] This
seeming arbitrariness disappears if the pragmatic level is taken into account.
As there are, at first sight, some differences between declarative, interrogative
and imperative sentences, I shall first deal with them separately:

a. Declarative clauses mostly open with a topic-constituent, usually the most thematic term of the sentence. It is less common, and thus marked, for the constituent bearing contrastive focus to occupy the first place; consider (12):

(12)   Een wandeling zou   ik willen maken
        a   walk   should I like   to-make
        'It's a WALK that I should like to take'

b. Interrogative clauses, as mentioned before, do not require any constituent before the verb, at least if the question concerns the SoA as a whole (yes/no-question). Even in this type of question, a thematic constituent may be put at the head; the question then gets a somewhat different implication: there is a clear suggestion that the thematic constituent gives rise to the question being asked. The clause thus assumes the character of a hypothesis; consider:

(13) a. Komt Peter morgen   ook?
        Comes Peter tomorrow too
        'Is Peter coming tomorrow too?'

   b. Peter komt morgen   ook?
        Peter comes tomorrow too
        'Peter is coming tomorrow too?'

Both (13a) and (13b) express uncertainty, but the speaker in (13b) gives an unmistakable hint that the SoA mentioned in the clause should be considered the 'normal' one, for whatever reason.

Questions with a specific focus (wh-questions) will always have either a thematic term or (usually) the focus itself in P1; cf.:

(14) a. Peter komt wanneer?
        Peter comes when
        'Peter is coming when exactly?'

   b. Wanneer komt Peter?
        when   comes Peter
        'When is Peter coming exactly?'

The difference between (14a) and (14b) is not so great, although it catches the eye that a. can hardly be answered by *nooit* (never). In other words: (14a) presupposes that the focus has a referent. A direct refutation, which is quite possible after (14b), is not very appropriate in (14a). (14b) may thus be called the unmarked construction, (14a) being marked for constructions in which the focus is contrasted with other (mostly implicit) referents.

c. Imperative clauses are similar to interrogative ones in that they may open
with a verb form; otherwise they behave like declarative sentences: P1 may be
occupied by a thematic constituent, as well as the term in focus; cf.:

(15) a. Peter breng je   mee   NAAR HUIS, hoor
         Peter bring you along to   home, hear
         'Do bring Peter HOME'

      b. PETER breng je   mee   naar huis, hoor
         Peter bring you along to   home, hear
         'Do bring PETER home'

   Recapitulating, we find that the first place in Dutch sentences can be taken
up by a clearly thematic or rhematic constituent; in this way theme and rheme
are put at quite a distance from each other in the sentence, thus emphasizing
the tension between them: thematic constituents in P1 stand out as the starting
point of the whole SoA; foregrounded focus constituents, on the other hand, call
forth an opposition to another referent that precisely does *not* fit into the
framework. Those sentence types that are easy to use without any term before the
verb form are especially subject to this strengthening of the theme-rheme tension.

3. *Filling P∅*

Languages with fundamental SOV-order do not necessarily require the verb in last
position in the sentence. There is of course, in these languages, as well as in
other ones, the phenomenon Dik has labelled 'tail', i.e. a constituent added to
the main part of the sentence, and separated from it by a clear break in the
intonation. Besides, Dutch sentences can have one (but in principle not more
than one)[3] constituent after the verb, without such a break. This means that
there is a difference between (16a) and (16b):

(16) a. Ik heb hem nog   gezien vanmorgen
         I   have him still seen   this-morning
         'I saw him this morning'

      b. Ik heb hem nog   gezien, vanmorgen
         I   have him still seen,   this-morning
         'I saw him, this morning'

We shall refer to the pragmatic position in (16a) as P∅, and that in (16b) as P3.
P∅ may be seen as the counterpart of P1 (Dik's 'topic'), and P3 (Dik's 'tail') as
the counterpart of P2 (Dik's 'theme').

   P∅-constituents may occur in all sentence types, including subordinate clauses;

in main clauses it is not always possible to state whether a constituent is in the SOV-part, or in PØ: this can only be established beyond doubt if a (main) verb or a term is inherently bound to the verb marks the end of the SOV-part. I will not go into this in any detail, but shall restrict the discussion to clear cases. My point is that the filling of PØ runs to a great extent parallel to that of P1. It thus may contain sentence modifiers, but not all sentence constituents.

3.1. Sentence modifiers

Examples of sentence modifiers in PØ are:

(16) a. Hij brengt het dus morgen   mee   misschien
        he brings it so tomorrow along possibly
        'So he'll bring it along tomorrow possibly'

     b. Brengt hij het morgen   mee   misschien?
        brings he it tomorrow along possibly
        'Will he bring it along tomorrow possibly?'

     c. Breng het morgen   mee   misschien!
        bring it tomorrow along possibly
        'Bring it along tomorrow, if possible!'

As was the case with sentence modifiers in P1, their positioning in PØ brings about considerable modifications in the speech-act values of utterances, and on the whole both sets of modifications (in P1 and PØ) run parallel. To be sure, quite a number of peculiar restrictions have to be stated, but this is far beyond the scope of this paper.

3.2. Sentence constituents

Contrary to P1, PØ excludes a number of syntactic categories: most types of adjectives/adverbs, and especially all nominal arguments that take up the syntactic functions of subject and object.

All other arguments and satellites may be put both inside and outside the SOV-part. A major question is whether, and if so, to what extent that choice is guided by functional principles. In order to get at least a partial answer, I shall confine myself to the treatment of prepositional phrases, the category that can be shifted most easily from the SOV-part of PØ, and back.

3.2.1. A quantitative analysis of a corpus of written language

From a corpus of 18,000 clauses,[4] all those with at least one PP were selected,
which yielded 3165 constructions. Of these, 1698 had at least one PP in the SOV-
part, and 1605 had at least one in P1 (besides possibly one or more in the SOV-
part: the latter was the case for 134 clauses). I will not go into prior attempts
at explaining 'extraposition' on the basis of the 'complexity' of the PP's themselves (their incorporating 'long' and 'intricate' constituents such as other
PP's, subclauses, etc.): however broadly we were to take the notion of 'complexity', it would account for at most 16.8% of the extraposed PP's in our corpus.
Another, though related, 'mechanistic' explanation tries to make use of a notion
'complexity of the pre-verbal part of the clause'. This, of course, is even less
transparent, as we have to take quite a number of factors into account: the
length of the constituents, semantic and pragmatic relations both among the constituents themselves and with elements in SOV and in P1, etc. As to our corpus,
we can readily assume that most PP's have a strong informative load: many of
them are satellites, not called up by the verb itself, and thus adding important
details (circumstances) to the sentence. It stands to reason that accumulating
PP's within the SOV-part should involve a sharp increase in the heterogeneity
and a decrease in the 'surveyability' of that part of the sentence. Pursuing
this point further, we should then expect an increase in the tendency toward
extraposing at least one of the PP's to PØ. This however is in utter contradiction with the material in my corpus;[5] consider Table 1, which lists the number
of instances with one, two and three PP's and shows whether PØ is occupied by
(one of) these PP's:

TABLE 1: PP's in PØ position in three clause types

	empty PØ position		filled PØ position	
clause with 1 PP	1334	(47.6%)	1467	(52.4%)
clause with 2 PP's	212	(61.8%)	131	(38.2%)
clause with 3 PP's	14	(66.7%)	7	(33.3%)

If anything, a strengthening of the SOV-part is the result of extending the
sentence with secondary relations. This fact is, to put it mildly, remarkable,
and very hard to explain. Getting far ahead of the present analysis, I venture
this explanation: sentences with quite a lot of information incorporated in

them do not display a clear theme/rheme-distinction, and so do not easily offer the condition for splitting the constituents according to their pragmatic values. I shall come back to this point in 4. What is at stake thus seems to be of a pragmatic, rather than a mechanistic-syntactic nature.

In this section I have hinted at the well-known theme/rheme-opposition that appears to dominate P1. How this could be interpreted is the topic of the following investigation.

3.2.2. *The grammaticality of sentences with PØ*

In order to investigate the acceptability of elements in PØ we carried out two experiments. In each experiment 30 students of Dutch had to evaluate sentences containing three PP's, with these PP's in different places with respect to each other and to the verb.

Each experiment contained a set of sentences with both a clearly thematic PP and a clearly rhematic one.[6] The experiments differed only in that in the first one[7] the third PP was a sentence constituent that was neither clearly thematic nor clearly rhematic, whereas in the second one the third PP was a sentence modifier (e.g. *naar mijn mening* (in my opinion)). Both experiments were alike in opposing two PP's with opposing pragmatic values to each other and to one 'neutral' PP. In experiment 1, subjects were asked to evaluate the acceptability (grammaticality) of 33 sentences, and in experiment 2 they had to rate the grammaticality of 48 sentences. Ratings could vary between 0 (= ungrammatical, not to be expected under any circumstance), and 4 (= 100% grammatical, can be used in all contexts). Subjects were asked to consider only the pronunciation with homogeneous slanting declination. All possible orderings were presented, and these are the average results:

TABLE 2: Evaluation of sentences with 3 PP's

(T = thematic PP, R = rhematic PP, N = pragmatically neutral PP, V = Verb)

	Experiment 1 (N = sentence const.)	Experiment 2 (N = sentence modifier)
TNRV	3.8	3.8
TRNV	0.9	0.9
NTRV	2.0	4.0
NRTV	0.5	1.2
RTNV	1.7	1.0
RNTV	0.4	0.7
TNVR	3.0	3.3
TRVN	1.8	3.2
NTVR	2.1	3.3
NRVT	3.3	3.7
RTVN	0.5	1.7
RNVT	0.8	0.7

The resulting picture is easy to interpret:

- The three PP's may be incorporated into the SOV-part of the sentence, but T
  has to precede R; the place of N is preferably between these two if it is a
  constituent, and before or after T (but before R) if it is a modifier.
- Both T and R may be put into PØ, the other two retaining their mutual ordering
  before V.
- Pragmatically neutral PP's cannot easily be placed in PØ if they are constituents, but they can if they are modifiers.

What is remarkable about these intuitions is that the sentences with thematic
constituents in PØ are judged at least as high as (in fact even slightly higher
than) those with rhematic PP's in PØ. This is surprising, because a general law
is for rhematic constituents, if possible, to be ordered *behind* thematic ones.

    At second sight this is less remarkable, considering that the evaluations
themselves do not tell us anything about the probability of these sentences
occurring in real life situations. To get some insight into what is at stake, we
go back to our first corpus of written sentences.

3.2.3. *Distribution of T, R and N in PØ-PP's*

I selected only those sentences containing two PP's (212 of them have both PP's in the SOV-part, 131 have one in PØ and stated the pragmatic value (T, R or N) of both PP's. This quantitative analysis is represented in Table 3:

TABLE 3: Pragmatic values of PP's in sentences with two PP's

Both PP's in SOV-part			One PP in SOV, one in PØ		
PP_1	PP_2	number	PP (in SOV)	PP (in PØ)	number
R	R	4	R	R	8
T	T	52	T	T	3
N	N	23	N	N	5
T	R	41	T	R	62
N	R	43	N	R	30
T	T	5	R	T	8
N	T	23	N	T	8
T	N	18	T	N	5
R	N	3	R	N	2

The most striking facts are:
- Fewer than half of the clauses with two PP's in the SOV-part have at least one rhematic PP (96 out of 212, i.e. 45.3%); on the other hand the vast majority of PP's in PØ are rhematic (100 out of 131, i.e. 76.3%).
- If neither PP is rhematic, extraposition is extremely rare (21 out of 137 instances, i.e. 15.3%), and can usually be explained on account of the length and/or complexity of the PP.

These figures seem to leave us with a fairly straightforward picture: if extraposition is not the result of a syntactic rule (as is the case with argument-clauses), the unmarked construction is the one where the most rhematic constituent ends up in PØ.

What strikes one immediately when analysing the few cases of T in PØ in our corpus is that they all contain propositional particles such as *ook* (= also), *zelfs* (= even), *alleen* (= only), etc. as focus markers attached to the rhematic constituent (cf. for this matter Verhagen 1979); one example, taken from a context about the historiography of Dutch literature:

(17)   Maar Van Duinkerkens poging om {[*ook* aan de regionalistische literatuur
        in Noord-Nederland een plaats in te ruimen] bij de beschrijving van de
        Nederlandse letterkundige geschiedenis} ...

        (structure: ... om {[(S) O V] PØ}

        'But Van Duinkerken's attempt to {[*also* find room for the regional
        literature of the northern Netherlands] in the description of Dutch
        literary history} ...'

Another well-known case in the literature about Dutch word order that displays
similar characteristics is that of attributive PP's split from their head, as
illustrated in (18):

(18)   Ik heb al heel wat romans van Vestdijk gelezen, maar *een essay* heb ik
        nog nooit in handen gehad *van die auteur*
        'I have read quite a number of Vestdijk's novels, but I have never
        tried an essay by that author'

Een essay (an essay) gets a very strong focus through being in plain opposition
with *romans* (novels), whereas *van die auteur* (by that author) clearly refers to
the same person that was mentioned in the first part of the coordination (and
probably had been discussed for some time before). We may safely conclude from
these and parallel cases that placement of a thematic PP in PØ (and probably
other types of thematic constituents as well) creates a special tension between
rhematic parts and the thematic constituent in PØ. Consequently such constructions have to be considered as rather strongly marked. This accounts for the
fact that their grammaticality is judged maximal on the one hand, whereas they
are extremely rare in everyday language (and even in written language) on the
other hand.

3.3. Conclusion of experiments

Apart from those constituents that are bound to PØ for syntactic reasons, the
following sentence parts may occupy this place:
- rhematic constituents
- thematic constituents in marked constructions, emphasizing the pragmatic
  theme/rheme-structure of the clause
- sentence modifiers.

4. The pragmatic functions of P1 and PØ

Pragmatic relations appear to play an important role in Dutch syntax. This is true to such an extent that we can apply the well-known syntactic typology that makes use of S, O and V to only part of the sentence. The resulting SOV-part may be followed by a position PØ, that is largely pragmatic in nature, and main clauses generally open with an equally pragmatic P1. This leaves us with the structural description represented in (4) above: [P1 [SOV] PØ].

The general tendency to order thematic and rhematic constituents on a left-right scale is reflected within the SOV-part (satellites are ordered before or after S and/or O according to their pragmatic value, cf. De Schutter and Van Hauwermeiren 1983: 192), as well as in the encompassing pragmatic structure (sentences with thematic constituents in P1, rhematic ones in PØ being unmarked). Moreover, the pragmatic order may very well be fundamentally connected with the speaker's or writer's wish to accentuate the theme-rheme tension inherent in most sentences. Some important facts mentioned in our discussion point to this:

- Sentences with thematic constituents in PØ are by no means odd, at least if they are in opposition with a rhematic constituent with strong contrastive focus.
- Sentences with rich informational content (hence usually a less prominent theme-rheme opposition between any two constituents) tend to avoid the structure with PØ.
- The strong theme/rheme-tension in wh-questions is reflected by the necessity to incorporate either a thematic or a rhematic constituent in P1.
- The parts of complex NP's, in which there is a strong tension between the thematic kernel term and a thematic PP may be split over P1 and/or PØ and/or the SOV-part (cf. examples (18), and (a1)-(a2) in footnote 8).

This fundamental function of the special positions P1 and PØ may very well account for the fact that P1 is sometimes occupied by rhematic constituents, and PØ by thematic ones. Leaving out wh-questions, we always get marked constructions in such cases.

5. The extended sentence in Dutch

Apart from P1 and PØ we may posit two more pragmatic positions: P2 and P3, corresponding to Dik's *theme* and *tail*. They are illustrated in (19) and (20) respectively:

(19) a. Peter(,) die   hebben we al   in maanden niet meer gezien
        Peter,   that-one have   we already in months   not   more seen
        'Peter, we haven't seen him for months'

     b. (Van) vakantie, daar droomt hij van
        (of) holidays, that dreams he   about
        'Holidays, that's what he dreams about'

(20) a. We hadden er niet meer op gehoopt, op die promotie
        we had   it not more for hoped,   for that promotion
        'We hadn't hoped for it any more, for that promotion'

     b. We hebben al   van alles   geplant in de tuin,
        we have   already of everything planted in the garden,

        bloemen, struiken, bomen
        flowers, bushes,   trees
        'We've already planted all kinds of things in the garden, flowers,
        bushes, trees'

Both P2 and P3 may again be occupied by thematic as well as rhematic constituents.
(19b) exemplifies that P2 may either be in the 'absolutive' form, or anticipate
the semantic and syntactic role it is going to have in the following predication
(cf. Dik 1981: 136), whereas the constituent in P3 will necessarily recapitulate
that role by taking over the preposition (see (20a)). The role of these constituents in the utterance is clearly to narrow down the listener's attention to one
specific part of the UoI. As described in Dik (1981), neither P2 ('Theme') nor
P3 ('Tail') need be a further 'spelling out' of information contained in the
predication: P2 may set up a situation in which one or more parts of the predication play a role; the constituent will then always be thematic, and requires a
special marking, see (21). P3 on the other hand may consist of additional (cir-
cumstantial) information, see (22):

(21)   Wat jou betreft, ik heb hier nog   een leuk werkje
        what you concerns, I have here still a   nice job
        'As for you, I have another nice little job'

(22)   We komen wel   terug hoor, morgen   of overmorgen
        we come indeed back hear, tomorrow or the-day-after
        'We'll be back, you know, tomorrow or the next day'

One final remark should be made here concerning P2 in subordinate clauses: P2
has of course to precede P1, which is occupied by the subordinating element. In
most types of subordinate clauses, then, P2 itself has to be preceded by that
same word(group); only if the clause is in front of the sentence to which it
belongs, or in some types of object clauses, can the subordinating word be dis-
pensed with; consider:

(23) a. (Als) die man, als die nog   eens belt, (dan ...)
        (if) that man, if he again once rings, (then ...)
        '(If) that man, if he calls again, ...'

     b. De eerste keer dat die man, dat die belde, ...
        the first time that that man, that he rang, ...
        'The first time that that man, that he rang, ...'

     c. Ik denk (dat) die vrouw, dat die nog   van zich   zal   laten spreken
        I think (that) that woman, that die still of herself shall let   speak
        'I think (that) that woman, that she will make her name known one day'

6. General conclusions

Our discussion of some basic facts of Dutch sentence structure leads to a number
of modifications to current FG-theory. First of all it appears that at least
SOV-languages may have up to four specific pragmatic positions, encompassing the
SOV-part, which itself is primarily of a syntactic nature. The sentence in such
languages (at least in Dutch) displays a symmetrical structure, which may be
represented in the formula ⌊P2, P1 SOV PØ, P3⌋. In this formula the commas stand
for breaks in the intonation pattern: P2 as well as P3 are stronger functional
markers than P1 and PØ respectively, but on the whole there is a striking functional parallelism between P1 and P2, and between PØ and P3. It is further argued
that the syntactic positions do not, as was put forward in Dik (1981), represent
simple pragmatic functions such as theme, topic, focus, but should be seen as
means to separate the members of a pragmatic relation on the basis of the general
theme-rheme-opposition present in most sentences (the occurrence of this relation
is signalled in Dutch main clauses by the appearance of a finite verb, which is
put in front of the SOV-part of the sentence.

As was suggested in De Schutter and Nuyts (1983), the best way to represent
the theme-rheme relation might very well be in an independent pragmatic component
stating the focal value of any constituent or term chosen to represent the situational network the sentence is to cover. If the focal values of thematic and
rhematic constituents do not differ considerably, P1 and/or PØ are chosen for the
thematic (T) and/or rhematic (R) term(s), thus leading to:
- neutral sentences: T in P1, R in SOV
                     T in P1, R in PØ
                     T in SOV, R in PØ
- less common, though by no means ungrammatical sentences:
                     R in P1, T in SOV
                     R in P1, T in PØ
                     R in SOV, T in PØ

If the theme-rheme relation is strong (e.g. if the speaker chooses a well-established thematic notion, or a very unexpected rhematic one, or both), this may be specially marked by putting one of the participants in the relation (or both of them) in P2 or/and P3, the most common way being with the thematic part in front of the sentence, the rhematic one following it; though again, the speaker may choose to put them the other way around.

NOTES

[1] We may refer to Kerstens (1981), who argues in favour of VSO-status, to Kooij (1973), who posits SVO, at least in main clauses, and to Koster (1975), who advocates SOV, both in main and in subordinate clauses.

[2] The fact that subjects are often placed in P1, for instance, can be attributed to speakers' and writers' preference for thematic terms or terms with contrast focus as subjects (cf. Dik 1981: 181).

[3] We cannot go into this problem here: Koster (1974) is right in stating that two constituents after V are perfectly possible, provided the more thematic constituent follows the more rhematic one, thus providing a mirror image of what is common when both constituents precede the verb. We have however to object to Koster's later analysis, allowing for no fewer than six constituents (3 of which may be PP's) following V (Koster 1978). This proposal would predict the grammaticality of such non-sentences as:

(i) *Hij heeft gewerkt voor zijn diploma met veel ijver gedurende die hele lange hete zomer
'He worked for his diploma with great zeal throughout the long, hot summer'

Sentences of this kind were put to the informants of the tests, along with the test-items discussed in this paper under 3.2.2. They were commonly rejected, achieving only between 0.4 and 0.8 on our scales.

[4] This corpus was taken from 18 different Dutch and Belgian authors, both literary and non-literary.

[5] This result is at least partly in accordance with the facts noted by Jansen (1978) in a corpus of spoken language: PP is rarely removed from SOV if it is the only non-verbal part of it; it is quite often removed if there are at least two other constituents in the clause, but the rate of placement in PØ does not increase proportionally to the number of these constituents.

[6] Our hypothesis about the thematic/rhematic nature of PP's was confirmed for each single instance by the fact that the order with the 'rhematic' constituent before the 'thematic' one within SOV was consistently rejected, cf. Table 2.

[7] The first experiment was carried out by L. Vandenbosch, and the results were reported in Vandenbosch (1982: 164-170).

[8] The same effects can be obtained in Dutch by distributing the parts of the NP (rhematic kernel term and thematic PP) over P1 and SOV:

(a1) Een roman heb ik van die auteur nog niet gelezen
(a2) Een roman heb ik nog niet gelezen van die auteur
(b) Van die auteur heb ik nog geen roman gelezen

It should be noted that (a1), with P1-placement of the focus constituent sounds slightly less common than (a2), with both P1-placement of the thematic part, and PØ-placement of the rhematic PP. This construction is discussed extensively in Kooij and Wiers (1977, 1978) and in Klein and Van den Toorn (1978).

Chapter 11

Topic and focus in Wambon discourse

Lourens de Vries
Seksi Linguistik ZGK, Irian Jaya, Indonesia

0. Introduction

This article describes the behavior of switch-reference[1] and focal suffixes in
Wambon[2], a Papuan tribal language spoken by about 3000 people in the southern
Lowlands of Irian Jaya along the banks of the Upper-Digul river. The major claim
of the article concerns the functionality of Topic and Focus (as defined in the
Functional Grammar framework of Dik 1978, 1980a) in Wambon discourse: Topic and
Focus mediate between discourse constraints of informational cohesion and the
syntactic form of linguistic expressions.

In trying to relate the description of sentence-grammar phenomena to discourse-
level phenomena I use some notions developed by Grimes (1975) on discourse-level,
viz. identification span and strength of identification. Cohesion constraints connected with identification spans have to do with establishing, maintaining and
re-establishing discourse-topics: for a discourse to be informationally cohesive
the speaker should first establish a discourse-topic ('This is the entity I want
to talk about') and then maintain and confirm it ('I am still talking about the
same entity'). These discourse-topics form the points at which the Addressee
integrates new information into his memory (Clark and Clark 1977: 95).

Switch-reference suffixes, triggered by the assignment of Topic, guide Wambon
Addressees as to how expressions fit into the development of discourse-topicality[3] in the preceding discourse. Same-Subject suffixes indicate that the Speaker
is still maintaining a previously well-established discourse-topic. Different-
Subject suffixes indicate that there will be a change of contextual perspective
from one well-established discourse-topic to another well-established discourse-
topic. Wambon distinguishes formally two types of Topic: Strong Topics and Weak
Topics. Strong Topics have to do with the act of establishing a topic, whereas
Weak Topics have to do with maintaining a previously well-established topic.

A Speaker should make clear not only what he is talking about (the dimension
of discourse-topicality) but also which information changes the pragmatic information of the Addressee most crucially (the dimension of discourse-saliency).
Wambon focal suffixes, triggered by Focus-assignment, guide the Addressee as to
how expressions fit into the development of saliency in the preceding discourse.

In this way Focus codes saliency constraints onto the form of linguistic expressions.

The article has the following structure: Section 1 contains theoretical pre-
liminaries concerning the definition of pragmatic functions (1.1.) and concerning
the notions of topical span, strong and weak topicality and strength of identification (1.2.); Section 2 deals with Topic in Wambon, 2.1. dealing with Weak
Topics and switch-reference, 2.2. with Strong Topics and their expression; Section
3 is about Focus in Wambon with 3.2. giving special attention to the relation
between Topic and Focus; and Section 4 presents some conclusions.

1. Theoretical preliminaries

1.1. Defining pragmatic functions

If we keep defining pragmatic functions on the level of general theory and in
terms of informational roles only, we will be defining and redefining them eter-
nally. I propose the following limitations on the definitions of pragmatic functions:

(i)   start by defining pragmatic functions on the level of individual languages;
      this provides a sound basis for a typologically adequate characterization
      of these functions in general theory.
(ii) define pragmatic functions also in terms of the expressive devices used to
      express them, and not only in terms of informational statuses or roles.

Along these lines the definition of pragmatic functions would be firmly tied to
the 'emic' distinctions languages themselves make, which is a typological advantage. A second advantage is the reduction in the vagueness of the definitions
because the definitions also refer to the expressive devices used. Thus Topic in
L is not only defined as the constituent presenting information the Speaker wants
to predicate something about (informational status) but also as the constituent
in linguistic expressions which attracts the suffix s or the position p or the
construction c (expressive devices).

An interesting consequence of this approach is that the definitions of pragmatic functions in individual languages differ not only in terms of the expressive devices used (which is to be expected) but also in terms of the informational
roles associated with the pragmatic functions: different languages appear to make
different 'emic' distinctions in the areas of topicality and saliency. Languages
like Wambon do not subdivide the saliency dimension into several types of saliency

on the level of sentence-grammar: Wambon uses the same formal means for the whole
area of saliency, thus neutralizing differences in the pragmatic conditions
causing the various types of saliency. Aghem, on the other hand (see 3.1.), distinguishes for example saliency caused by newness from saliency caused by contrast
with a previous assertion by treating the salient constituents differently in the
different pragmatic conditions. Thus the definitions of Focus in Aghem and Wambon
differ in both expressive devices and informational roles involved. On the other
hand Wambon distinguishes formally two types of Topic where other languages use
the same expressive device for the whole area of topicality.

   If we define pragmatic functions along the lines proposed here, we define them
on the level of the constituents of linguistic expressions and not on the level
of conceptual structures as proposed by De Schutter and Nuyts (1983: 393). Dik
(1982: 199) defines the optimal level of abstractness of linguistic theory as
the most concrete level at which it is still possible to capture the typological
differences among natural languages. This is a very important methodological
principle, which protects linguistic theory on the one hand from losing itself in
irrelevant and empirically almost empty abstractions and on the other hand from
becoming a trivial enumeration of facts. Any proposal in the direction of a more
abstract theory of pragmatic functions than the theory of Dik (1978), which defines pragmatic functions on the relatively concrete level of constituents of
linguistic expressions, should make clear first of all that that theory is too
concrete to capture the typological differences among natural languages. By defining pragmatic functions on the level of constituents in terms of both the informational roles and the expressive characteristics of these constituents we can
arrive at concrete and concise definitions of pragmatic functions, which enable
us to compare individual languages, thus making a typological sound general
theory of pragmatic functions possible.

1.2. Some discourse notions

Discourse-constraints on topical cohesion can be formulated in terms of Grimes'
(1975: 92) notions of strength of identification and identification span. Grimes
defines these notions as follows (1975: 92): 'An identification span consists of
a series of identifications of the same participant, not necessarily in contiguous clauses, in which no identification is stronger than the one before it.
Strength of identification is a ranking that goes from proper names like *George
Washington Carver* to explicit descriptives like *the mechanic who fixed our
generator in Arkansas* to common nouns like *the teacher* to nouns used generically

like *the fellow* to pronouns like *him*, and from there to reference without identification.'

To facilitate the description of Wambon in terms of the Functional Grammar
model I insert the notion of Topic into this definition: a topical span consists
of a series of identifications of the same Topic, not necessarily in contiguous
clauses, in which no identification is stronger than the one before it. Furthermore, I make a distinction between discourse-topics and sentence-topics.
Sentence-topics are discourse-topics that have been formally expressed as Topics
by the expression rules of sentence-grammar.

To illustrate the idea of topical span analysis consider the following stretch
of discourse from English:

(1) A : Yesterday I met *your brother John*

(2) A : *He* looked very pale

(3) B : Yes, *he* has not been well for a couple of weeks now

(4) A : *John* had better consult a doctor the way *he* looks

(1)-(4) contains two topical spans with *John* as the discourse-topic. In (1) this
topic is introduced by the strong identification *your brother John*. In (2) this
topic is treated as a well-established topic and it is given a weak identification by *he*. In the same way the topic is maintained in (3) by weak, pronominal
identification. In (4) the topic is re-established by the identification *John*,
which is stronger than the one before it (*he* in (3)); thus a new topical span is
started with the same topic.

Usually there is a gradual decrease in strength of identification from the
beginning of a topical span towards the end. Initially in topical spans, the
Speaker uses as much identification as is needed given the pragmatic information
of the Addressee. Medially and finally in topical spans the Speaker uses as
little identification as possible while still maintaining the discourse-topic.
Every now and then the Speaker will, in the middle of a topical span, give in-
sufficient identification of a topic (because of over-estimating the pragmatic
information of the Addressee), which is then corrected by a marked strong identification finally in the topical span, resulting in a Predication, Tail-con-
struction like (5):

(5)   *She* is a beautiful woman, *your sister*

There are at least two cases in which, within one topical span, an identification of a topic is stronger than the one before it, resulting in a strong-weak-
strong identification sequence. The first case concerns the usage of Tails like
your sister in (5), which we discussed above. This use of a strong expression
finally in a topical span is clearly connected with identificational strategies.
The second case concerns strong expressions which contain markedly more descriptive information than is needed for identificational purposes. In these cases
the use of a strong expression is not at all connected with identification.
Consider (6):

(6) a. *Ronald Reagan* again stressed the importance of a strong NATO
    b. *He* reminded his European guests of what the Russians were doing in
        Afghanistan and *he* brought the situation in Poland to their attention
    c. *The President* furthermore expressed *his* worries about the growing
        influence of pacifism in Western Europe

The use of the strong expression *the President* in (6c) is a clear case of identificational redundancy. If the weak pronominal identification *he* had been used
instead of *the President* in (6c), it would have been perfectly clear who the
Speaker was talking about. The Ronald Reagan topical span, started in (6a), is
continued in (6c).

Generally, identificational redundancy will be unacceptable as it will '...
unnecessarily hold up the course of the communicative interaction' (Dik 1978: 55).
However, sometimes the demands of identificational efficiency are ignored in
favor of the demands of stylistic variety, and this is what happens in (6c).
Although formally *the President* is a strong identification, following a weak one
in (6b) (*he*), functionally this strong expression is not used as part of referring strategies but as part of style strategies aimed at keeping readers interested. The repetitive use of weak pronominal identification is especially avoided
in newspaper and broadcasting language.

This second case leads us to modify the definition of topical span given above
as follows: a topical span consists of a series of identifications of the same
Topic, not necessarily in contiguous clauses, in which no identification is
stronger than the one before it, unless the strong expression is used as part of
stylistic strategies of variation and not as part of referring strategies.[4]

Strongly identified Topics occurring initially in topical spans in the phase
of establishing topicality, I will label Strong Topics. Weakly identified Topics
occurring medially and finally in topical spans in the phase of maintaining

topicality I will call Weak Topics. Wambon as we will see below formally distinguishes these two types of Topics by applying different expression-rules to them.

2. Topic in Wambon

2.1. Weak Topics

2.1.1. Switch-reference morphology

Compare (7) and (8):

(7)   Nukhe oye hetag-mbelo topkeka-lepo
        I   pig see-SS   flee-past1sgfinal
        'I saw a pig and I fled'

(8)   Nukhe oye hetakha-levo topkeka-tbo
        I   pig see-NF1sgDS   flee-past3sgfinal
        'I saw a pig and it fled'

        (NF = non-future)

Both (7) and (8) consist of two clauses. In (7) both clauses have the same Subject
(*nukhe*, 'I'). In (8) the second clause has a different Subject from the first
clause. Wambon, like many other Papuan and some American Indian languages, uses a
system of verbal suffixes to signal sameness or change of Subject with regard to
the following clause. If the Subject of the following clause has a different referent from the Subject of the preceding clause, Different-Subject (DS) suffixes
appear on the verb of the preceding clause (e.g. *-levo* in (8)). If the Subject
stays the same, Same-Subject (SS) suffixes appear on the verb (e.g. *-mbelo* in
(7)). This monitoring of subjects in consecutive clauses is commonly called
switch-reference (SR) (see Reesink 1983a for an overview).

Connected with switch-reference phenomena is the distinction between final and
medial verbs. Final verbs (like *topkekalepo* in (7)) occur only in the last clause
of a sentence. They cannot be marked for SS or DS; they are independent verbs,
i.e. they can stand on their own and are not dependent on other verbs for the interpretation of their tense and other verb-bound categories. Medial verbs occur
only in non-final clauses; they must carry SR-morphology and they are dependent
on the final verbs for their tense and person/number interpretation.

To carry the SR-monitoring of Subjects across sentence-boundaries the final
verb of the preceding sentence is typically repeated as the first verb of the
following sentence. This repeated verb being medial, it is obligatorily marked
for SS or DS. In this way the SR-monitoring of two sentence-domains is linked.

Medial verbs come in three sorts: participle SS-verbs, finite SS-verbs and

finite DS-verbs. Participle SS-verbs are the most frequent medial verbs; they
are morphologically very simple as they consist of the stem of the Present tense
with the optional addition of the SS suffix -*mbelo* or -*lo*. Finite SS-verbs occur
mainly as repeated final verbs after sentence-boundaries to link SR-domains.
They are derived from the final verb forms by adding the SS suffix -*o* to the
final forms; the repeated final verb mostly occurs in the Present tense, which
functions also as the Neutral tense. Finite DS-verbs can express only two tenses,
Non-Future (NF) and Future (F).

When the final verb of the sentence has Past or Present tense the DS-verb
consists of the Past-stem plus the following suffixes:

- levo   NF1sgDS
- lo   NF2/3sgDS
- levano   NF1plDS
- leno   NF2/3plDS

When the tense of the final verb is Future, Uncertain Future or Intentional
Present, the DS-verb consists of the Future-stem plus the following suffixes:

- vo   F1sgDS
- no   F2/3sgDS
- vano   F1plDS
- nano   F2/3plDS

Sentences in Wambon, especially in narrative discourse, typically consist of
long series of rather simply structured clauses with the Subjects often not expressed but identified by SR-monitoring. As regards the interclausal relationships with these long sequences of clauses (Reesink 1983a: 226 speaks of
'clause chaining'), from a semantic point of view one can agree with Reesink's
(1983a: 226) remark that '...I prefer to see "clause chaining" with the help of
medial verbs as a case of coordination, rather than as subordination. This would
make it more understandable that clauses in such sequences can stand in almost
any semantic relation to each other, because addition, or "collection" (as
Grimes 1975 calls it) is the most neutral semantic relationship.'

However, from a syntactic point of view - and is the distinction subordination/
coordination not primarily a syntactic one? - medial clauses are subordinated to
final clauses because medial verbs are dependent on final verbs for their person/
number and tense interpretation. Even medial DS-verbs which express person and

number independently of their final verbs, have two distinct subordinative qual-
ities:

(i) they can express only two tenses whereas final verbs can express all the
five Wambon tenses; this neutralization of verb-bound morphological categories
is typical of verbs in subordinated domains, whereas verbs in independent clauses
typically express the full range of these oppositions;

(ii) the choice of these two tenses in medial DS-verbs depends on the tense of
the final verb, as we have seen above.

Furthermore final clauses can occur all by themselves, whereas medial clauses
cannot; medial clauses depend on final ones.

2.1.2. Topicality and switch-reference

Reesink (1983a: 240, 242) has argued that topicality factors play an important
role in the SR-mechanisms of several Papuan languages. Above I have formulated
the distribution of SS and DS suffixes in Wambon in terms of the notion of Subject; and indeed this formulation is valid as long as one takes isolated sentences as data. However, when one starts to study the SR-mechanism as it operates
in discourse, the notion of Topic appears to be crucially involved in the distribution of SR-morphology (see Dik 1978: 141 for this notion of Topic). Consider
the following stretch of discourse, taken from a travel narrative, in which the
Speaker[5] tells about a journey he made a year ago. On the way he met some men,
from whom he had tried to buy sago:

(9)   jakhove : 'woyo, ndune tembet!' nde-leno
        they   : 'No,   sago not be   say-NF3plDS
        'They said: 'No, there is no sago...''

(10)   et-mbelo   epka nda-gndev-o
        leave-behind-SS there come-pres1sgSS
        '... (and) leaving (them) behind there I travelled on ...'

(11)   sale inolapngelimo
        sun go down (SS) (present tense stem)
        '...till the sun went down'

(12)   ot   numbum-ke-tbo
        stomach empty-become-past3sgfinal
        '...(and) (my) stomach felt empty (I got hungry)'

In the transition from clause (9) to (10) the switch of Subject (from *jakhove* in
(9) to the 1sg Subject identified in (10) by person/number suffix only) is reflected in the -*leno* NF3plDS suffix on the verb in (9). In the transition from
(10) to (11) there is a switch of Subject (to *sale*, 'the sun', in (11)) but the

verb in (10) carries an SS-marking. Another 'false' SS-marking occurs in (11),
because the Subject of (12), *ot*, 'stomach', is different from that of (11).

The 'false' SS-markings in Wambon narrative discourse can be explained as follows: every time there is a change of Subject, but the Subject of the following
clause presents information that is not previously well-established as a discourse-topic, the 'false' SS-markings occur. That is, the 'false' SS-markings
occur whenever the Subject of the following clause is not a Weak Topic. For
example 'the sun' in (11) has not been established in the preceding discourse as
a topic; 'the sun' does not occur medially in a topical span. On the other hand
the Subject of (10), 'I', refers to a previously well-established discourse-
topic. The 'I'-topic occurs medially in a topical span, and is a maintained topic.

The SR-mechanism in Wambon is connected with keeping track of or maintaining
discourse-topics medially in topical spans. In the first clause of the story of
which (9)-(12) is a part the Speaker had introduced himself as the topic of the
travel narrative as follows:

(13)   Koiwo-talome nukhe Mboma ka-lepo-n-o
         last-year   I   Boma go-past1sg-TN-SS
         'Last year I travelled to Boma ...'

         (TN = transitional nasal)

Since this initial introduction in (13) the 'I'-topic has been identified only
by person/number suffixes and SR-morphology on the verbs. It is not all uncommon
to find a topic maintained this way throughout dozens of clauses before re-establishing takes place. The occurrence of very long topical spans is certainly
a typical characteristic of Wambon narrative discourse.

Different Subject markings occur when the Subject of the following clause
refers to a different Weak Topic from the Subject of the preceding clause. The
notion of Subject is essentially involved in the SR rules because DS-markings do
not simply occur whenever there is a change of Weak Topics between two clauses,
but only when there is a change of *Subject*Topic. The notion of Topic is also
essentially involved because DS-markings do not occur simply whenever there is a
change of Subjects between two consecutive clauses but only when there is a
change of Subject*Topic* constituents.

False SS-markings are not at all rare exceptions; on the contrary they are
rather frequent in Wambon texts. The most frequent 'false' SS-markings occur in
clauses preceding a time-clause which specifies the temporal background of an
event, such as (11). The Subjects of such temporal clauses ('*the morning* came',

'when *the evening* fell', 'till *the sun* went down', 'when *the morning bird* sang') are never well-established discourse-topics. And because of this there is no change of SubjTop but only of Subj in the transitions into and out of these time-setting clauses. The same holds for predications about the weather ('*the rain* came down') and experiential clauses ('*the stomach* gave me an empty feeling'). The Subjects of these temporal, meteorological and experiential clauses are never Weak Topics and this fact explains the occurrence of the SS-marking in clauses preceding them.

However, 'false' SS-markings are not restricted to these three types of clauses, which typically have non-human and inanimate Subjects, but they also occur preceding clauses with human Subjects which have not been previously es-tablished as topics. Consider the following example, also taken from a travel narrative; the travelling party (the 'we'-topic) arrives by canoe at the village Bi on the Upper-Digul river:

(14)   hitulovo-sale lavi-lo   ko-gndeva-n-o
         fourth-day   go down-SS go-pres1pl-TN-SS
         'On Thursday we travelled down(-river)...'

(15)   Mbi-kambom-nga te-mbelo tu-lo
         Bi-village-loc tie-SS   go up-SS
         '...(and) in the village Bi we tied (our canoes) and went up
         (the river-bank)'

(16)   ola na ep-kuva   nokho-nela   mba-khe-kot
         and PM there-also our-brother-in-law stay-pres3sg-perf
         '...and there our brother-in-law stayed already...'

(17)   tu-lo   ep-ka
         go up-SS there-loc
         '...there we went up (the river-bank)'

         (PM = pause marker)

In (15) the verbs carry-SS markings because the Subject of (16), *nokhonela*, has not been established as a discourse-topic in the preceding discourse. It is not a Weak Topic. In fact in (16) the weak discourse-topic is the same as in (14) and (15), viz. the travelling party referred to as 'we', which is identified in (16) by the possessive prefix *nokho-* and in all other clauses by person/number and SR suffixation.

An interesting class of 'false' SS-markings is formed by cases where the Sub-ject switches in number only, from 1pl to 1sg and back, but also from 2 and 3sg to 2 and 3pl and back. Consider the following stretch of discourse:

(18)   la-levambo-n-o   jat-ke-lo
         sleep-past1pl-TN-SS day-become-SS
         '...and we slept till the day came ...'

(19)   Mbulungop ka-lepo
         Burunggop go-past1sgFinal
         '...(and) I went to Burunggop'

(20)   Kwoip-ka mba-gndev-o   minggu hane
         there-loc stay-pres1sg-SS week   one
         'There I stayed one week ...'

(21)   kwoip-ka mba-gndeva-n-o
         there-loc stay-pres1pl-TN-SS
         '...there we stayed ...'

(22)   osakha hali senine ndave-lepo
         and   day Monday return-past1sgfinal
         '...and on Monday I returned'

From (18) to (19) there is a shift from 1pl to 1sg; from (20) to (21) there is a
shift back from the 1sg Subject to the 1pl Subject; from (21) to (22) there is
again a shift from 1pl to 1sg. Throughout this stretch of discourse the verbs
carry SS-markings. In the discourse (18)-(22), the travelling party ('we') is a
set of participants treated as one topic. The shifts to one of the members of
the set and back are not considered as a change of topic.

   Generally in Wambon number-shifts of this type are not considered as a switch
of reference, i.e. 'I' is thought to be included in the reference of 'we'. However, in the data which formed the basis for this article[6] there is one case in
which a number-shift from 1sg to 1 pl does count as a switch of reference, marked
by DS suffixation. Consider the following discourse which belongs to the same
travel story as (14)-(17); (14)-(17) immediately preceded (23)-(26):

(23)   nukhe eve nomboneve ndayonge-ka-lepo-n-o
         I   STM STM   oar-go-past1sg-TN-SS
         '...and as far as I am concerned, I had travelled by canoe ...'

(24)   kinum-ngup-ma-lo   kinumla-lepo
         sleep-with-verbaliser-SS sleep-past1sgfinal
         '...till I became sleepy and slept.'

(25)   ep-ka   la-levo
         there-loc sleep-NF1sgDS
         'There I slept ...'

(26)   nduno ene-mo-gndeva-n-o
         sago eat-durative-pres1pl-TN-SS
         '...and we were eating sago ...'

         (STM = strong Topic marker)

In (25) there is a DS-marking registering the shift from the 1sg Subject in (25) to the 1pl Subject in (26). As a possible explanation for this DS suffix I suggest the following.

(14)-(17)/(23)-(26) are part of a travel narrative in which the travelling party ('we') is the main topic. This topic was introduced in the first sentence of the story as follows:

(27)   Koiwo-talome nukho Wemba Mbitemovo Lorelo
         last-year   I   Wemba Bitemop   Lores
         'Last year I, Wemba, Bitemop and Lores, ...'

         nokhove hitulopkup lavi-lo   ka-levambo
         we   four   go down-SS go-past1plfinal
         '...the four of us, we went down river'

Although the individual members are mentioned separately, the set as a whole (*nokhove hitulopkup*, 'the four of us') is introduced and maintained as one discourse-topic. This topical span is broken, but not ended in (23), because the 'we' topical span is continued in (26) by weak identification (person/number and SR identification). Now in (23) one of the members of the set of participants mentioned in (27) is re-introduced and re-established as a separate topic by the explicit mentioning of the participant (*nukhe*, 'I') followed by the markers of strong topicality ('this is the entity I am now going to talk about') *eve* and *nomboneve* (see 2.2.). Thus in (23) a new topical span begins with the 'I'-topic which ends in (25), where the DS-marking on the verb signals the return to the 'we'-topic. So it could be the case that when one member of a set is explicitly singled out and re-introduced as a new topic, this participant counts as a different referent, causing DS-markings. (In (17), the clause preceding (23), we find an SS-marking because the Subject of the following clause is a Strong Topic, whereas the SR mechanism monitors only *Weak* Topics.)

In the data collected thus far there are no instances of 'false' DS-marking, i.e. every DS-suffix corresponds to a change of SubjectTopic in the following clause. There are, however, three instances of 'false' SS-marking in the data which cannot readily be explained within the theory of SR proposed above. Consider the following discourse, which presents one of these instances:

(28)   nda-gndev-o
         return-pres1sg-SS
         '...I returned ...'

(29)   wamip-ka kave ngaluma-lepo
         way-loc man meet-past1sgfinal
         '...(and) on the way I met a man'

(30)   ngalu-mbelo
         meet-SS
         '...I met (a man)...'

(31)   evo   kave : 'Nguve avoko-kap-ndekhe?' ne-mbelo
         that man   You   who-man-quotemarker say-SS
         '...(and) that man said: 'Who are you?''

Although (31) has a different Subject(Weak)Topic from the preceding sentences
(*evo kave* 'that man'), there is a SS-suffix on the verb in (30). The *kave*-topical
span starts in (29) where *kave* 'a man' is introduced as topic. The 'I'-topic is
maintained from (28) on by person/number and SR identification.

    One could 'save' the theory proposed here by claiming that *evo kave* in (31)
is not a *Weak* Topic but a *Strong* Topic, because a relatively strong expression
is used (the definite NP *evo kave*) and because *evo kave* is arguably used within
the phase of establishing topicality. The crucial question is then of course:
how far does the initial phase of topical spans extend? As I have not given
clear criteria for distinguishing the topic-establishing phase from the topic-
maintaining phase, it seems fair to accept cases like (30)/(31) as counterexamples with regard to the theory defended here.

2.1.3. Contextual perspective and switch-reference

Not all discourse-topics have the same importance. Discourse-topics which are
maintained and re-established in long stretches of discourse and which have a
high degree of involvement in the events of the story, I will label major
discourse-topics and discourse-topics which are maintained in relatively short
topical spans and which are not or only once or twice re-established and which
have a relatively low degree of involvement in the events, I will label minor
discourse-topics.

    For example, in the discourse (14)-(17)/(23)-(26) discussed above, the travel-
ling party 'we' introduced in (27) is the major discourse-topic, whereas the
'I'-topic, introduced in (23), is the minor one. Whereas the 'we'-topic is maintained throughout the whole story, the 'I'-topical span extends only for four
clauses, and is not re-established afterwards. Now one of the rules for telling
stories in Wambon culture is that the narrator presents the main discourse-topic
in the very first sentence of the story and then narrates the events that follow
from the perspective of the main discourse-topic. Thus in (14)-(17)/(23)-(26)
the story is told from the perspective of the 'we'. This 'we'-topic is the main
target of the contextual perspective of the story (see Itagaki and Prideaux
1983: 329-330) for this notion of contextual perspective and its statistical

relation to the sentence-grammar process of Subject-selection).

In an overwhelming majority of clauses in Wambon narratives the main discourse-topic is selected as Subject. This fits into the Functional Grammar interpretation of Subjects as presenting the point of view or perspective on the state of affairs designated by predications (cf. Dik 1978: 71). In this way the narrator expresses on the level of sentence-grammar the dominant contextual perspective of the discourse.

Above I tried to show that both the notion of Subject and that of Topic are indispensable in the formulation of SR rules as they operate in discourse. Now we can formulate the involvement of Subject and Topic as follows: DS-markings signal that the contextual perspective (Subject-notion) is going to switch to another well-established entity about which the speaker is still talking (Weak Topic-notion).

2.2. *Strong Topics*

Weak Topics trigger rules of SR that help the hearer to keep track of well-established discourse-topics medially in topical spans. In this section we will look at discourse-topics which occur initially in topical spans and which are strongly identified (Strong Topics). Wambon has two expressive devices to express Strong Topics: the Strong Topic-construction and the Strong Topic markers (STM's) *eve* and *nomboneve*.

2.2.1. *The Strong Topic-construction*

Consider the following examples:

(32)   Nguve nga-hile keno-nde
         you   your-name what-Focus
         'What is your name?'

(33)   Evo kave nekhon-oye ndominuk
         that man his-pig   one
         'That man has one pig'

(32) can be paraphrased as: 'I am going to ask something about you, viz. what is your name?' and (33) as: 'I am going to say something about that man, viz. that he has one pig.' In this construction the speaker first establishes his (Strong) Topic and then goes on to make a statement or a question about that Topic. In Indonesian we find a similar construction, which is very frequent in that language, and also in Dutch. In Dutch the construction is very rare in the written,

formal language, but very frequent in colloquial spoken language.

Indonesian:

(34)   Perempuan itu anak-nya sakit
         woman   that child-her ill
         'That woman's child is ill'

Dutch:

(35)   Die man z'n vrouw is ziek
         that man his wife is ill
         'That man's wife is ill'

In Wambon, Indonesian and Dutch the Strong Topic is intonationally very firmly
integrated in the following expression.

     In Wambon the Strong Topic-construction contrasts with the Theme-Predication-
construction exemplified by (36):

(36)   Evo kave eve na nekheve jambolokup
         that man ThM PM he   ill
         'That man, he is ill'

         (ThM = Theme-marker)

The Theme in (36), *evo kave*, is separated from the following predication by
pause-intonation, by the conventional pause marker *na* and by the Theme-marker
eve. In the Strong Topic-construction these markers are absent; the Strong Topic
is weakly identified by a possessive prefix on the Subject. In Wambon the Strong
Topic-construction is restricted to stative clauses and has the following functional pattern:

(37)   Strong Topic x_i+ [poss pro x_i + Subj] + Predicate

The Predicate has often, but not obligatorily, the Focus-suffix *-nde* attached to
it. I call pattern (37) a Topic-construction because the pattern intrinsically
defines the first constituent as the (Strong) Topic.

2.2.2. The Strong Topic-markers eve and nomboneve

Strong Topichood can also be expressed by special markers (STM's). These markers
are *eve* and *nomboneve*, which sometimes occur together as in (23). Consider the
following example:

(38)   Takhimo-gambat nomboneve Tuhan okh   ha-lo   ip   ha-lo
         third-picture STM   Lord water make-SS land make-SS
         'On the third picture the Lord creates water and land'

(38) could be insightfully paraphrased as 'About the third picture: it shows how the Lord created water and land.'

If *eve* and *nomboneve* are followed by the pause-marker *na* and if the constituent marked by *eve* and *nomboneve* is intonationally separated from the following predication, then that constituent is a Theme. In this respect Wambon resembles Usan, another Papuan language (cf. Reesink 1983b: 228).

The Strong Topic-marker *eve* is also used as independent demonstrative pronoun:

(39)   Eve   ngulum-nde
         that teacher-Focus
         'That is a teacher'

In colloquial Dutch there is a similar frequent use of the resumptive pronouns *die* and *dat* after Strong Topics:

(40)   Jan   *die*   is gek
         John that is crazy
         'John, he's crazy'

Nomboneve cannot be used in the function of independent pronoun:

(41)   *Nomboneve ngulum-nde
         that   teacher-Focus
         'That is a teacher'

The clustering of *eve* and *nomboneve*, possible after Strong Topics, is not possible in the independent pronominal use:

(42)   *Nomboneve eve   ngulum-nde
         that   that teacher-Focus
         'That is a teacher'

Thus *nomboneve* clearly only functions as Strong Topic-marker, although its pronominal origin is clear, because *nombo* functions (only) as a pronoun:

(43)   Nombo ngulum-nde
         this   teacher-Focus
         'This is a teacher'

Nomboneve is composed of *nombo* 'this' plus *eve* 'that' (with a transitional nasal in between).

3. Focus in Wambon discourse

3.0. Introduction

Wambon has a focal suffix *-nde* which is not frequent in narrative discourse but very frequent in conversational dialogues. The fact that the development of saliency is generally more complex in dialogues could explain why *-nde* is so frequent in such discourse: the speaker thinks the hearer needs more guidance as to what information he should pick up as salient. On the other hand, in narrative discourse the speaker is more concerned to make clear how the topicality is developing, especially when there is more than one discourse-topic to trace throughout the narrative. This could explain why SR markings play a central role in narrative but a minor role in dialogues, where sentences are much shorter and often consist of one final clause only.

3.1. Neutralization and diversification

In discourse the speaker should make clear not only what he is talking about (the topicality dimension) but also which information is the most important given the pragmatic information of the hearer (the saliency dimension). To change the pragmatic information of the hearer is certainly one of the major goals of language-use.

In the topicality dimension there is a certain continuity (the speaker establishes his topic and maintains it for a certain time) which is completely lacking in the saliency dimension. Which information is salient and which not changes constantly, this saliency being completely dependent on the context, situation and general information at the time of the utterance. Even constituents which are sometimes regarded as inherently salient, such as Q-words, are qua saliency essentially dependent on the pragmatic factors just mentioned.

Take for example the exchange (44)-(47) which Hannay (1983: 211) gives to show that Q-words lose their saliency in certain contexts.

(44)   A : I hear you have been to London and New York recently?
(45)   A : Why did you go to London?
(46)   B : I went there for my sister's wedding
(47)   A : And New York?

In (47) the Q-word is left out because it is contextually given and non-salient, whereas in (45) the Q-word is salient. To guide the hearer as to how an express- ion fits into the development of saliency in the discourse the speaker can assign Focus function to the salient constituents in expressions. This Focus function then triggers expression rules which give the constituent with Focus a specific form or position. Often the informational make-up of the discourse is so trans- parent that the speaker does not need to assign Topic and Focus, i.e. only a minority of the discourse-topics get sentence-level expression as Topic and only a minority of the constituents which present salient information are treated as Focus constituents.

In Dik et al. (1981) six types of pragmatic conditions are mentioned which create six types of saliency. One of the contexts they discuss is that of the Q-word question and its answer. Consider the following Wambon exchange:

(48)   Jakhove kenonop-nde takhim-gende?
        they   what-Focus buy-pres3plfinal
        'WHAT do they buy?'

(49)   Ndu-nde   takhim-gende
        sago-Focus buy-pres3plfinal
        'They buy SAGO'

The constituent in (49) that presents the information that fills the blank in the pragmatic information of the speaker of (48) is of course the relatively most salient constituent in this context: that is why *ndu-nde* 'sago' in (49) is marked for Focus by *-nde*. Dik et al. (1981: 63) apply the label 'completive' to this type of pragmatic condition.

In Wambon the same suffix *-nde* appears in another context which Dik et al. (1981: 63) label 'replacing' contexts:

(50)   A : Mbitemop ndune ande-tbo
            Bitemop sago eat-past3sgfinal
            'Bitemop ate sago'

(51)   B : Woyo, nekheve ndu-nde   e-nogma-tbo
            No,   he   sago-Focus eat-Neg-past3sgfinal
            'No, he did not eat SAGO'

(52)   B : Nekheve ande-nde   ande-tbo
            he   bananas-Focus eat-past3sgfinal
            'He ate BANANAS'

In (51) B rejects a piece of information received from A and in (52) B corrects A's statement by replacing that wrong piece of information and substituting the correct information.

Thus by using the same expressive device (-nde) in Q-word questions, their answers, rejections and corrections, Wambon neutralizes the different pragmatic conditions underlying the different types of saliency. As we shall see in 3.2., the suffix -nde also marks salient constituents in parallel contexts (cf. Dik et al. 1981: 66 for a discussion of Parallel Focus).

Not all languages code saliency-constraints onto the form of expressions in such a strongly neutralizing fashion. An example of a language which allows a considerable degree of diversification by distinguishing several types of saliency caused by different pragmatic conditions is Aghem, a Grassfields Bantu language of Cameroon. Watters (1979) has described the complicated and elaborate Focus mechanism of this language in detail, and Dik et al. (1981: 48) give a useful summary of his findings.

According to Watters (1979: 177), Aghem distinguishes six types of Focus, each having a specific informational role. Five of these types have their own expressive devices. Thus different expressive devices are used in completive and replacing contexts: the salient constituents in completive contexts get a different treatment in terms of positioning from those in replacing contexts (cf. Watters 1979: 77). In completive contexts Watters (1979: 177) speaks of Assertive Focus: 'that information which the speaker believes, assumes or knows the hearer does not share with him or her.' In replacing contexts he speaks of Counter-assertive Focus: 'that information which the speaker substitutes for information which the hearer asserted in a previous utterance.'

The functionality of Focus assignment in Wambon conversational discourse manifests itself most clearly in the very strong negative reactions of speakers when one deliberately places the Focus suffix -nde on the wrong constituent, thereby creating a contextual misfit in terms of saliency-constraints:

(53)   A : Sanop kenonop-nde takhim-ge?
             Sanop what-Focus buy-pres3sgfinal
             'WHAT does Sanop buy?'

(54)   B : Sanop-nde   ndune takhim-ge
             Sanop-Focus sago buy-pres3sgfinal
             'SANOP buys sago'

The context of (53) constrains (54) informationally in such a way that only expressions with a specific distribution of saliency are acceptable. Now the form of the expression (54) reflects an informational make-up that clashes with the development of saliency in the preceding discourse. Although (54) gives the

information asked for in (53), native speakers reject (54) as an answer to (53).
The wrong Focus assignment in (54) creates an unacceptable lack of informational
cohesion in the conversational discourse.

3.2. *The relation of topicality to saliency*

In discourse the dimensions of topicality and saliency operate independently and
that is why the two dimensions can and do co-occur in one constituent; in certain contexts a discourse-topic becomes informationally important or salient.
For example, when weak discourse-topics become involved in contrasts the dimensions of topicality and saliency coincide. Consider the following Wambon exchange:

(55)   A : Nombone ndu-ngup ande-ngup?
             this   sago-and bananas-and
             'What about this sago and bananas?'

(56)   B : Wembane ndu-nde   takhima-tbo,   Karolule ande-nde
             Wemba   sago-Focus buy-past3sgfinal Karolule bananas-Focus

             takhima-tbo
             buy-past3sgfinal
             'Wemba bought SAGO, and Kalorus BANANAS'

In (56) *ndu-nde* and *ande-nde* are weak discourse-topics, introduced as the topics
of conversation in (55). At the same time they are involved in the parallel contrast of (56) (cf. Dik et al. 1981: 66 for this notion of parallel contrastive
saliency). *Wemba* and *Karolule* are also involved in the parallel contrast and they
are also salient constituents in (56). However, their saliency is not formally
expressed, because in Wambon only one constituent per predication can receive
Focus function. In the context of (55) the contrast between the sago and the
bananas is in the center of attention: they, and not the pair *Wemba/Karolulu*,
form the main contrast.

In contrastive saliency the given-new informational opposition is completely
irrelevant. For example the following English parallel contrast can be used in
various types of contexts:

(57)   JOHN bought a CAR and MARY a BIKE

(57) can be used as an answer to the following questions:

(58)   WHAT did John and Mary buy?
(59)   I know John and Mary bought a car and a bike but WHO bought WHAT?

As an answer to (58) CAR and BIKE in (57) are new, and as an answer to (59) they
are given information. Hannay (1983: 210) distinguishes Assertive Focus (saliency
caused by newness of information) from Emphatic Focus (saliency caused by other
factors such as contrast) and then specifies CAR and BIKE in (57) as an answer to
(58) as both Assertive Focus and Emphatic Focus. As we have seen, however, the
given-new opposition is irrelevant in these cases. Therefore the specification
Assertive Focus is superfluous.

Because of the strong association of Focus with new information (an important
class of Focus assignments having to do with saliency caused by newness) and of
Topic with given information (an important class of Topic assignments having to
do with topicality caused by prior mentioning (Weak Topics)), it is tempting to
interpret Topic and Focus in terms of the dichotomous given-new distinction, or
at least to define them in such a way that they can never coincide on one constituent. Hannay (1983) for example suggests redefining Focus in such a way that
it is restricted to new information; for cases of saliency caused by other factors such as emphasis and contrast he proposes the introduction of a third
predication-internal pragmatic function Emphasis.

As we have seen, however, the dimensions of saliency and topicality operate
independently in discourse and this means that Topic and Focus as reflections of
these discourse-dimensions on sentence-level in principle have a non-dichotomous
relation. If we define pragmatic functions (as proposed in 1.1.) in terms of both
informational role and expressive devices, we have a clear case of coincidence of
Topic and Focus whenever the expressive devices of both functions co-occur in one
constituent. If one interprets the use of anaphoric pronouns to maintain topics
medially in topical spans as a sentence-grammar-determined process to express
Weak Topics (and not as a discourse-level phenomenon), then there is a coincidence
of the expression of Topic and Focus in the following examples:

(60)   What about Rebecca?   (= Hannay 1983: 214, no. 34/35)
(61)   It was to HER that John gave his most precious painting

In (61) *HER* is a Weak Topic; established in (60), expressed as Weak Topic by the
use of pronominal identification. At the same time *HER* is a salient constituent
(emphatic saliency), its saliency being expressed by the use of a Focus-construc-
tion and by intonational prominence.

Consider also the following example from Indonesian:

(62)   Memang dari semua abdi dalem yang paling menarik   ada-lah   mereka
         really of   all   serf royal who most   attractive are-Focus they

         yang ber-tugas   melayani keluarga raja
         who to-have-as-task to-serve family   king
         'Really of all the royal serfs those who serve the royal family have
         the most attractive position'

(63)   MEREKA-LAH yang paling dekat dengan raja
         they-Focus who most   close to   king
         'THEY are the ones that are most close to the king'

In (62) *abdi dalem* has been established as topic. In (63) this topic becomes
salient, its saliency being expressed by the Focus-suffix *-lah*. The topicality
is expressed by the use of weak pronominal identification. Hannay (1983: 220)
proposes to give constituents like *mereka-lah* in (63), *HER* in (61) and *ndu-nde*
in (56) the functional specification Topic/Emphasis. For Wambon and Indonesian,
and probably also for English, this proposal would mean the grammar distinguishing two functions Emphasis and Focus, both expressed by the same devices (Wambon
uses *-nde* in *all* saliency contexts, and Indonesian uses *-lah* analogously),
whereas at the same time the informational roles associated with Emphasis and
Focus would have a striking feature in common, which neither shares with Topic,
viz. the informational property of saliency. Thus the introduction of the function Emphasis would mean a considerable complication of the grammars of Wambon
and Indonesian.

   Hannay (1983: 219) notes as a consequence of accepting the possibility of
Topic and Focus coinciding on one constituent 'that one would have to make explicit that only the specific combination of Topic and emphatic Focus was possible, which further necessitates the acknowledgement of two levels, or layers,
of Focus assignment.' I have argued above (cf. the examples (57)-(59)) that in
the examples Hannay adduces to support the two-level distinction of Assertive
Focus and Emphatic Focus the specification Assertive Focus is superfluous because
of the irrelevance of the given-new distinction in contrastive saliency. That
(Weak) Topics and Assertive Focus (newness-Focus) never coincide is simply a
consequence of the fact that information cannot be at the same time given and
new, and for the same reason there is no need to state specifically in the grammar the possibility of Topic and Emphatic Focus coinciding, because *any* type of
information (topical or not, given or new) can become salient in emphatic and
contrastive contexts. The given-new distinction is thus not essential to the
nature of Topic and Focus; that the dimensions of topicality and saliency do not
interact when the topical information is given and the salient information new

does not mean that it is inherent to the nature of topicality and saliency not
to interact.

Although the given-new opposition is clearly relevant to the description of
the informational make-up of discourse, it remains to be seen whether this dis-
course-distinction is systematically reflected in sentential structures and
syntactico-morphological processes. And even if we did find languages which express the given-new dichotomy on clause-level by breaking up clauses (by intonation, markers, etc.) into new and given parts, this would not affect the
notions of Topic and Focus; rather we would have to add a pragmatic notion
Given-New to the sentence-grammar. Only if Topic or Focus assignment were
restricted to either the New or Given domain of the clause, would the theory of
Topic and Focus be affected.[7]

4. Concluding remarks

The subject of this article has been the dimensions of topicality and saliency
in Wambon discourse, their interrelation and their reflection in Wambon sentence-
grammar.

Cohesion constraints connected with topicality have been formulated in terms
of the notion of topical span; topical spans reflect the cycle of establishing,
maintaining and re-establishing topics in discourse. Discourse-topics occurring
medially in topical spans which are weakly identified (for example by pronouns
or person/number-suffixation on verbs or switch-reference morphology) have been
labeled 'Weak Topics' and those which occur initially in topical spans and are
strongly identified (full NP's, proper names), 'Strong Topics'.

We have seen that Wambon grammar formally distinguishes Weak Topics and Strong
Topics. Weak Topics can be defined as constituents which present information
that has previously been established as topic and that is now maintained as such
(the informational role of Weak Topics can be paraphrased as: 'I am still speaking about the same entity I established a few utterances ago as my topic.'). In
terms of expressive devices, Weak Topics are constituents that are monitored by
SR-suffixes. Strong Topics are constituents which present information that the
speaker establishes or introduces as his topic ('this is the entity I want to
say something about'), and occur initially in topical spans; they are signalled
as Strong Topics by the Strong Topic-construction and the Strong Topic-markers.

SR suffixes, triggered by the assignment of Weak Topic and Strong Topic-
markers, and the Strong Topic-construction, triggered by the assignment of Strong
Topic, now guide the hearer as to how expressions fit into the development of

topicality in the preceding discourse. The distribution of SR suffixes is the result of the interaction of pragmatic and syntactic factors. The Functional Grammar model, which distinguishes the notion of Topic from that of Subject, can formulate this interaction in a straightforward way by giving constituents which are monitored by SR-suffixation the functional specification SubjectTopic (= Weak Topic); these constituents are then distinguished from constituents with the specification Subject or Topic which do not trigger SR-suffixation. Both notions, Subject and Topic, are essential to the formulation of the Wambon SR mechanism: in functionalist terms the contribution of Topic is the maintenance of discourse-topics and that of Subject the expression of the contextual perspective on sentence-level. Thus DS suffixes indicate that there will be a change of contextual perspective from one well-established discourse-topic to another in the following clause.

As far as the dimension of saliency is concerned, the Wambon Focus-suffix -nde guides the hearer as to how the expression fits into the development of saliency of the preceding discourse. The differences in pragmatic conditions causing the saliency are all neutralized by the Wambon Focus system: the suffix -nde marks Focus constituents in completive, replacing and parallel contexts. In this respect Wambon and Aghem form two typological extremes: Aghem distinguishes formally five types of Focus in five different pragmatic conditions.

The following general picture of pragmatic functions emerges from the present article. The development of the pragmatic information in the discourse preceding an utterance constrains the informational make-up of that utterance in terms of two dimensions: saliency and topicality. These dimensions operate independently in discourse. Topic and Focus trigger rules of sentence-grammar which reflect, in a largely neutralizing fashion, informational discourse-constraints on the form of linguistic expressions. Pragmatic functions thus have a mediating position between discourse and sentence-grammar: on the one hand their assignment depends completely on the discourse-factors of context, situation and general information, on the other hand they trigger the expression-rules of sentence-grammar.

In this respect the present position of pragmatic functions in the model of Functional Grammar is the right one. If the proposal of Nuyts (1983: 384) to remove the pragmatic functions to 'a deeper position in the grammar' were to mean positioning these functions outside sentence-grammar proper (and in the light of De Schutter and Nuyts 1983a, 392, 393 who speak of a pre-verbal pragmatics this seems to be the case), this point of contact between discourse and sentence-grammar would be destroyed.

As far as the relation between saliency and topicality is concerned, every now and then these dimensions coincide on one constituent, for example when a discourse-topic gets involved in contrast. This means that these dimensions have a non-dichotomous relation: utterances cannot simply be broken into salient and topical parts. It also means that Topic and Focus have in principle a non-dichotomous relation. However, if these functions are also defined in terms of the expressive devices connected with them, a clear case of coincidence of Topic and Focus will be found when a constituent exhibits the expression of both Topic and Focus. Of course when Topic is assigned to given information and Focus to new information, the two cannot possibly coincide, but since the given-new distinction is not essential to Topic and Focus, this is not a consequence of their being Topic and Focus.

Many problems have been left untouched in this article. Among these are the following: the interesting question how to formalize SR rules in the Functional Grammar formalism, the consequences of SR phenomena for the theory of processing sentences (cf. the fact that the speaker in producing verb forms in Wambon already has to decide on the selection of a SubjectTopic of the following clause), the formalization of Strong Topic rules, the problem of the pragmatic and syntactic relations between Strong Topic-constructions like (64) and constructions like (65):

Indonesian:

(64)   Perempuan itu anak-nya sakit
        woman   that child-her ill
        'That woman's child is ill'

(65)   Anak perempuan itu sakit
        child woman   that ill
        'The child of that woman is ill'

NOTES

[1]   Switch-reference is the commonly-used label in Papuan linguistics for the widespread phenomenon in Papuan languages whereby, in consecutive clauses, the verbs carry affixes that indicate that the Subject of the following clause is the same or different from the Subject of the preceding clause.

[2]   In the classification of Voorhoeve (1975), Wambon is as a member of the (non-Austronesian) Trans-New Guinea Phylum, more specifically a member of the Awyu-Dumut family. It has two main dialects, Digul-Wambon and Yonggom. There is a low degree of mutual intelligibility between speakers from the centers of these two dialects.

      Lexico-statistically there is 47% cognatic correspondence between Digul-Wambon and Yonggom. There are striking differences in the grammars of both dialects. Possibly Yonggom should be classified as member of the Dumut-sub-family and Digul-Wambon as member of the Awyu-subfamily (Voorhoeve 1975: 27, 28). In this article it is Digul-Wambon that is described. Drabbe (1959) sketches the grammar and phonology of Yonggom, which he terms Wambon.

[3]   See section 1.2. for the distinction between discourse-topic and sentence-topic.

[4]   Examples like (6) which show the influence of stylistic factors were brought to my attention by Simon Dik, who was kind enough to offer some comments on an earlier version of this article.

[5]   This speaker was Ahitup Kerenggere, a Wambon native speaker from Manggelum, who helped me to learn and describe his language. Having had six years of Indonesian primary school, he was sufficiently bilingual to assist in the task of recording and transcribing the travel narratives discussed in the present article.

[6]   The corpus consisted of about 300 clauses of travel narrative.

[7]   In my discussion of Hannay (1983), I have concentrated on the relation be-tween Focus and given-new, but the same line of reasoning can be applied to the relation between Topic and given-new:
a. Topics can be either given or new (cf. the Strong Topic examples (34), (35) and (38), all of which can be used to refer to newly introduced infor-mation about which the speaker wants to say something);
b. just as an important subclass of Focus assignments is related to new in-formation (Assertive Focus), so a frequent subclass of Topic assignments is related to given information (Weak Topics).

Chapter 12
Parentheticals and functional grammar
Yael Ziv
Department of English, Hebrew University of Jerusalem

1. Background and introduction

Despite occasional references to parenthetical entities, the notion 'parenthetical' has not, in fact, been explicitly defined in the linguistic literature. This
notion is implicitly regarded as representing either one general conceptual entity or, alternatively, a few such entities characterized by a common pragmatic
discourse function, namely, the expression of a comment on or a qualification of
that which is communicated in the co-occurring sentence. Formally, the parenthetical unit is conceived of as representing an entity which in some significant
sense is external to the sentence. This pretheoretical characterization will
serve as the point of departure for the current investigation.

This paper will concentrate on two major issues: (a) an initial delimitation
of the class(es) of parentheticals and (b) an attempt to account for at least
some parentheticals within the theory of Functional Grammar. It seems particularly
appropriate to try to incorporate a treatment of parentheticals within Functional
Grammar (FG) since FG is by its very essence a theory which regards language as a
means of communication and which takes into account language use. As a theory
which, in addition, strives for pragmatic and psychological adequacy, FG ought to
be able to account for parentheticals. Within the existing framework of FG, however, there is, to the best of my knowledge, no available treatment of parentheticals; consequently, I will proceed from a pretheoretical working definition
and examine its consequences for the theory.

2. General characterization

Formally, the class of parentheticals seems to include such varied entities as
adverbials (*however*), adverbial clauses (*as you know*), infinitival clauses (*to be
honest*), *-ing* clauses (*speaking as a layman*), nominal relative clause-like
clauses (*what's more*) and main clause-like clauses (*I believe*, *inter alia*) (cf.
Quirk et al. 1972).

Phonologically, it has been claimed that parentheticals constitute a separate
tone unit from the sentence in which they occur. However, this need not be the
case, as is evident from:

(1)   He will be late of course

which Reinhart (1975, 1983) has shown to be capable of phonological assimilation. In this case the [t] of *late* could be flapped. In fact, Reinhart distinguishes clearly between two types of parentheticals, speaker-oriented and subject-oriented, which she shows to differ crucially with respect to intonation. The speaker-oriented parenthetical does not involve a necessary intonational pause and hence need not constitute a separate tone unit, while the subject-oriented parenthetical requires an obligatory intonational break and hence constitutes a distinct tone unit.[1] The characterization in terms of tone-units is, thus, non-exhaustive.

Pragmatically, parentheticals are assumed to display a uniform nature expressing a comment by the speaker which, in some way, qualifies that which is expressed by the sentence to which they are appended. The parentheticals may strengthen or weaken the force, or specify the form, of the speaker's attitude towards the content of the expression with which they co-occur.[2] Examples are:

(2) a.   The Labour Party will lose power in the foreseeable future, I am told

    b.   The Labour Party, I'm sure, will gain power in the coming elections

    c. $\begin{Bmatrix} \text{To be brief} \\ \text{To cut a long story short} \end{Bmatrix}$, she decided to quit her job

    d.   To put it bluntly, I didn't like your book

Syntactically, this class is characterized by the lack of a specified position in the sentence. The parenthetical may occur in several locations in the sentence; some may occur in initial, medial or final position and they seem to be barred from such positions only where their occurrence would break an otherwise inseparable sequence.[3] Compare, in this context (3a-c) with (3d-e):

(3) a.   As far as I know, Bill sent her a lot of money

    b.   Bill sent her a lot of money, as far as I know

    c.   Bill, as far as I know, sent her a lot of money, but Jack ...

    d.   *Bill sent, as far as I know, her a lot of money

    e.   *John should write the address, I would say, down (Emonds 1976: 49, his 69)

An additional syntactic characteristic seems to be the 'extraneous' nature of parentheticals. Accordingly, parentheticals are regarded as constructions which show no dependence on other elements in the sentence and which do not partake in any sentential syntactic process.[4]

Thus, it is evident that parentheticals cannot be adequately characterized morphologically or phonologically. The syntactic and functional properties seem to be more promising in an attempt to delineate the class(es) of parentheticals. In what follows I will examine the consequences of adopting the syntactic and pragmatic characterizations presented in this section.

3. Syntactic and pragmatic properties - implications

3.1. Predictions of the syntactic characterization

3.1.1. Lack of dependency

Describing parentheticals as syntactically extraneous to the sentence with which they co-occur, namely, as showing no dependency relations of any type,[5] would predict that such entities as *however*, *so to speak*, *in fact*, *of course* are parenthetical, but the question would then remain whether such a characterization would account for cases like *I know*, *I believe*, *I think*, which might be claimed to normally govern 'complement objects' as parenthetical. First, there is the problem of their occurrence in non-initial position, either medially or finally. If no discontinuous dependencies are included in the determination of the various dependencies, then they would count as parenthetical, since their complements would not exhibit the required adjacency. If, however, discontinuous dependencies are to be taken into account when examining the relation of dependency, then we may invoke precedence as a requirement, such that adjacency may not be relevant for dependency but a relative precedence relation will be. Accordingly, sentences with medial or final *I believe* would not show the necessary dependence of the 'complement object' on the verb since in them the verb follows the complement in question and thus violates the precedence requirement on dependency. The phrase in question would thus count as a parenthetical. Sentence-initially *I believe* would show the necessary precedence relation and would consequently be judged to exhibit dependency, which in turn would imply that it is non-parenthetical.

Alternatively, a different conception of dependency may be adopted which would predict that the relevant phrases and clauses do not exemplify control on any of the elements with which they co-occur in the sentence. This approach would, correctly, predict the parenthetical status of the entities under discussion in medial or final position but, if continuity is irrelevant, it will also necessarily imply that they are parentheticals when occurring sentence-initially. The question to be asked in this context is whether this prediction is borne out, namely, whether sentence-initial *I think, I believe, I suppose*, are parenthetical.

The views on this point differ. Urmson (1952) speaks of parenthetical vs. non-parenthetical senses of assertive verbs. For him a verb in the main clause which introduces the sentence can have a parenthetical reading. So sentence-initial *I think* may be parenthetical. Quirk et al. (1972) consider such sentence-initial sequences as parentheticals only if they display an intonational pause to distinguish them from the main assertion of the sentence. Thus compare the following sentences from Quirk et al. (1972: 779):

(4) a.   You know I think you're wrong
    b.   You know | I think you're wrong (| designates a pause)

Only *you know* in (4b) functions parenthetically according to this view. For the purposes of this paper I will adopt a similar approach and refer to such syntactic main clauses as parentheticals only when there is an intonational pause between them and the rest of the sentence. The pause would, thus, count as a partition (in the sense of Taglicht 1984), making what follows it non-dependent on the verb in question.

3.1.2. No relevant sentential syntactic processes

The claim that parentheticals do not participate in sentential syntactic processes is supported by such data as discussed in McCawley (1982). In this article McCawley shows that VP deletion operates in VPs including a parenthetical as if the parenthetical were not there. Consider:

(5)   John talked, of course, about politics and Mary did too
        (= Mary talked about politics too ≠ Mary talked too ≠
        Mary talked, of course, about politics too) (McCawley's 5a)

Several counterexamples are evident which should be considered carefully to see whether they are just apparent or whether they necessitate a modification of this generalization. One such exception to the transparency of the parenthetical to sentential syntactic processes appears in the form of subject-oriented parentheticals. Reinhart (1975, 1983) discusses two types of parentheticals, subject-oriented and speaker-oriented, exemplified by (6) and (7) respectively (Reinhart's (24a) and (24b) in both versions):

(6)   He$_i$ would be late to her$_j$ party, John$_i$ told Mary$_j$ (subject-oriented);
and
(7)   John$_i$ will be late to Mary$_j$'s party, he$_i$ told her$_j$ (speaker-oriented)

The subject-oriented sentence containing the parenthetical would have obligatory backward anaphora and obligatory tense agreement, whereas the speaker-oriented sentence containing the parenthetical has regular forward anaphora and no tense agreement. (The tense is determined by the time of the utterance of the sentence with respect to the time of the reported events.) The obligatory cataphoric relationship as well as the tense agreement or back-shift tense rule in the case of the subject-oriented parentheticals could be regarded as an indication (a) that our characterization of parentheticals as not involved in any sentential syntactic process is wrong; or (b) that the subject-oriented sequence in question is not a parenthetical; or (c) that the syntactic processes in question, namely, anaphoric-cataphoric processes and back-shift tense assignment, are part of discourse rather than sentence grammar, and as such do not affect our generalizations about the class of parentheticals as not partaking in any sentential syntactic processes. There is a fourth possibility, namely, that the phenomena evident in the sentence with the parenthetical follow from general and independent principles and hence their occurrence need not bear on the question at hand. I will discuss the last two alternatives in some detail.

Support for the suggestion that anaphoric processes need not necessarily be just part of sentence grammar would come from any consideration of texts where anaphoric references occur across sentences, or, in fact, across the whole text. Cataphoric references are found in instances of detective stories or suspense-type texts, where the author wishes to be less than fully specific about the referent in question at the relevant point in the narration. A detective story may, thus, open the following way:

(8)   It was 3 a.m. when he$_i$ returned home. It was raining heavily ...
         John Smith$_i$ hung up his wet coat and ...

In fact, anaphoric relations are considered the prime instance of discourse grammar rules (cf. Williams 1977). If this approach is adopted with respect to the subject-oriented parentheticals at hand and if a non-ad-hoc account is given for the sequence of tenses, then the entities in question would not violate the restriction on involvement in sentential syntactic processes and could, thus, count as parentheticals.

In this context I would like to mention Reinhart's (1975, 1983) account of
the anaphoric-cataphoric relations in the case at hand. Reinhart suggests that
the backward anaphora in the subject-oriented parentheticals is a consequence of
independently motivated performance constraints. The relevant constraint is based
on the convention that in our culture a speaker refers to himself only by use of
a pronoun and not by use of the full name. Reinhart formulates this convention
and suggests that it applies in a wide range of cases, some covered by Kuno
(1972) in his observation that backward anaphora is obligatory where the second
NP is understood to be the assertor of the first, and others exemplified by instances like subject-oriented parentheticals.

The suggestion that there is a general pragmatic basis for the backward anaphora in the parentheticals at hand seems not to affect our position that ana-
phora-cataphora are discourse, rather than sentence, processes. This suggestion
simply provides the rationale for the syntactic phenomenon which seems to be
shared by longer sequences than the sentence and is realized in the case of the
subject-oriented parentheticals within the domain of a single sentence. Next I
shall discuss the tense-agreement phenomenon in the parentheticals in question.

A consideration of the back-shift of tense indicates that such a syntactic
process is required across large segments of texts and is not restricted to
intra-sentential domains. The natural environment in which this is the case is
the free indirect discourse context (cf. Banfield 1973), where there is no explicit reporting verb but the reported activities all have to follow the same
sequence of tenses and they may constitute rather large segments of the text. In
this case, then, as in the case of the backward anaphora, the syntactic processes
in question seem to apply within the realm of the discourse rather than within
the sentence and hence the parenthetical in question can, in fact, be said not to
partake in any sentential syntactic process.

Another potential problem with the characterization of parentheticals as un-
affected by sentential syntactic processes is the occurrence of negative or
interrogative parentheticals as in:

(9)   It is not very important, I don't think
(10)   Is he coming, do you know?

and negative interrogative parentheticals as in:

(11)   Isn't that a bit of an imposition, don't you think?
        (cf. Mittwoch 1979: 409)

The occurrence of such parentheticals is severely restricted. The negative declarative parenthetical, as in (9), can only occur when the sentence to which
it is appended is negative. Hence, the ill-formedness of (12):

(12)   *It is very important, I don't think[6]

However, such negative sentences as in (9) do not require that the parenthetical
be negative, as is evident from the well-formedness of (13):

(13)   It is not very important, I think

The occurrence of the negative parenthetical in (9) could count as a problem in
this context under the assumption that 'agreement in negation' is an optional
sentential syntactic process. If, however, this distribution of negative parentheticals could be attributed to independently motivated pragmatic principles
not restricted in their application to a sentential domain, then it need not
count as violating the restriction on parentheticals. In fact, I would like to
make just this point.

My suggestion is that whichever explanation is provided for the negative
parentheticals the same explanation would be required independently in an account
of the non-occurrence of such non-parenthetical negative verbs in a distinct
sentence. Consider (9a):

(9)   a. It is not very important. I don't think so

Sequence (9a) shows the same semantic transparency with respect to negation as
does (9); cf. also the ill-formed sequence in (12a):

(12) a.*It is very important. I don't think so[7]

which mirrors the ill-formedness in (12). Thus the semantic (syntactic?) and
pragmatic properties associated with the parentheticals in (9) and (12) seem not
to be merely sentential properties but rather discourse properties. Hence, the
negative parentheticals would seem to exhibit no violation of the constraint on
parentheticals.

Sentences (10) and (11) display interrogative parentheticals. Interrogative
parentheticals seem to be restricted to interrogative sentences. Hence the ill-
formedness of:

(14)   *John is going, do you think?

Mittwoch (1979) points out that interrogative parentheticals may occur with
declarative sentences only when the latter function as questions and display the
characteristic rising intonation as in:

(15)   John is coming do you think?

In her interesting study on this topic, Mittwoch (1979) suggests that the interrogative parenthetical forms a distinct sentence from the interrogative with
which it co-occurs and that discourse rules produce strings where the interrogative parenthetical functions as part of the utterance of which the non-
parenthetical is the other part. According to Mittwoch, any process connected
with the interrogative is, thus, inter-sentential. If we adopt Mittwoch's position we would have no problem with our characterization of parentheticals as not
involving any sentential syntactic process. The interrogative is pragmatically
conditioned, asking for confirmation or correcting the preparatory rules for the
previous illocutionary act and hence is restricted in its context to questions.
Thus, the pragmatics and the communicative function of the sentence determine
the following string as an interrogative.

Negative interrogatives, as in (11), are not restricted to co-occurring with
interrogatives. Their function is not so much that of a question as that of a
confirmation (cf. Mittwoch 1979) and they do not seem to involve any syntactic
process. We may thus conclude that so far we can maintain the generalization
that parentheticals are not involved in any sentential syntactic process. Next I
shall consider the communicative functions of parentheticals.

3.2. Communicative properties

Parentheticals are conceived of as expressions of comments by the speaker on
that which is expressed by the sentences with which they co-occur. The parenthetical may reinforce or modify the force of that which was uttered in the sentence to which it is appended or it may specify the form of the communication,
or express the speaker's attitude towards its content (cf. 2a-d). Mittwoch (1979)
cites interesting examples of interrogative parentheticals the function of which
is to correct the speech act performed in the sentence with which they co-occur.
In (16):

(16)   Where is he going do you know (Mittwoch's A_2)

the parenthetical 'retroactively soften[s] the act performed in asking the question', by suggesting that perhaps the speaker shouldn't have assumed that the
hearer knew the answer. Likewise in:

(17)   Is he going do you think?   (Mittwoch's B_1)

the parenthetical signals that the hearer 'is not expected to have definite knowledge of the answer but only an opinion'.

Mittwoch's characterization of such parentheticals as correcting the speech
act of the sentences with which they co-occur suggests that what look like different types of function - the speaker's comment on a statement and an invitation
to the hearer to say something with respect to it - may be two manifestations of
the same basic 'modification' function. What may be modified is, then, the force
of the utterance or the preparatory rules for this utterance.[8]

Next I will examine the predictions that the functional and formal characteristics make with respect to a variety of grammatical entities.

3.3. Potential parentheticals - speculations

In this section I will briefly sketch some observations on the potential parenthetical nature of grammatical entities such as tag questions, interjections,
vocatives and non-restrictive relative clauses.

3.3.1. Tag questions

Tag questions seem to invite the addressee to confirm (or disconfirm) that which
the speaker has communicated. This appeal for the hearer's confirmation indicates
that the speaker is not fully certain of the facts. Functionally, then, the tag
exhibits similarity to parentheticals, especially the interrogative parentheticals. Characterizing tag questions as parentheticals would involve showing that
they are external to the sentence and are not involved in any sentential process.
Tags are distinct from other parentheticals in that they are restricted to
sentence-final position. The syntactic phenomena evident in the tag include a
pronoun which is co-referential with the subject of the clause to which it acts
as a tag as in:

(18) $John_i$ is coming tonight, isn't he_i?

Anaphoric processes, however, were shown to constitute part of discourse rather than merely sentence grammar. Negativity is another such syntactic factor to be taken into account. The tag has to occur with the opposite value of negativity from the clause to which it acts as a tag (cf. (18)). The function of the negative or positive interrogative is identical: inviting the hearer's confirmation. This is achieved by simply suggesting: 'isn't it the case' via the interrogative sentence with the opposite value of negativity. The negative value of the tag is, thus, pragmatically conditioned by presenting the opposite option. This is clearly a pragmatic factor not restricted to sentence grammar and tags may, consequently, count as parentheticals.

3.3.2. Interjections

Interjections like *Oh, Ah, Oho, Wow,* are clearly external to the sentence. They constitute emotive devices expressing surprise *(Oh)*, satisfaction or recognition *(Ah)* and great surprise *(Wow)*, *inter alia*. They may occur without an accompanying sentence and when they co-occur with a sentence they seem to be restricted to initial position. Functionally, the interjection does not comment on the clause but rather the clause seems to function as the rationale for the interjection. Thus (19a) is functionally (19b):

(19) a. Ah, you are a vegetarian

    b. Ah, I'm surprised. Why? Answer: You are a vegetarian

Such functional characterization would make the interjection parenthetical-like. However, interjections are clearly a non-productive and severely restricted class, unlike the other parentheticals.

It is worth noting in this context that some interjections were shown in James (1972) to be sensitive to Island constraints (cf. Ross 1967). This could constitute an argument for their inclusion in sentence grammar and their non-inclusion as parentheticals. However, on the one hand, Ross' constraints have been shown to affect sentence fragments and question-answer sequences (Morgan 1973), and on the other hand, Island constraints have been shown (Erteschik-Shir and Lappin 1979) to be expressible and explainable in discourse-functional terms like Dominance, so that sensitivity to Ross' Island constraints need not serve as criterial in the case at hand.

3.3.3. *Vocatives*

Like parentheticals, vocatives are external to the sentence and can occupy
several positions in it. Vocatives are severely restricted to proper names and
epithets. They function in expressing the speaker's attempt to capture the
hearer's attention or to direct it to that which is uttered. This function has
to do with the pragmatics of the speech situation more than with the content or
form of the utterance. For these reasons they are marginal parentheticals, at
best.

3.3.4. *Non-restrictive relative clauses*

Non-restrictive relative clauses may display the functional characteristics
associated with parentheticals in some instances:

(20)   John, who I suspect is a drug addict, is going to be the chairman

(21)   He married her, which was a stupid thing to do

The non-restrictive relative clause is a syntactic construction offering the
option of introducing information which constitutes a separate speech act about
the whole sentence (21) or parts of it (20). Syntactically, it is more of an
entity in the sentence than any of the parentheticals examined so far. Its position in the sentence is relatively fixed, immediately following its antecedent.[9]
The occurrence of the relative pronouns is the most disturbing syntactic factor
which would raise problems for a parenthetical hypothesis. If, however, we adopt
a different analysis of relative clauses (cf. Morgan 1972) then the relative
pronoun may not constitute such an insurmountable obstacle. Emonds (1979) suggests that non-restrictive relative clauses do not manifest any syntactic properties as a class and that whatever restrictions they have to obey follow from more
general principles. If this argument is carried through, it may be the case that
non-restrictives would count as parentheticals after all.

4. *Semantic and pragmatic restrictions*

We have so far maintained that parentheticals are basically a functionally defined class lacking obvious positive grammatical characteristics other than their
non-involvement in sentential syntactic processes and the relatively free position in the sentence. In addition, parentheticals are sometimes claimed to be restricted with respect to their concatenation with other parentheticals. I would like
to suggest that such restrictions need not be stated syntactically but rather

semantically and/or pragmatically. Thus, ill-formed sentences like:

(22) a.*John, to be sure, Bill thinks, is not the best man for the job
   b.*Bill, I believe, it seems, is a drug addict
   c.*The vice president will have to resign after all, as I understand it,
      they tell me
   d.*Jerry will be our next chairman, I heard, so they say

would be ruled out not on syntactic but rather on semantic or pragmatic grounds
and the prediction would be that in cases where there was no semantic or pragmatic clash between the two consecutive parentheticals the sentence would be
well-formed.[10]

   First let us examine the sentences in (22). In (22a) we have both *to be sure*,
an indication of the speaker's certainty about the truth of the assertion made
in the main clause, and *Bill thinks*, which is a way of absolving responsibility
for the truth or certainty of what is being communicated. Thus we find a pragmatic clash which no arbitrary syntactic account will explain. Sentence (22b) is
ill-formed in the concatenated reading, where both parentheticals refer to the
whole sentence, because the parentheticals seem to exhibit a semantic and pragmatic clash between a personal point of view (*I believe*) and a neutral expression
of observation. (22c) is ill-formed in the intended reading due to a semantic-
pragmatic clash of the type found in (22b) between the personal conclusion as the
source of information and an attribution of the content of the communication to
an unnamed source and (22d) seems to be odd, if not ill-formed, due to a semantic
redundancy evident in the double expression of the unknown, impersonal source of
information.[11]

   Next we will examine the prediction that we made, namely, that a sentence with
concatenated parentheticals is well-formed if no semantic/pragmatic conflict results from this concatenation. The prediction seems to be borne out, as is evident
from the well-formedness of the sentences in (23):

(23) a. John, in fact, I must admit, has never been my favorite candidate
   b. John, of course, you must realize, wouldn't write such a letter
   c. To be honest, as I understand it, the committee is not really
      interested in this issue
   d. Senator Baker: '... You gained the impression, I believe you said,
      to paraphrase your testimony, that the President knew that there
      was an ongoing effort ...' (Watergate Hearings IV, 1481)
(This last example may also be construed as an instance of embedded parentheticals

The parentheticals in (23) do not exhibit the semantic/pragmatic clashes that were evident in (22). It thus seems that there need not be any formal restriction on the occurrence of concatenated parentheticals. There are, however, other restrictions worth mentioning briefly in the present context.

First, it is evident that there are semantic and pragmatic restrictions on the occurrence of parentheticals, depending on the context. Consider (24a-d), where ill-formedness, inappropriateness and oddity are apparent.

(24) a. *As you say, I loved his book
     b. *I loved his book, they tell me
     c. *Roughly speaking, it is exactly 3 a.m.
     d.??To be absolutely honest, I loved his book

Sentences (24a-b) are hard to contextualize due to the apparently inexcusable pragmatic clash between an expression of an idea by an individual and attribution of this same idea simultaneously to somebody else. In sentence (24c), there is an impossible semantic contradiction between a promise of rough presentation of the facts and an exact statement of these facts in practice.

Sentence (24d) seems to be questionable on pragmatic grounds, under our regular assumptions about the world. The parenthetical 'to be absolutely honest' is used in cases where the state-of-affairs expressed by the sentence to which it is appended is embarrassing or unpleasant, and disclosing it could, potentially, hurt the listener or the person to whom the property in question is being attributed or anyone connected with these people. In (24d) the state-of-affairs in question is pleasant and, under normal assumptions, could not embarrass anyone, hence the oddity of prefacing it with 'to be absolutely honest'. We may, however, dream up a set of circumstances where (24d) would be fully acceptable. One such potential context could be the following: the author is known for his extreme conservative positions on a variety of social and political issues and the conversation takes place between two liberals.

It would appear that such pragmatic requirements need not be stated in an ad-hoc fashion, but that they would rather follow from the general requirements on relevance and coherence between the parenthetical and the sentence with which it co-occurs as part of these general requirements on discourse sequences (cf. Grice 1975; Sperber and Wilson 1982).[12]

5. The theoretical status of parentheticals

5.1. Generative-Transformational Grammar

Several attempts to account for parentheticals have been made within the theory of Generative Transformational Grammar. Ross (1973) offered a Slifting approach, whereby a parenthetical like *I think* would originate from a main clause and via lifting of the subordinate clause and further nichings would land in all possible positions in the sentence. Problems with this approach abound, as is shown, for example, in Reinhart (1975, 1983). Jackendoff (1982) and Bresnan (1968) suggest a sentential adverb source for parentheticals. Lakoff (1974) suggests an amalgamation derivation which is not worked out in detail, whereby two separate sentences one of which is the parenthetical, are amalgamated into one. Mittwoch (1979), too claims that the underlying structure of sentences containing parentheticals consists of two sentences. For her they remain two distinct sentences in the syntactic surface structure as well but they form one discourse unit which she refers to as 'utterance'.

In all of the preceding treatments the underlying assumption seems to be that all parentheticals are derived the same way. The only explicit mention of the possibility that they may have more than one source occurs in Reinhart (1975, 1983), where two sources are offered, one adverbial for the speaker-oriented parentheticals and the other consisting of some version of Banfield's (1973) adoption of Partee's (1973) analysis of direct quotes where E(xpression) is the initial non-recursive symbol and the sentence with the parenthetical constitutes one E made up of two E's, the parenthetical and the non-parenthetical.

In the remainder of this paper I will investigate the consequences of incorporating parentheticals into the theoretical framework of Functional Grammar.

5.2. Functional Grammar

As a theory of language which attempts to characterize language as a means of communication and to account for its formal system within the framework of language use, Functional Grammar ought to incorporate a coherent treatment of parentheticals. In this section I will raise some suggestions to be taken into account in future research on parentheticals within FG.

The major question in the present context is whether, having realized that parentheticals exhibit a variety of formal properties not necessarily shared by all the other members of the class (e.g. intonational pauses, backward vs. forward anaphora, sequence of tenses, position in the sentence, morphological characteristics), we still want to capture them under one unified account. If commu-

nicative considerations are of primary importance within the theory of FG then
the common discourse-functional properties would seem to advocate a unified
account. The formal differences between the various parentheticals might then
either follow from independently motivated principles, in the best case, or, in
the worst of cases, be stated arbitrarily. Such an account, despite its proble-
maticity, seems to be more in line with FG than an approach whereby the discourse-
functional similarities between the various parentheticals would be accounted for
by some rules of discourse or Expression interpretation of the type advocated in
Mittwoch (1979) and to an extent in Verhagen (1979), which are, so far, missing
from the theory of FG.

The most appropriate approach to parentheticals within the current framework
of FG seems to involve regarding them as instances of the pragmatic function
Tail. As a pragmatic function, Tail seems most suitable as the host of parentheticals, especially if they are to be positively defined in terms of their
communicative discourse functions (cf. 3.2.). However, the current conception of
Tail would have to be altered for this notion to be able to accommodate parentheticals.

In Dik (1978) the Tail function is characterized the following way: it presents, as an 'afterthought' to the predication 'information meant to clarify or
modify (some constituent contained in) it' and 'is assigned to material which is
produced outside of the predication proper' (Dik 1978: 153). Its typical position,
it is claimed, is after the predication, in the right-dislocation position P3 and
it is set off from the predication by an intonational break. The only examples of
constituents with the Tail function are right dislocations as in:

(25)   He's a nice chap, your brother (Dik's 82)

belated satellites as in:

(26)   John gave that book to a girl, in the library (Dik's 85)

where the locative expression follows a distinct intonational pause, and corrections as in:

(27)   John won't even be invited, eh ... Bill I mean (Dik's 87)

all of which are presented as instances of afterthoughts. The nature of these
instances of afterthoughts is explained on behavioral grounds. Accordingly, the

speaker is claimed to have neglected to mention or to specify some part of the information and then, having realized his performance error, he supplies the missing pieces of information.

Tail constituents are claimed to be 'partially independent of the predication'. According to Dik the dependence lies in further specifying or modifying the preceding predication and the partial independence in the fact that 'it does not necessarily contain a further "spelling out" of material already contained in the Predication' (1978: 155). In addition, it is claimed that Tails 'which further specify constituents of the predication must have the corresponding marking' (1978: 155). Hence, they are semantically and syntactically equivalent in function to the term marked by the pronoun in the preceding predication.

I will now suggest some changes in the conception of Tails just presented, in order to incorporate 'parentheticals' within the theory of FG.

(a)   The concept of 'afterthought' seems to be built into the definition of the pragmatic function Tail. However, it is not clear to me that all instances of parentheticals are afterthoughts. In fact, it seems safe to assert that many sentence-medial parentheticals are not, and to the extent that we have sentence-initial parentheticals they can clearly never count as afterthoughts. We may, thus, require that 'afterthought' be removed from the definition of Tail as a necessary requirement for Tail to be able to characterize non-afterthought parentheticals. It could, of course, still be the case that many instances of Tail including various parentheticals would function like afterthoughts, but if this concept is not built into the notion 'Tail' necessarily, we could account for both afterthought and non-afterthought parentheticals in the same manner.[13]

(b)   The discourse-functional characterization of Tail seems to require modification. The Tail is claimed to clarify or modify the predication or parts of it. As pointed out in the course of this paper, Mittwoch (1979) has shown that the parenthetical may function in correcting (the preparatory rules for) the speech act performed in the preceding sentence. If parentheticals are to be accounted for by the pragmatic function Tail, then we would need to incorporate this change in the discourse-functional characterization of the Tail.

(c)   Although Tails are claimed to occur typically following the predication, the possibility of their occurrence in medial position is raised by Dik (1978: 153). This theoretical possibility should be materialized if parentheticals are to be accounted for by Tail. If, in addition, we have sentence-initial parentheticals we might need to incorporate this position too into Tail. Here we would have to require that Theme always precede Tail, to account for the distinction between the well-formed (28) where Theme precedes Tail, and the ill-formed (29), where this order is violated:

(28)   As for John, as far as I know, he is leaving town tomorrow
(29)   *As far as I know, as for John, he is leaving town tomorrow

(d)   The 'comma intonation' claimed to characterize Tails would have to be presented as an option rather than an absolute requirement, if we are to incorporate those parentheticals into this framework which do not exhibit the relevant intonational break.

(e)   The worst problem, so far, with respect to the existing characterization of Tail seems to originate from instances where the Tail is marked in a manner corresponding to the relevant constituent in the predication. This morphological, semantic and syntactic dependence of the Tail on the preceding predication is clearly foreign to the strict requirement on parentheticals that they not be involved in any sentential syntactic process. Case marking is one of the prime examples of such a sentential process.

At this point we may either abandon the attempt to characterize parentheticals as instances of Tail, a very unsound move on pragmatic and discourse-functional grounds, or attempt to claim that right dislocations of the type which display case marking are not, in fact, instances of Tail, but, rather, belong in the realm of actual performance and thus constitute part of the predication on psychological grounds. As such they seem to present the revised form in question in place of the entity in the predication by assigning the same case to it. It is as if the speaker erases the under-specified or erroneous entity in the original predication and supplies a new one *in its place in the predication* (cf. fn. 13 in this context).

Alternatively, we could conceive of it as an instance of ellipsis whereby all the preceding elements have been deleted under identity with the previous sentence. If this line of argument is adopted, the case assignment would indeed be an instance of a syntactic operation and the entity so marked would not violate any constraint on the operation of syntactic processes.

Another way out of this dilemma may be to relax the requirement that parentheticals be uninvolved in any sentential syntactic process, which is clearly hard to maintain in view of the evidence examined so far.

The second option seems to me to be worth pursuing.

It is hoped that such modifications to the notion *Tail* will pave the way for future research towards incorporating parentheticals into the framework of Functional Grammar.

NOTES

*   I wish to thank the participants in the Conference on Functional Grammar for their comments and suggestions. I am especially grateful to Judith Junger for help in preparing the draft and to Erhard Voeltz for his encouragement.

1   I will come back to Reinhart's distinction later in this paper.

2   This functional characterization may require some modifications which will be considered in the course of this paper.

3   There are differences in this respect between the various members of the class of parentheticals. Some parentheticals are more restricted with respect to position than others.

4   Taglicht (1984) expresses this 'extraneous' nature of the parentheticals by referring to them as neither thematic nor rhematic, where these terms are structurally rather than functionally defined. In Taglicht's framework the thematic element is the initial segment of the sentence, the rhematic element constitutes the final element and the only other element in the sentence is the mobile segment which he calls 'operator'. The operator is usually realized by the finite auxiliaries and the non-auxiliary uses of finite forms of *be*. Parentheticals are, therefore, not considered elements in the sequential (= textual) organization of the sentence.

5   It is interesting to note in this context that it follows from the 'extraneous' property that omission of the parenthetical results in syntactic well-formedness. This prediction is borne out.

6   The ill-formedness of (12) appears to constitute a problem for such analyses of parentheticals as Ross' (1973) Slifting (cf. 5.1.), whereby sentences like: (i) *I don't think it is very important*, would serve as its underlying structure. An approach along these lines with ad-hoc conventions designed to maintain the negative element in the complement sentence following negative raising is presented by Lawler (1974).

7   The reason for the ill-formedness of (12a) seems to be pragmatic; specifically, you cannot negate that which you have just positively asserted.

8   Such a characterization would seem to leave out adverbials like *of course, in fact* and *however*. A closer look, however, would show that *of course* may be used to indicate that the speaker (S) wants the hearer (H) to realize that S does not think that he is saying anything new or unexpected under the circumstances - a clearly parenthetical function. Likewise, *in fact* and *however* seem to indicate something like: despite what may be expected. The speaker, thus, signals that he is describing the real state-of-affairs.
      There are suggestions for a variety of additional discourse functions for parentheticals, such as corrections, filling in gaps, capturing the hearer's attention and possibly also keeping the communication going. I will not discuss these suggestions here.

9   Extraposition is very restricted, if possible at all, with such appositive, non-restrictive relative clauses. Cf. Ziv (1973, 1976).

10 Note that the sentences in (22a-d) are judged as instances of concatenation only. There is no denial that a sequence of parentheticals may occur where one refers to the other as in:

(i) John, the doctors say, so I hear, will recover from his heart
     attack after all
or
(ii) Bill, Jim_i said, if I understood him_i correctly, had a serious
     drinking problem

[11] A nice example of concatenation of parentheticals comes from the Israeli TV
program 'Carousella' (= carrousel) where the character, Hanan-Anan (= Hanan
the Cloud) a stupid and naive fellow, tentatively ventures his opinion on
various matters by attaching the sequence of parentheticals ... *I think, if
I'm not mistaken* ... His sentences always sound funny because of the conflict
between a report of the content of his thought, his opinion, and a simulta-
neous modification, 'if I'm not mistaken'. It could also sound funny in the
reading where the second parenthetical modifies the first. However, the intonation - pause between the two parentheticals - would seem to argue for the
concatenation reading.

[12] An additional type of pragmatic restriction which might be required involves
processing. Accordingly, a certain sequence of consecutive parentheticals in
one sentence would result in ill-formedness, even in those cases where the
parentheticals are compatible, simply due to the break of the flow of the
main sentence. I will not pursue the issue here.

[13] The right dislocation examples in the original treatment of 'Tail', as well
as its characterization in terms of concrete behavioral characteristics (Dik
1978: 154) seem to raise the theoretical question as to the distinction between competence and performance in the case at hand. What are we dealing
with when we are dealing with 'afterthoughts'? If these are purely matters
of performance, why not account for a variety of possible hesitation phenomena, memory limitations and the like? It is obvious that we are dealing with
the competence of speakers to fill in information, for whatever reason, in
permissible locations in the sentence in accordance with a variety of
semantic, syntactic and pragmatic generalizations. The notion 'Tail' might,
consequently, require some further reformulation to make this theoretical
point explicit.

References

ABRAHAM, W. & W. SCHERPENISSE
1983   'Zur Brauchbarkeit von Wortstellungstypologien mit Universalanspruch'.
        Sprachwissenschaft 8, 291-355.

ALLERTON, J.D.
1980   'Grammatical Subject as a psycholinguistic category'. *TPS*, 40-61.

AUWERA, J. van der
1981   *What do we talk about when we talk?* Amsterdam: John Benjamins.

BACQUET, P.
1962   *La structure de la phrase verbale à l'époque Alfrédienne*. Publications
        de la faculté des lettres de l'Université de Strasbourg, fasc. 145
        (en dépot Belles Lettres, Paris).

BANFIELD, A.
1973   'Grammar of quotation, free indirect style and implications for a theory
        of narrative'. *Foundations of Language* 9, 1-39.

BATES, E. & B. MacWhinney
1982   'Functionalist Approaches to Grammar'. In: L. Gleitman & E. Wanner (eds.)
        Language Acquisition: The State of the Art. Cambridge: CUP.

BEAN, M.C.
1983   *The development of word order patterns in English*. London: Croom Helm.

BENTIVOGLIO, P.
1983   'Topic continuity and discontinuity in discourse: a study of spoken
        Latin-American Spanish'. In: Givón ed. (1983), 255-312.

BEVER, T.G.
1970   'The cognitive basis for linguistic structures'. In: J.R. Hayes (ed.)
        Cognition and the development of language, 279-362. New York: Wiley.

1971   'The integrated study of language behaviour'. In: J. Morton (ed.)
        Biological and Social Factors in Psycholinguistics, 158-209. London:
        Logos Press.

1975   'Psychologically Real Grammar emerges because of its role in language
        acquisition'. In: Dato ed. (1975), 63-75.

BOLINGER, D.
1977   'Another glance at main clause phenomena'. *Language* 53, 511-519.

BOLKESTEIN, A.M.
1981   'Embedded predications, displacement and pseudo-argument formation in
        Latin'. In: Bolkestein et al. (1981), 63-112.

1983   'The role of discourse in syntax: Evidence from the Latin Nominativus
        cum Infinitivo'. In: K. Ehlich & H. van Riemsdijk (eds.) *Connectedness
        in Sentence, Discourse and Text*, 111-140. TSLL-4, Dept. of Language and
        Literature, Tilburg University.

1984   'Discourse and case-marking; three-place predicates in Latin'. In: Touratier ed. (1984).

BOLKESTEIN, A.M., H.A. COMBÉ, S.C. DIK, C. de GROOT, J. GVOZDANOVIĆ, A. RIJKSBARON & C. VET
1981   *Predication and Expression in FG*. London & New York: Academic Press.

BOLKESTEIN, A.M., C. de GROOT & J.L. MACKENZIE eds.
1985   *Predicates and Terms in Functional Grammar*. Dordrecht: Foris.

BOSSUYT, A.
1982   *Aspekten van de geschiedenis van de negatieve zin in het Nederlands*. VUB-dissertation, Brussels.

1983   'Historical Functional Grammar: an outline of an integrated theory of change'. In: Dik ed. (1983), 301-325.

in preparation
        Principles of Historical Functional Grammar.

BRESNAN, J.W.
1968   Remarks on Adsententials. Unpublished paper, MIT.

BRÖMSER, B.
1984   Completive verb formation and incorporation in English: two aspects of wordformation in Functional Grammar. Paper read at the first Colloquium on Functional Grammar, Amsterdam, June 1984.

BROWN, C.
1983   'Topic continuity in written English narrative'. In: Givón ed. (1983), 313-341.

BROWN, D.R.
1984   Terms and term operators. Paper, SIL Nairobi.

1985   'Term operators'. In: Bolkestein, de Groot & Mackenzie eds. (1985).

BROWN, G. & G. YULE
1983   *Discourse analysis*. Cambridge: CUP.

BRUNER, J.
1974   'From communication to language'. *Cognition* 3, 255-287.

BUBENIK, V.
1983   'Impersonal constructions in FG'. In: Dik ed. (1983), 183-204.

BUUREN, L. van
1980   'On Dutch Intonation'. In: S. Daalder & M. Gerritsen (eds.), *Linguistics in the Netherlands*, 1-9. Amsterdam/Oxford/New York: North-Holland.

1981   'On English vs. Dutch Intonation'. In: Daalder & Gerritsen eds. (1981), 1-11.

CAIRNS, H.S. & C.E. CAIRNS
1976   *Psycholinguistics*. New York: Holt.

CALBOLI, G.
1962   *Studi grammaticali*. Studi pubblicati dall'Istituto di Filologia Classica XI. Bologna: Nicola Zanichelli.

CALLAWAY, M.
1889   *The absolute participle in Anglo-Saxon*. Baltimore: John Hopkins Diss.

1901   'The appositive participle in Anglo-Saxon'. *Publications of the Modern Language Association of America* 16, 141-360.

1918   *Studies in the Syntax of the Lidnisfarne Gospels*. Baltimore: John Hopkins.

CHAFE, W.L.
1976   'Givenness, contrastiveness, definiteness, subjects, topics and point of
        view'. In: Li ed. (1976), 25-55.

CHOMSKY, N.
1959   'Review of verbal behaviour by B.F. Skinner'. *Language* 35, 26-58.

1964   'The logical basis of linguistic theory'. *Proc. of the 9th Int. Congress
        of Ling.*, 914-1008.

1965   *Aspects of the theory of syntax.* Cambridge: MIT Press.

1972   *Language and Mind.* New York: Harcourt.

1975a   *Reflections on Language.* London: Temple Smith [1976].

1975b   *The Logical Structure of Linguistic Theory.* New York: Plenum Press.

1980   *Rules & Representations.* New York: Columbia UP.

1981   *Lectures on government and binding.* Dordrecht: Foris.

CLARK, H.H. & E.V. CLARK
1977   *Psychology & Language.* New York: Harcourt.

CLARK, H.H. & S.E. HAVILAND
1977   'Comprehension and the Given New contract'. In: R.O. Freedle (ed.)
        Discourse production and comprehension, 1-40. Norwood, N.J.: Ablex
        Publishing.

COMRIE, B.
1983   'Switch-reference in Huichol: a typological study'. In: Haiman & Munro
        eds. (1983), 17-37.

COOREMAN, A.
1983   'Topic continuity and the voicing system of an ergative language:
        Chamorro'. In: Givón ed. (1983), 425-489.

in preparation
        Functional analysis of passives in Chamorro (Chapter 4 of doctoral dis-
        sertation).

COOREMAN, A., B. FOX & T. GIVÓN
1984   'The discourse definition of Ergativity'. *Studies in Language*, 1-39.

DAALDER, S. & M. GERRITSEN eds.
1981   *Linguistics in the Netherlands.* Amsterdam/Oxford/New York: North-Holland.

DANEŠ, F.
1974   'FSP and the organisation of the text'. In: F. Daneš (ed.) *Papers on
        Functional Sentence Perspective.* Prague: Academia.

1976   'Zur semantischen und thematischen Struktur des Kommunikats'. In:
        F. Daneš & F. & D. Viehweger (eds.) *Probleme der Textgrammatik*, 29-40.
        Berlin: Academie-Verlag.

DATO, D.P. ed.
1975   *Developmental Psycholinguistics.* Washington: Georgetown U.P.

DELBRÜCK, B.
1909   *Zu den Germanischen Relativsätzen.* Leipzig: B.G. Teubner.

DES TOMBE, L.
1976   'Competence and Performance'. In: G. Koefoed & A. Evers (eds.) *Lijnen
        van taaltheoretisch onderzoek*, 111-141. Groningen: Tjeenk Willink.

DIK, S.C.
1968   *Co-ordination*. Amsterdam: North-Holland.

1978   *Functional Grammar*. North-Holland Linguistic Series 37. Amsterdam: North-Holland. (Third printing, 1981, Dordrecht: Foris).

1980a   *Studies in Functional Grammar*. London: Academic Press.

1980b   'Seventeen sentences: basic principles and application of Functional Grammar'. In: Moravcsik & Wirth eds. (1980), 45-75.

1982   'Taalbeschouwing en Taaltheorie'. *Forum der Letteren* 23, 3, 184-200.

1983   'Two constraints on relators and what they can do for us'. In: Dik ed. (1983), 267-298.

DIK, S.C., M.E. HOFFMANN, J.R. de JONG, SIE ING DJIANG, H. STROOMER & L. de VRIES
1981   'On the typology of Focus Phenomena'. In: Hoekstra et al. eds. (1981), 41-74.

DIK, S.C. ed.
1983   *Advances in Functional Grammar*. Dordrecht: Foris.

DINGWALL, W.O.
1975   'The Species-Specifity of Speech'. In: Dato ed. (1975), 17-62.

1979   'The evolution of human communication systems'. In: H. Whitaker & H.A. Whitaker (eds.) *Studies in Neurolinguistics* 4, 1-95. New York: Academic Press.

DOBZHANSKY, Th. et al.
1977   *Evolution*. San Francisco: Freeman.

DOOREN, K. van & K. van den EYNDE
1982   'A structure for the intonation of Dutch'. *Linguistics* 20, 203-236.

DRABBE, P.
1959   *Kaeti en Wambon*. The Hague: Nijhoff.

DRESSLER, W. & R.A. BEAUGRANDE
1981   *Introduction to Text Linguistics*. London: Longman.

DULAY, H. & M. BURT
1979   'You can't learn without goofing'. In: J.C. Richards (ed.) *Error Analysis* 95-123. London.

EMONDS, J.
1979   'Appositive relatives have no properties'. *Linguistic Inquiry* 10, 2, 211-243.

ERNOUT, A.
1908-9 'Recherches sur l'emploi du passif Latin à l'époque républicaine'. *MSL* 15, 273-333.

ERTESCHIK-SHIR, N. & S. LAPPIN
1979   'Dominance and the functional explanation of island phenomena'. *Theoretical Linguistics* 6, 1, 41-86.

EYNDE, K. van den & K. van DOOREN
1983   'Intonation and syntactic structure in Dutch'. *ITL* 60-61, 27-42.

EYNDE, K. van den & K.B. KYOTA
1984   'Procédés tonals de construction syntaxique en Yaka (Zaire)'. In: pre-prints 5th International Phonology Meeting, June 1984, Eisenstadt, Austria.

FILLMORE, C.
1977   'The case for case reopened'. In: P. Cole & J. Sadock (eds.) *Syntax and Semantics 8: Grammatical relations*, 59-81. New York: Academic Press.

FLOBERT, P.
1975   *Les Verbes Déponents Latins*. Paris: Les Belles Lettres.

FODOR, J. & H. GARRETT
1966   'Some reflections on competence and performance'. In: J. Lyons & R.J. Wales (eds.) *Psycholinguistics Papers*, 135-179. Edinburgh: EUP.

GERRITSEN, M.
1978   'De opkomst van SOV patronen in het Nederlands in verband met de woordvolgordeveranderingen in de Germaanse talen'. In: Kooij ed. (1978), 3-39.

GILLIS, S.
1983   Van pretalige naar talige interactie. Antwerp Papers in Linguistics 30.

1984   *De verwerving van talige referentie.* Ph.D. Dissertation. Wilrijk: Universitaire Instelling Antwerpen.

GIVÓN, T.
1979   *On understanding grammar.* New York: Academic Press.

1982   'Transitivity, Topicality and the Ute Passive'. In: Hopper & Thompson eds. (1982), 143-160.

1983a   'Topic continuity in discourse: an introduction'. In: Givón ed. (1983), 1-41.

1983b   'Topic continuity in discourse: the functional domain of switch reference'. In: Haiman & Munro eds. (1983), 51-82.

1984a   *Syntax: A Functional-Typological Introduction I*. Amsterdam: John Benjamins.

1984b   'Direct Object and dative shifting: semantic and pragmatic case'. In: F. Plank (ed.) *Objects*, 151-182. New York: Academic Press.

GIVÓN, T. ed.
1983   *Topic Continuity in Discourse: A Quantitative Cross-language Study.* Amsterdam: John Benjamins.

GOODMAN, N.
1969   'The Emperor's New Ideas'. In: S. Hook (ed.) *Language & Philosophy*, 138-142. New York: NYUP.

GRANGER, S.
1983   *The 'be + past participle' Construction in Spoken English with Special Emphasis on the Passive*. Amsterdam: North-Holland.

GREENBERG, J.H.
1958   *Essays in Linguistics*. Chicago: Univ. of Chicago Press.

GREENE, J.
1972   *Psycholinguistics*. Harmondsworth: Penguin.

GRICE, P.
1975   'Logic and conversation'. In: P. Cole & J.L. Morgan (eds.) *Syntax and Semantics 3: Speech Acts*, 41-58. London & New York: Academic Press.

GRIMES, J.
1975   *The Thread of Discourse*. The Hague: Mouton.

GROOT, C. de
1981a   'Sentence-intertwining in Hungarian'. In: Bolkestein et al. (1981), 41-62

1981b   'The structure of predicates and verb agreement'. In: Daalder & Gerritsen eds. (1981), 149-158.

1981c   'On Theme in FG: an application to some constructions in spoken Hungarian In: Hoekstra et al. eds. (1981), 75-88.

GVOZDANOVIĆ, J.
1984   The role of semantic and pragmatic factors in determining 'deviant' con- gruence in Serbo-Croatian. Paper read at the first Colloquium on Functiona Grammar, Amsterdam, June 1984.

HAHN, E.A.
1930   *Coordination of Non-coordinate Elements in Vergil*. New York: W.F. Humphrey

HAIMAN, J. & P. MUNRO eds.
1983   *Switch reference and Universal Grammar*. Amsterdam: John Benjamins.

HALLIDAY, M.A.K.
1967   *Intonation & Grammar in British English*. The Hague: Mouton.

HALLIDAY, M.A.K. & R. HASAN
1976   *Cohesion in English*. London: Longman.

HANNAY, M.
1982   'On the definiteness and predicate restrictions in existential sentences i English'. *Free University Studies in English* 2, 57-90.

1983   'The Focus function in Functional Grammar: questions of contrast and con- text'. In: Dik ed. (1983), 207-224.

to appear
        Existentials in Functional Grammar. Ph.D. Diss., University of Amsterdam.

HARNAD, S.R., H.D. STEKLIS & J. LANCASTER eds.
1976   *Origins and Evolution of Language and Speech*. New York: New York Academy of Sciene.

Hearings before the Select Committee on Presidential campaign activities of the U.S. Senate (1973). Watergate Investigation Book IV. Washington D.C.

HIRT, H.
1934   *Handbuch des Urgermanischen, III: Abriss der Syntax*. Heidelberg: Carl Winter.

HOEKSTRA, T.
1978   'Funktionele Grammatika'. *Forum der Letteren* 19, 293-312.

HOEKSTRA, T., H. van der HULST & M. MOORTGAT eds.
1981   *Perspectives on Functional Grammar*. Dordrecht: Foris.

HÖHLE, T.N.
1978   *Lexikalistische Syntax: Die Aktif-Passif-Relation und andere Infinitiv- konstruktionen im Deutschen*. Tübingen: Niemeyer.

HOPPER, P.J.
1975   *The syntax of the simple sentence in Proto-Germanic*. The Hague: Mouton.

1979   'Aspect and foregrounding in discourse'. In: T. Givón (ed.) *Syntax and Semantics 12: Discourse and Syntax*, 213-241, New York: Academic Press.

HOPPER, P. & S. THOMPSON
1980   'Transitivity in grammar and discourse'. *Language* 56, 251-299.

HOPPER, P.J. & S.A. THOMPSON eds.
1982   *Syntax and Semantics 15: Studies in Transitivity.* New York: Academic
        Press.

HÖRMANN, H.
1978   *Meinen und Verstehen.* Frankfurt: Suhrkamp.

ITAGAKI, N. & G.D. PRIDEAUX
1983   'Pragmatic constraints on Subject and Agent Selection'. In: Dik ed.
        (1983), 329-342.

JACKENDOFF, R.
1972   *Semantic interpretation in generative grammar.* Cambridge, Mass.: MIT
        Press.

JAMES, D.
1972   'Some aspects of the syntax and semantics of interjections'. *Papers from
        the eighth regional meeting, Chicago Linguistic Society,* 162-172.

JANSEN, F.
1978   'Hoe krijgt een spreker zijn woorden op een rijtje?' In: Kooij ed.
        (1978), 70-104.

1981   *Syntaktische konstrukties in gesproken taal.* Ph.D. Diss., University of
        Amsterdam.

JONG, J. de
1981   'On the treatment of focus phenomena in FG'. In: Hoekstra et al. eds.
        (1981), 89-115.

KATZ, J.
1964   'Mentalism in Linguistics'. *Language* 40, 124-137.

KEENAN, E.L.
1981   Passive in the World's Languages. Trier: LAUT.

KEENAN, E. & B. COMRIE
1977   'Noun phrase accessibility and universal grammar'. *LI* 8, 63-99.

KEMPEN, G.
1978   'Sentence Construction by a Psychologically Plausible Formulator'. In:
        R.N. Campbell & P.T. Smith (eds.) *Recent Advances in the Psychology of
        Language,* vol. b, 103-123. New York: Plenum Press.

KERSTENS, J.
1981   'Structure & Structure Assignment. Dutch as a VSO-Language'. In: Daalder
        & Gerritsen eds. (1981), 103-113.

KEYSPER, C.E.
1983   'Comparing Dutch & Russian Pitch Contours'. *Russian Linguistics* 7, 101-
        154.

1984   'Vorm en betekenis in Nederlandse toonhoogte contouren'. *Forum der
        Letteren* 25, 20-37, 113-126.

KILBY, D.
1984   *Descriptive Syntax and the English Verb.* London: Croom Helm.

KIRKWOOD, H.W.
1979   'Information structure, sentence order and intonation in British English'.
        SMIL 3-4, 5-28.

KLEIN, M. & M. van den TOORN
1978   'Vooropplaatsing van PP's in het Nederlands'. *Spektator* 7, 423-433.

KOOIJ, J.
1973   *Is Nederlands een SOV-Taal?* Amsterdam: North-Holland.

KOOIJ, J. ed.
1978   *Aspekten van de woordvolgorde in het Nederlands.* Leiden: publikaties van de vakgroep Nederlandse taal- en letterkunde.

KOOIJ, J. & E. WIERS
1977   'Vooropplaatsing van PP's in het Nederlands'. *Spektator* 6, 445-449.

1978   'Vooropplaatsing, verplaatsingsregels en de interne struktuur van nominale groepen'. In: Kooij ed. '1978).

KOSTER, J.
1974   'Het werkwoord als spiegelcentrum'. *Spektator* 3, 601-618.

1975   'Dutch as an SOV-language'. *Linguistic Analysis* 1, 111-136.

1978   *Locality Principles in Syntax.* Dordrecht: Foris.

KUNO, S.
1972   'Pronominalization, reflexivization and direct discourse'. *Linguistic Inquiry* 3, 2, 161-196.

LAKOFF, G.
1974   Syntactic amalgams. *Papers from the tenth regional meeting, Chicago Linguistic Society,* 321-344.

LALLEMAN, J.
1983   'The Relationship between Formal and Content Properties of Speech'. In: Dik ed. (1983), 343-366.

LAMENDELLA, J.T.
1976   'Relations between the Ontogeny and Phylogeny of Language'. In: Harnad et al. eds. (1976), 396-412.

1977   'General Principles of Neurofunctional Organization'. *Language Learning* 27, 155-196.

LAWLER, J.
1974   Ample negatives. *Papers from the tenth regional meeting, Chicago Linguistic Society,* 357-377.

LENNEBERG, E.H.
1967   *Biological Foundation of Language.* New York: Wiley.

LEVELT, W.J.M.
1973   *Formele Grammatica's in Linguistiek en Taalpsychologie, 3 vol.* Deventer: Van Loghum Slaterus.

1975   'What became of LAD?' In: W. Abraham (ed.) *Ut Videam,* 171-190. Lisse: P. de Ridder.

LEVINSON, S.C.
1983   *Pragmatics.* Cambridge: CUP.

LI, C. ed.
1976   *Subject and Topic.* New York: Academic Press.

LONGACRE, R.E.
1983   *The Grammar of Discourse.* New York: Plenum.

LYONS, J.
1977   *Semantics.* Cambridge: CUP.

MACKENZIE, J.L.
1983   'Nominal predicates in a Functional Grammar of English'. In: Dik ed.
        (1983), 31-51.

1984   'Communicative functions of subordination'. In: Mackenzie & Wekker eds.
        (1984), 67-84.

MACKENZIE, J.L. & H. WEKKER eds.
1984   English language research: the Dutch contribution I. Amsterdam: Free
        University Press.

MARIN, O.S.M.
1976   'Neurobiology of Language'. In: Harnad et al. eds. (1976), 900-912.

MAYR, E.
1974   'Behaviour Programs and Evolutionary Strategies'. American Scientist
        62, 650-659.

McCAWLEY, J.
1982   'Parentheticals and discontinuous constituent structure'. Linguistic
        Inquiry 13, 1, 91-106.

McNEILL, D.
1979   The Conceptual Basis of Language. Hillsdale: Erlbaum.

MILLER, G.A. & P.N. JOHNSON-LAIRD
1976   Language & Perception. Cambridge: CUP.

MILLER, J. & P. TENCH
1982   'Aspects of Hausa Intonation (2)'. Journal of the International Phonetic
        Association 12, 2, 78-93.

MITTWOCH, A.
1979   'Final parentheticals with English questions: their illocutionary function
        and grammar'. Journal of Pragmatics 3, 401-412.

MORAVCSIK, E. & J. WIRTH eds.
1980   Syntax and Semantics 13: Current Approaches to Syntax. London/New York:
        Academic Press.

MORGAN, J.L.
1972   'Some aspects of relative clauses in English and Albanian'. In: The
        Chicago Which Hunt. Papers from the Relative Clause Festival. Chicago
        Linguistic Society, 63-72.

1973   'Sentence fragments and the notion 'sentence''. In: B. Kachru, R.B. Lees,
        Y. Malkiel, A. Pietrangeli & S. Saporta (eds.) Issues in Linguistics,
        719-751. Urbana: University of Illinois Press.

MOUTAOUAKIL, A.
1983a   Le Focus en Arabe: vers une analyse fonctionelle. Paper, University of
        Rabat. (To appear in Lingua).

1983b   Le thème en Arabe: analyse fonctionelle. Paper, University of Rabat.
        (Arabic version has appeared in Dirasat falsafiyya wa Padabiyya).

MUNRO, P.
1983   'When same is "not different".' In: Haiman & Munro eds. (1983), 223-243.

NAGEL, E.
1979   Teleology Revisited and other Essays in the Philosophy and History of
        Science. New York: Columbia UP.

NUYTS, J.
1982a   Een psycho-linguistische benadering van de fonologische aspekten van
        afasie. Antwerp Papers in Linguistics 26.

1982b 'Afasie en Linguistiek: een status quo'. *De Psycholoog* 17, 377-383.

1983a 'On the methodology of a functional language theory'. In: Dik ed. (1983), 369-386.

1983b 'Functional Grammar: een notationele variant?' *De Nieuwe Taalgids* 76,19-26.

1984   Sprachfunktionen. Trier: LAUT A 128.

forthcoming
       'On Mentalism and Functional Grammar'. In: J. Nuyts (ed.) *Antwerp Studies in Functional Grammar*. Antwerp Papers in Linguistics.

in preparation
       Principes van een funktionalistische taaltheorie. Antwerpen: UIA.

O'CONNOR, J.D. & G.F. ARNOLD
1973   *Intonation of Colloquial English* (2nd ed.). London: Longman.

PANHUIS, D.G.
1982   *The Communicative Perspective in the Sentence. A Study of Latin Word Order*. Amsterdam: John Benjamins.

PAPE-MÜLLER, S.
1980   *Textfunktionen des Passifs*. Tübingen: Niemeyer.

PARRET, H.
1979   *Filosofie en Taalwetenschap*. Assen: Van Gorcum.

PARTEE, B.
1973   'The syntax and semantics of quotation'. In: S.R. Anderson & P. Kiparsky (eds.) *A festschrift for Morris Halle*, 410-418. Holt: Reinhart & Winston.

PAUL, H.
1920   *Deutsche Grammatik: IV Syntax*. Halle a.S.: Max Niemeyer.

PERLMUTTER, D.
1980   'Relational Grammar'. In: Moravcsik & Wirth eds. (1980), 195-229.

PINKSTER, H.
1984   'Het Latijnse Passief'. *Lampas* 17, 5.

PRINCE, E.F.
1981   'Towards a taxonomy of given-new information'. In: P. Cole (ed.) *Radical Pragmatics*, 223-255. New York: Academic Press.

QUIRK, R., S. GREENBAUM, G. LEECH & J. SVARTVIK
1972   *A Grammar of Contemporary English*. New York: Seminar Press.

REESINK, G.P.
1983a 'Switch-reference and topicality hierarchies'. *Studies in Language* 7, 215-246.

1983b 'On subordination in Usan and other Papuan languages'. In: Dik ed. (1983), 225-243.

1984   *Structures and their functions in Usan*. Ph.D. Diss., University of Amsterdam.

REINHART, T.
1975   'Whose main-clause-point of view in sentences with parentheticals'. In: S. Kuno (ed.) *Harvard Studies in syntax and semantics I*, 127-171.

1983   'Point of view in language: the use of parentheticals'. In: G. Rauh (ed.) *Essays on Deixis*, 169-194. Tübingen: Günter Narr Verlag.

RESEARCH GROUP FUNCTIONAL GRAMMAR
forthcoming
       The Typology of Embedded Predications. University of Amsterdam.

ROSS, J.R.
1967   *Constraints on Variables in Syntax*. Unpublished MIT dissertation.

1973   'Slifting'. In: M. Gross, M. Halle & M.P. Schützenberger (eds.) *Proceed-
        ings of the first International Conference on the formal analysis of
        natural languages*, 133-165. The Hague: Mouton.

RYLE, G.
1949   *The concept of mind*. Harmondsworth: Penguin [1980].

SADOCK, J.M.
1984   'The pragmatics of subordination'. In: W. de Geest & Y. Putseys (eds.)
        Sentential complementation, 205-213. Dordrecht: Foris.

SANFORD, A.J. & S.C. GARROD
1981   *Understanding Written Language*. Chichester: Wiley.

SCHACHTER, P.
1976   'The Subject in Philippine languages: topic, actor, actor-topic, or none
        of the above'. In: Li ed. (1976), 491-518.

1984   'Semantic-role based syntax in Toba Batak'. In: Schachter ed. (1984),
        122-149.

SCHACHTER, P. ed.
1984   *Studies in the structure of Toba Batak*. UCLA occasional papers in lin-
        guistics, no. 5. Los Angeles.

SCHAERLAEKENS, A.W.
1977   *De Taalontwikkeling van het Kind*. Wolters-Noordhoff.

SCHANK, R.C. & Y. WILKS
1974   'The Goals of Linguistic Theories Revisited'. *Lingua* 34, 301-326.

SCHLESINGER, I.M.
1977   *Production & Comprehension of Utterances*. Hillsdale: Erlbaum.

1982   *Steps to Language*. Hillsdale: Erlbaum.

SCHOENTHAL, G.
1976   *Das Passiv in der deutschen Standardsprache*. München: Hueber.

SCHUTTER, G. de
1981a   'Werkwoordelijke tempuskategorieën'. *Handelingen van het 33e Vlaams
        Filologencongres*, 107-112.

1981b   'Beschouwingen over het Nederlandse tempussysteem vanuit een universalis-
        tische gezichtshoek'. In: L. Goossens (ed.) *Bijdragen over semantiek van
        het 33e Vlaams Filologencongres*, 21-47. Antwerp Papers in Linguistics 23.

1983   'Modaliteit en andere modificaties in de Nederlandse grammatica'. In:
        Fr. Daems & L. Goossens (eds.) *Een Spyeghel voor G. Jo Steenbergen*,
        277-291. Leuven: Acco.

SCHUTTER, G. de & P. van HAUWERMEIREN
1983   *De Structuur van het Nederlands*. Malle: de Sikkel.

SCHUTTER, G. de & J. NUYTS
1983   'Towards an integrated model of a Functional Grammar'. In: Dik ed. (1983),
        387-404.

SEUREN, P.A.M.
1977   'On Linguistic Awareness'. *Gramma* I, 4.

SMITH, N. & D. WILSON
1979   *Modern Linguistics: the Results of Chomsky's Revolution*. Harmondsworth: Penguin.

SMYTH, R.H., G.D. PRIDEAUX & J. HOGEN
1979   'The effect of context on dative position'. *Lingua* 47, 27-42.

SPERBER, D. & D. WILSON
1982   'Mutual knowledge and relevance in theories of comprehension'. In: N.V. Smith (ed.) *Mutual Knowledge*, 61-85. Academic Press.

STEIN, G.
1979   *Studies in the function of the passive*. Tübingen: Narr.

STEINBERG, D.
1975   'Chomsky: From Formalism to Mentalism and Psychological Invalidity'. *Glossa* 9, 218-252.

1982   *Psycholinguistics*. London: Longman.

STOCKWELL, R.P.
1977   'Motivations for exbraciation in Old English'. In: C. Li (ed.) *Mechanisms of Syntactic Change*, 291-316. Austin: University of Texas Press.

STRAIGHT, S.H.
1976   'Comprehension versus Production in Linguistic Theory'. *Foundations of Language* 12, 525-540.

SUGAMOTO, N.
1984   'Reflexives in Toba Batak'. In: Schachter ed. (1984), 150-171.

SVARTVIK, J.
1966   *Voice in the English verb*. The Hague: Mouton.

SVOBODA, A.
1968   'The hierarchy of communicative units and fields as illustrated by English attributive constructions'. *Brno Studies in English* 7, 49-99.

TAGLICHT, J.
1984   *Message and Emphasis: On Focus and Scope in English*. London: Longman.

TOULMIN, S.
1972   *Human Understanding 1*. Princeton: PUP.

TOURATIER, C. ed.
1984   *Syntaxe et Latin*. Marseille: Université de Provence, Lafitte.

TUUK, H.N. van der
1867   *Tobasche spraakkunst II*. Translated as: Teeuw, A. & R. Roolvink eds. (1971) *A grammar of Toba Batak*. The Hague: Nijhoff.

URMSON, J.O.
1952   'Parenthetical Verbs'. *Mind* 61, 480-496.

VANDENBOSCH, L.
1982   De SOV-hypothese toegepast op het Nederlands. Unpubl. Lic. thesis, UIA, Antwerp University.

VERHAGEN, A.
1979a   'Fokusbepalingen en grammatikale theorie'. *Spektator* 8, 372-402.

1979b   'On the E-hypothesis of dislocation and conditions on discourse grammar'. *Recherches Linguistiques*. Paris: Vincennes.

VOORHOEVE, C.L.
1975   Languages of Irian Jaya: checklist, preliminary classification, language
        maps, wordlists. Pacific Linguistics Series B, no. 31.

VOOYS, C. de
1960   *Nederlandse Spraakkunst*. Groningen: Wolters.

VRIES, L. de
1983   'Three passive-like constructions in Indonesian'. In: Dik ed. (1983),
        155-173.

WACKERNAGEL, J.
1892   'Über ein Gesetz der indogermanischen Wortstellung'. *Indogermanische
        Forschungen* 1, 333-435.

WATT, W.C.
1974   'Mentalism in Linguistics, II'. *Glossa* 8, 3-40.

WATTERS, J.R.
1979   'Focus in Aghem: a study of its formal correlates and typology'. In:
        L.M. Hyman (ed.) *Aghem Grammatical Structure*. SCOPIL 7, 137-197.
        Los Angeles: UCLA.

WEINER, E.J. & W. LABOV
1983   'Constraints on the agentless passive'. *JoL* 19, 29-58.

WERTH, P.N.
forthcoming
        Focus, coherence and emphasis. London: Croom Helm.

WEYNEN, A.A. *Schets van de Geschiedenis van de Nederlandse Syntaxis*. Assen:
        Van Gorcum.

WHITAKER, H.A.
1973   'Comments on the Innateness of Language'. In: R.W. Shuy (ed.) *Some New
        Directions in Linguistics*, 95-120. Washington: Georgetown UP.

WILLIAMS, E.S.
1977   'Discourse and logical form'. *Linguistic Inquiry* 8, 1, 101-139.

WINOGRAD, T.
1972   *Understanding Natural Language*. New York: Academic Press.

WOUK, F.
1984   'Scalar transitivity and trigger choice in Toba Batak'. In: Schachter ed.
        (1984), 195-219.

WÜLFING, J.E.
1897   *Die Syntax in den Werken Alfreds des Grossen*, II. Bonn: Hanstein's Verlag.

WUNDERLICH, H.
1894   *Unsere Umgangssprache*.

ZIV, Y.
1973   'Why can't appositives be extraposed?' *Papers in Linguistics* 6, 2, 243-
        254.

1976   On the communicative effect of relative clause extraposition in English.
        Unpublished dissertation University of Illinois.

Index of authors

Index of languages and language-families

Index of subjects